Microsoft® Office

Publisher 2007

Introductory Concepts and Techniques

Gary B. Shelly

Thomas J. Cashman

Joy L. Starks

THOMSON COURSE TECHNOLOGY   25 THOMSON PLACE   BOSTON MA 02210

SHELLY CASHMAN SERIES®

Australia • Canada • Denmark • Japan • Mexico • New Zealand • Philippines • Puerto Rico • Singapore • South Africa • Spain • United Kingdom • United States

Microsoft Office Publisher 2007
Introductory Concepts and Techniques

Gary B. Shelly

Thomas J. Cashman

Joy L. Starks

Executive Editor Alexandra Arnold	**Director of Production** Patty Stephan	**Art Director** Bruce Bond
Senior Product Manager Reed Curry	**Senior Content Project Manager** Jennifer Goguen McGrail	**Cover and Text Design** Joel Sadagursky
Associate Product Manager Klenda Martinez	**Developmental Editor** Jill Batistick	**Cover Photo** Jon Chomitz
Editorial Assistant Jon Farnham	**Proofreader** Kim Kosmatka	**Compositor** GEX Publishing Services
Senior Marketing Manager Joy Stark-Vancs	**Indexer** Liz Cunningham	**Printer** Banta Menasha
Marketing Coordinator Julie Schuster	**QA Manuscript Reviewers** John Freitas, Serge Palladino, Chris Scriver, Danielle Shaw, Marianne Snow, Teresa Storch	
Print Buyer Denise Powers		

Microsoft® Office
Publisher 2007
Introductory Concepts and Techniques

Contents

CHAPTER THREE
Publishing a Tri-Fold Brochure

E-MAIL FEATURE

Creating an E-Mail Letter Using Publisher

Appendices

APPENDIX A

Project Planning Guidelines

APPENDIX B

Introduction to Microsoft Office 2007

APPENDIX C

Microsoft Office Publisher 2007 Help

APPENDIX D

Publishing Office 2007 Web Pages to a Web Server

APPENDIX E

Customizing Microsoft Office Publisher 2007

APPENDIX F

Steps for the Windows XP User

Preface

The Shelly Cashman Series® offers the finest textbooks in computer education. We are proud of the fact that our series of Microsoft Office 4.3, Microsoft Office 95, Microsoft Office 97, Microsoft Office 2000, Microsoft Office XP, and Microsoft Office 2003 textbooks have been the most widely used books in education. With each new edition of our Office books, we have made significant improvements based on the software and comments made by instructors and students.

Microsoft Office 2007 contains more changes in the user interface and feature set than all other previous versions combined. Recognizing that the new features and functionality of Microsoft Office 2007 would impact the way that students are taught skills, the Shelly Cashman Series development team carefully reviewed our pedagogy and analyzed its effectiveness in teaching today's Office student. An extensive customer survey produced results confirming what the series is best known for: its step-by-step, screen-by-screen instructions, its project-oriented approach, and the quality of its content.

We learned, though, that students entering computer courses today are different than students taking these classes just a few years ago. Students today read less, but need to retain more. They need not only to be able to perform skills, but to retain those skills and know how to apply them to different settings. Today's students need to be continually engaged and challenged to retain what they're learning.

As a result, we've renewed our commitment to focusing on the user and how they learn best. This commitment is reflected in every change we've made to our Office 2007 books.

Objectives of This Textbook

Microsoft Office Publisher 2007: Introductory Concepts and Techniques is intended for a course that includes an introduction to Publisher 2007. No experience with a computer is assumed, and no mathematics beyond the high school freshman level is required. The objectives of this book are:

- To teach the fundamentals of Microsoft Office Publisher 2007
- To expose students to practical examples of the computer as a useful tool
- To acquaint students with the proper procedures to create documents suitable for coursework, professional purposes, and personal use
- To help students discover the underlying functionality of Publisher 2007 so they can become more productive
- To develop an exercise-oriented approach that allows learning by doing

The Shelly Cashman Approach

Features of the Shelly Cashman Series Microsoft Office Publisher 2007 books include:

- **Project Orientation** Each chapter in the book presents a project with a practical problem and complete solution in an easy-to-understand approach.

- **Plan Ahead Boxes** The project orientation is enhanced by the inclusion of Plan Ahead boxes. These new features prepare students to create successful projects by encouraging them to think strategically about what they are trying to accomplish before they begin working.

- **Step-by-Step, Screen-by-Screen Instructions** Each of the tasks required to complete a project is clearly identified throughout the chapter. Now, the step-by-step instructions provide a context beyond point-and-click. Each step explains why students are performing a task, or the result of performing a certain action. Found on the screens accompanying each step, call-outs give students the information they need to know when they need to know it. Now, we've used color to distinguish the content in the call-outs. The Explanatory call-outs (in black) summarize what is happening on the screen and the Navigational call-outs (in red) show students where to click.

- **Q&A** Found within many of the step-by-step sequences, Q&As raise the kinds of questions students may ask when working through a step sequence and provide answers about what they are doing, why they are doing it, and how that task might be approached differently.

- **Experimental Steps** These new steps, within our step-by-step instructions, encourage students to explore, experiment, and take advantage of the features of the Office 2007 new user interface. These steps are not necessary to complete the projects, but are designed to increase the confidence with the software and build problem-solving skills.

- **Thoroughly Tested Projects** Unparalleled quality is ensured because every screen in the book is produced by the author only after performing a step, and then each project must pass Thomson Course Technology's Quality Assurance program.

- **Other Ways Boxes and Quick Reference Summary** The Other Ways boxes displayed at the end of most of the step-by-step sequences specify the other ways to do the task completed in the steps. Thus, the steps and the Other Ways box make a comprehensive reference unit. A Quick Reference Summary at the end of the book contains all of the tasks presented in the chapters, and all ways identified of accomplishing the tasks.

- **BTW** These marginal annotations provide background information, tips, and answers to common questions that complement the topics covered, adding depth and perspective to the learning process.

- **Integration of the World Wide Web** The World Wide Web is integrated into the Publisher 2007 learning experience by (1) BTW annotations that send students to Web sites for up-to-date information and alternative approaches to tasks; (2) a Quick Reference Summary Web page that summarizes the ways to complete tasks (mouse, shortcut menu, and keyboard); and (3) the Learn It Online section at the end of each chapter, which has chapter reinforcement exercises, learning games, and other types of student activities.

- **End-of-Chapter Student Activities** Extensive student activities at the end of each chapter provide the student with plenty of opportunities to reinforce the materials learned in the chapter through hands-on assignments. Several new types of activities have been added that challenge the student in new ways to expand their knowledge, and to apply their new skills to a project with personal relevance.

Q&A

What is a maximized window?

A maximized window fills the entire screen. When you maximize a window, the Maximize button changes to a Restore Down button.

Other Ways

1. Click Italic button on Mini toolbar
2. Right-click selected text, click Font on shortcut menu, click Font tab, click Italic in Font style list, click OK button
3. Click Font Dialog Box Launcher, click Font tab, click Italic in Font style list, click OK button
4. Press CTRL+I

BTW

Toolbar Rows

The Standard and Connect Frames toolbars are preset to display on one row, immediately below the menu bar. The Publisher Tasks and Formatting toolbar are displayed below that. If the resolution of your display differs from that in the book, some of the buttons that belong on these toolbars may not appear. Use the **Toolbar Options button** to display these hidden buttons.

Organization of This Textbook

Microsoft Office Publisher 2007: Introductory Concepts and Techniques consists of three chapters on Microsoft Office Publisher 2007, one special feature, six appendices, and a Quick Reference Summary.

End-of-Chapter Student Activities

A notable strength of the Shelly Cashman Series Microsoft Office Publisher 2007 books is the extensive student activities at the end of each chapter. Well-structured student activities can make the difference between students merely participating in a class and students retaining the information they learn. The activities in the Shelly Cashman Series Office books include the following.

Figure 1–84

CHAPTER SUMMARY A concluding paragraph, followed by a listing of the tasks completed within a chapter together with the pages on which the step-by-step, screen-by-screen explanations appear.

LEARN IT ONLINE Every chapter features a Learn It Online section that is comprised of six exercises. These exercises include True/False, Multiple Choice, Short Answer, Flash Cards, Practice Test, and Learning Games.

APPLY YOUR KNOWLEDGE This exercise usually requires students to open and manipulate a file from the Data Files that parallels the activities learned in the chapter. To obtain a copy of the Data Files for Students, follow the instructions on the inside back cover of this text.

EXTEND YOUR KNOWLEDGE This exercise allows students to extend and expand on the skills learned within the chapter.

MAKE IT RIGHT This exercise requires students to analyze a document, identify errors and issues, and correct those errors and issues using skills learned in the chapter.

IN THE LAB Three all new in-depth assignments per chapter require students to utilize the chapter concepts and techniques to solve problems on a computer.

CASES AND PLACES Five unique real-world case-study situations, including Make It Personal, an open-ended project that relates to student's personal lives, and one small-group activity.

Instructor Resources CD-ROM

The Shelly Cashman Series is dedicated to providing you with all of the tools you need to make your class a success. Information about all supplementary materials is available through your Thomson Course Technology representative or by calling one of the following telephone numbers: Colleges, Universities, and Continuing Ed departments, 1-800-648-7450; High Schools, 1-800-824-5179; and Career Colleges, Business, Government, Library and Resellers, 1-800-477-3692.

The Instructor Resources CD-ROM for this textbook include both teaching and testing aids. The contents of each item on the Instructor Resources CD-ROM (ISBN 1-4239-1233-0) are described on the following page.

INSTRUCTOR'S MANUAL The Instructor's Manual consists of Microsoft Word files, which include chapter objectives, lecture notes, teaching tips, classroom activities, lab activities, quick quizzes, figures and boxed elements summarized in the chapters, and a glossary page. The new format of the Instructor's Manual will allow you to map through every chapter easily.

LECTURE SUCCESS SYSTEM The Lecture Success System consists of intermediate files that correspond to certain figures in the book, allowing you to step through the creation of a project in a chapter during a lecture without entering large amounts of data.

SYLLABUS Sample syllabi, which can be customized easily to a course, are included. The syllabi cover policies, class and lab assignments and exams, and procedural information.

FIGURE FILES Illustrations for every figure in the textbook are available in electronic form. Use this ancillary to present a slide show in lecture or to print transparencies for use in lecture with an overhead projector. If you have a personal computer and LCD device, this ancillary can be an effective tool for presenting lectures.

POWERPOINT PRESENTATIONS PowerPoint Presentations is a multimedia lecture presentation system that provides slides for each chapter. Presentations are based on chapter objectives. Use this presentation system to present well-organized lectures that are both interesting and knowledge based. PowerPoint Presentations provides consistent coverage at schools that use multiple lecturers.

SOLUTIONS TO EXERCISES Solutions are included for the end-of-chapter exercises, as well as the Chapter Reinforcement exercises.

TEST BANK & TEST ENGINE In the ExamView test bank, you will find our standard question types (40 multiple-choice, 25 true/false, 20 completion) and new objective-based question types (5 modified multiple-choice, 5 modified true/false and 10 matching). Critical Thinking questions also are included (3 essays and 2 cases with 2 questions each) totaling the test bank to 112 questions for every chapter with page number references, and when appropriate, figure references. A version of the test bank you can print also is included. The test bank comes with a copy of the test engine, ExamView, the ultimate tool for your objective-based testing needs. ExamView is a state-of-the-art test builder that is easy to use. ExamView enables you to create paper-, LAN-, or Web-based tests from test banks designed specifically for your Thomson Course Technology textbook. Utilize the ultra-efficient QuickTest Wizard to create tests in less than five minutes by taking advantage of Thomson Course Technology's question banks, or customize your own exams from scratch.

DATA FILES FOR STUDENTS All the files that are required by students to complete the exercises are included. You can distribute the files on the Instructor Resources CD-ROM to your students over a network, or you can have them follow the instructions on the inside back cover of this book to obtain a copy of the Data Files for Students.

ADDITIONAL ACTIVITIES FOR STUDENTS These additional activities consist of Chapter Reinforcement Exercises, which are true/false, multiple-choice, and short answer questions that help students gain confidence in the material learned.

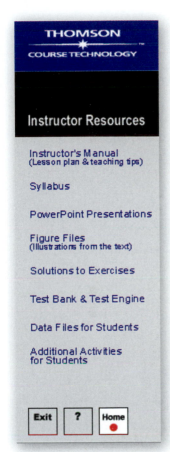

Assessment & Training Solutions
SAM 2007

SAM 2007 helps bridge the gap between the classroom and the real world by allowing students to train and test on important computer skills in an active, hands-on environment.

SAM 2007's easy-to-use system includes powerful interactive exams, training or projects on critical applications such as Word, Excel, Access, PowerPoint, Outlook, Windows, the Internet, and much more. SAM simulates the application environment, allowing students to demonstrate their knowledge and think through the skills by performing real-world tasks.

Designed to be used with the Shelly Cashman series, SAM 2007 includes built-in page references so students can print helpful study guides that match the Shelly Cashman series textbooks used in class. Powerful administrative options allow instructors to schedule exams and assignments, secure tests, and run reports with almost limitless flexibility.

Student Edition Labs

Our Web-based interactive labs help students master hundreds of computer concepts, including input and output devices, file management and desktop applications, computer ethics, virus protection, and much more. Featuring up-to-the-minute content, eye-popping graphics, and rich animation, the highly interactive Student Edition Labs offer students an alternative way to learn through dynamic observation, step-by-step practice, and challenging review questions.

Online Content

Blackboard is the leading distance learning solution provider and class-management platform today. Thomson Course Technology has partnered with Blackboard to bring you premium online content. Instructors: Content for use with *Microsoft Office Publisher 2007: Introductory Concepts and Techniques* is available in a Blackboard Course Cartridge and may include topic reviews, case projects, review questions, test banks, practice tests, custom syllabi, and more.

Thomson Course Technology also has solutions for several other learning management systems. Please visit http://www.course.com today to see what's available for this title.

CourseCasts Learning on the Go. Always Available…Always Relevant.

Want to keep up with the latest technology trends relevant to you? Visit our site to find a library of podcasts, CourseCasts, featuring a "CourseCast of the Week," and download them to your portable media player at http://coursecasts.course.com.

Our fast-paced world is driven by technology. You know because you are an active participant — always on the go, always keeping up with technological trends, and always learning new ways to embrace technology to power your life.

Ken Baldauf, a faculty member of the Florida State University (FSU) Computer Science Department, is responsible for teaching technology classes to thousands of FSU students each year. He knows what you know; he knows what you want to learn. He is also an expert in the latest technology and will sort through and aggregate the most pertinent news and information so you can spend your time enjoying technology, rather than trying to figure it out.

Visit us at http://coursecasts.course.com to learn on the go!

CourseNotes

Course Technology's CourseNotes are six-panel quick reference cards that reinforce the most important and widely used features of a software application in a visual and user-friendly format. CourseNotes will serve as a great reference tool during and after the student completes the course. CourseNotes for Microsoft Office 2007, Word 2007, Excel 2007, Access 2007, PowerPoint 2007, Windows Vista, and more are available now!

To the Student . . .   Getting the Most Out of Your Book

Welcome to *Microsoft Office Publisher 2007: Introductory Concepts and Techniques*. You can save yourself a lot of time and gain a better understanding of the Office 2007 programs if you spend a few minutes reviewing the figures and callouts in this section.

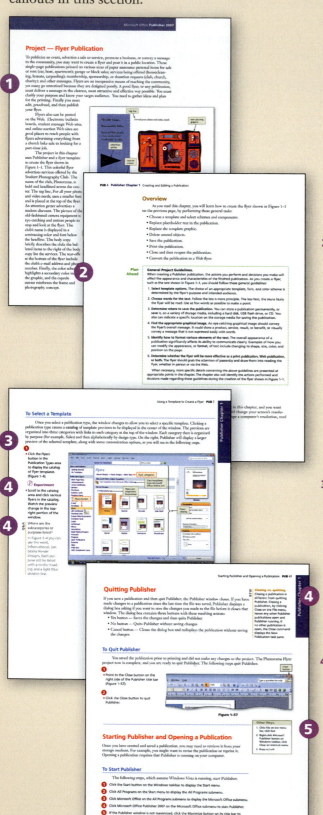

1 PROJECT ORIENTATION

Each chapter's project presents a practical problem and shows the solution in the first figure of the chapter. The project orientation lets you see firsthand how problems are solved from start to finish using application software and computers.

2 PROJECT PLANNING GUIDELINES AND PLAN AHEAD BOXES

Overall planning guidelines at the beginning of a chapter and Plan Ahead boxes throughout encourage you to think critically about how to accomplish the next goal before you actually begin working.

3 CONSISTENT STEP-BY-STEP, SCREEN-BY-SCREEN PRESENTATION

Chapter solutions are built using a step-by-step, screen-by-screen approach. This pedagogy allows you to build the solution on a computer as you read through the chapter. Generally, each step includes an explanation that indicates the result of the step.

4 MORE THAN JUST STEP-BY-STEP

BTW annotations in the margins of the book, Q&As in the steps, and substantive text in the paragraphs provide background information, tips, and answers to common questions that complement the topics covered, adding depth and perspective. When you finish with this book, you will be ready to use the Office programs to solve problems on your own. Experimental steps provide you with opportunities to step out on your own to try features of the programs, and pick up right where you left off in the chapter.

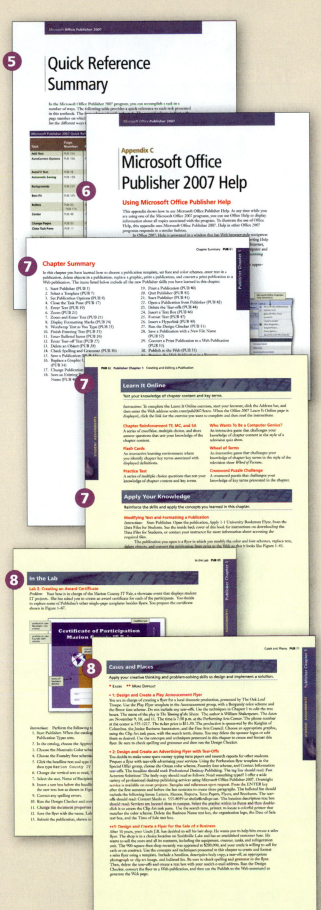

5 OTHER WAYS BOXES AND QUICK REFERENCE SUMMARY

Other Ways boxes that follow many of the step sequences and a Quick Reference Summary at the back of the book explain the other ways to complete the task presented, such as using the mouse, Ribbon, shortcut menu, and keyboard.

6 EMPHASIS ON GETTING HELP WHEN YOU NEED IT

The first project of each application and Appendix C show you how to use all the elements of Office Help. Being able to answer your own questions will increase your productivity and reduce your frustrations by minimizing the time it takes to learn how to complete a task.

7 REVIEW, REINFORCEMENT, AND EXTENSION

After you successfully step through a project in a chapter, a section titled Chapter Summary identifies the tasks with which you should be familiar. Terms you should know for test purposes are bold in the text. The Learn It Online section at the end of each chapter offers reinforcement in the form of review questions, learning games, and practice tests. Also included are exercises that require you to extend your learning beyond the book.

8 LABORATORY EXERCISES

If you really want to learn how to use the programs, then you must design and implement solutions to problems on your own. Every chapter concludes with several carefully developed laboratory assignments that increase in complexity.

About Our New Cover Look

Learning styles of students have changed, but the Shelly Cashman Series' dedication to their success has remained steadfast for over 30 years. We are committed to continually updating our approach and content to reflect the way today's students learn and experience new technology.

This focus on the user is reflected in our bold new cover design, which features photographs of real students using the Shelly Cashman Series in their courses. Each book features a different user, reflecting the many ages, experiences, and backgrounds of all of the students learning with our books. When you use the Shelly Cashman Series, you can be assured that you are learning computer skills using the most effective courseware available.

We would like to thank the administration and faculty at the participating schools for their help in making our vision a reality. Most of all, we'd like to thank the wonderful students from all over the world who learn from our texts and now appear on our covers.

Microsoft Office Publisher 2007

1 Creating and Editing a Publication

Objectives

You will have mastered the material in this chapter when you can:

- Start and quit Publisher
- Describe the Publisher window
- Choose Publisher template options
- Create a flyer from a template
- Replace Publisher template text
- Edit a synchronized object
- Delete objects
- Check spelling

- Save a publication
- Replace a graphic
- Print a publication
- Change publication properties
- Open and modify a publication
- Convert a print publication to a Web publication
- Use Publisher Help

1 | Creating and Editing a Publication

What Is Microsoft Office Publisher 2007?

Microsoft Office Publisher 2007 is a powerful desktop publishing (DTP) program that assists you in designing and producing professional, quality documents that combine text, graphics, illustrations, and photographs. DTP software provides additional tools over and above those typically found in word processing packages, including design templates, graphic manipulation tools, color schemes or libraries, advanced layout and printing tools, and Web components. For large jobs, businesses use DTP software to design publications that are camera ready, which means the files are suitable for outside commercial printing. In addition, DTP software is becoming a tool of choice for Web pages and interactive Web forms.

Microsoft Publisher is used by people who regularly produce high-quality color publications, such as newsletters, brochures, flyers, logos, signs, cards, and business forms. Saving publications as Web pages or complete Web sites is a powerful component in Publisher. All publications can be saved in a format that easily is viewed and manipulated using a browser.

Publisher has many features designed to simplify production and make publications look visually appealing. Using Publisher, you easily can change the shape, size, and color of text and graphics. You can include many kinds of graphical objects, including mastheads, borders, tables, images, pictures, charts, and Web objects in publications.

While you are typing, Publisher performs many tasks automatically. For example, Publisher detects and corrects spelling errors in several languages. Publisher's thesaurus allows you to add variety and precision to your writing. Publisher also can format text, such as headings, lists, fractions, borders, and Web addresses, as you type.

This latest version of Publisher has many new features to make you more productive. For example, Publisher has many new predefined templates and graphical elements designed to assist you with preparing publications and marketing strategies. Publisher also includes new e-mail, charting, and diagramming tools; uses themes so that you can coordinate colors, fonts, and graphics; and enables you to convert a publication to the PDF format. Publisher's tracking tools help determine the effectiveness of marketing mailings.

To illustrate the features of Publisher, this book presents a series of projects that create publications similar to those you will encounter in academic and business environments.

Project Planning Guidelines

The process of developing a publication that communicates specific information requires careful analysis and planning. As a starting point, establish why the publication is needed. Once the purpose is determined, analyze the intended audience and its unique needs. Then, gather information about the topic and decide what to include in the publication. Define a plan for printing, including color, type of paper, and number of copies. Finally, determine the publication design, layout, and style that will be most successful at delivering the message. After editing and proofreading, your publication is ready to print or upload to the Web. Details of these guidelines are provided in Appendix A. In addition, each project in this book provides practical applications of these planning considerations.

Project — Flyer Publication

To publicize an event, advertise a sale or service, promote a business, or convey a message to the community, you may want to create a flyer and post it in a public location. These single-page publications printed on various sizes of paper announce personal items for sale or rent (car, boat, apartment); garage or block sales; services being offered (housecleaning, lessons, carpooling); membership, sponsorship, or donation requests (club, church, charity); and other messages. Flyers are an inexpensive means of reaching the community, yet many go unnoticed because they are designed poorly. A good flyer, or any publication, must deliver a message in the clearest, most attractive and effective way possible. You must clarify your purpose and know your target audience. You need to gather ideas and plan for the printing. Finally you must edit, proofread, and then publish your flyer.

Flyers also can be posted on the Web. Electronic bulletin boards, student message Web sites, and online auction Web sites are good places to reach people with flyers advertising everything from a church bake sale to looking for a part-time job.

The project in this chapter uses Publisher and a flyer template to create the flyer shown in Figure 1–1. This colorful flyer advertises services offered by the Student Photography Club. The name of the club, Photorama, is bold and headlined across the center. The tag line, For all your photo and video needs, uses a smaller font and is placed at the top of the flyer. An attention getter advertises a student discount. The picture of the old-fashioned camera equipment is eye-catching and entices people to stop and look at the flyer. The club's name is displayed in a contrasting color and font below the headline. The body copy briefly describes the club; the bulleted items to the right of the body copy list the services. The tear-offs at the bottom of the flyer include the club's e-mail address and phone number. Finally, the color scheme highlights a secondary color in the graphic, and the capsule cutout reinforces the frame and photography concept.

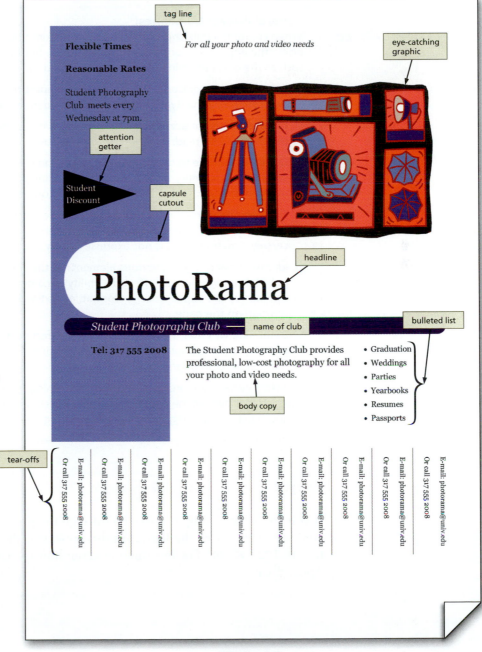

Figure 1–1

Overview

As you read this chapter, you will learn how to create the flyer shown in Figure 1–1 on the previous page, by performing these general tasks:

- Choose a template and select schemes and components.
- Replace placeholder text in the publication.
- Replace the template graphic.
- Delete unused objects.
- Save the publication.
- Print the publication.
- Close and then reopen the publication.
- Convert the publication to a Web flyer.

Plan Ahead

> **General Project Guidelines.**
>
> When creating a Publisher publication, the actions you perform and decisions you make will affect the appearance and characteristics of the finished publication. As you create a flyer, such as the one shown in Figure 1–1, you should follow these general guidelines:
>
> 1. **Select template options.** The choice of an appropriate template, font, and color scheme is determined by the flyer's purpose and intended audience.
>
> 2. **Choose words for the text.** Follow the less is more principle. The less text, the more likely the flyer will be read. Use as few words as possible to make a point.
>
> 3. **Determine where to save the publication.** You can store a publication permanently, or **save** it, on a variety of storage media, including a hard disk, USB flash drive, or CD. You also can indicate a specific location on the storage media for saving the publication.
>
> 4. **Find the appropriate graphical image.** An eye-catching graphical image should convey the flyer's overall message. It could show a product, service, result, or benefit, or visually convey a message that is not expressed easily with words.
>
> 5. **Identify how to format various elements of the text.** The overall appearance of a publication significantly affects its ability to communicate clearly. Examples of how you can modify the appearance, or **format**, of text include changing its shape, size, color, and position on the page.
>
> 6. **Determine whether the flyer will be more effective as a print publication, Web publication, or both.** The flyer should grab the attention of passersby and draw them into reading the flyer, whether in person or via the Web.
>
> When necessary, more specific details concerning the above guidelines are presented at appropriate points in the chapter. The chapter also will identify the actions performed and decisions made regarding these guidelines during the creation of the flyer shown in Figure 1–1.

Starting Publisher

If you are using a computer to step through the project in this chapter, and you want your screen to match the figures in this book, you should change your screen's resolution to 1024 × 768. For information about how to change a computer's resolution, read Appendix E.

To Start Publisher

The following steps, which assume Windows Vista is running, start Publisher, based on a typical installation. You may need to ask your instructor how to start Publisher for your computer.

Note: If you are using Windows XP, see Appendix F for alternate steps.

- Click the Start button on the Windows Vista taskbar to display the Start menu.

- Click All Programs at the bottom of the left pane on the Start menu to display the All Programs list.

- Click Microsoft Office in the All Programs list to display the Microsoft Office list (Figure 1–2).

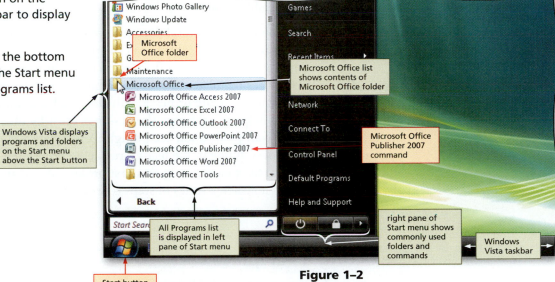

Figure 1–2

- Click Microsoft Office Publisher 2007 to start Publisher (Figure 1–3).

- If the Publisher window is not maximized, click the Maximize button next to the Close button on its title bar to maximize the window.

Q&A

What is a maximized window?

A maximized window fills the entire screen. When you maximize a window, the Maximize button changes to a Restore Down button.

Other Ways

1. Double-click Publisher icon on desktop, if one is present
2. Click Microsoft Office Publisher 2007 on Start menu

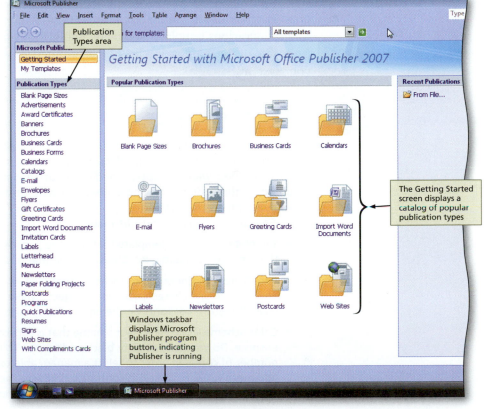

Figure 1–3

Using a Template to Create a Flyer

Publisher provides many ways to begin the process of creating and editing a publication. You can:

- Create a new publication from a design template
- Create a new publication or a Web page from scratch
- Create a new publication based on an existing one
- Open an existing publication

Choosing the appropriate method depends upon your experience with desktop publishing and how you have used Publisher in the past.

Because composing and designing from scratch is a difficult process for many people, Publisher provides templates to assist in publication preparation. Publisher has hundreds of templates to create professionally designed and unique publications. A **template** is a tool that helps you through the design process by offering you publication options and changing your publication accordingly. A template is similar to a blueprint you can use over and over, filling in the blanks, replacing prewritten text as necessary, and changing the art to fit your needs. In this first project, as you are beginning to learn about the features of Publisher, a series of steps is presented to create a publication using a design template.

Selecting a Template

In the Getting Started with Microsoft Office Publisher 2007 window (Figure 1–3 on the previous page), Publisher displays a list of publication types on the left side of the screen. **Publication types** are typical publications used by desktop publishers. The more popular types also are displayed in the center of the window. Each publication type is a link to display various templates and blank publications from which you may choose. On the right side of the window is a list of recent publications that have been created or edited on your system.

BTW

Starting Publisher
When you first start Publisher, the Getting Started with Microsoft Office Publisher 2007 window usually is displayed. If it is not displayed, click Options on the Tools menu, and then click Show Publication Types when starting Publisher on the General sheet. See Appendix E for additional customization features.

Plan Ahead

> **Select template options.**
> Publisher flyer templates are organized by purpose. A good flyer must deliver a message in the clearest, most attractive and effective way possible. The purpose is to communicate a single concept, notion, or product in a quick, easy-to-read format. The intended audience may be a wide, nonspecific audience, such as those who walk by a community bulletin board, or the audience may be a more narrowly defined, specialized audience, such as those who visit an auction Web site.
>
> Four primary choices must be made:
>
> - **Template** – Choose a template that suits the purpose with headline and graphic placement that attracts your audience. Choose a style that has meaning for the topic.
>
> - **Font Scheme** – Choose a font scheme that gives your flyer a consistent professional appearance and characterizes your subject. Make intentional decisions about the font style. Repetition of fonts on the page adds consistency to flyers.
>
> - **Color Scheme** – Choose a color scheme that is consistent with your company, client, or purpose. Do you need color or black and white? Think about the plan for printing and the number of copies in order to select a manageable color scheme. Remember that you can add more visual interest and contrast by bolding the colors in the scheme; however, keep in mind that too many colors can detract from the flyer and make it difficult to read.
>
> - **Contact Information Object** – Decide if you need a contact information tear-off. Is there something specific that may be difficult for your audience to remember? What kind of tear-off makes sense for your topic and message?

To Select a Template

Once you select a publication type, the window changes to allow you to select a specific template. Clicking a publication type causes a **catalog** of template previews to be displayed in the center of the window. The previews are organized into three categories with links to each category at the top of the window. Each category then is organized by purpose (for example, Sales) and then alphabetically by design type. On the right, Publisher will display a larger preview of the selected template, along with some customization options, as you will see in the following steps.

1
- Click the Flyers button in the Publication Types area to display the catalog of flyer templates (Figure 1–4).

🔍 Experiment

- Scroll in the catalog area and click various flyers in the catalog. Watch the preview change in the top-right portion of the window.

Q&A

Where are the subcategories or purposes listed?

In Figure 1–4 you can see the word, Informational, just below Newer Designs. Each purpose will be listed with a similar heading and a light blue division line.

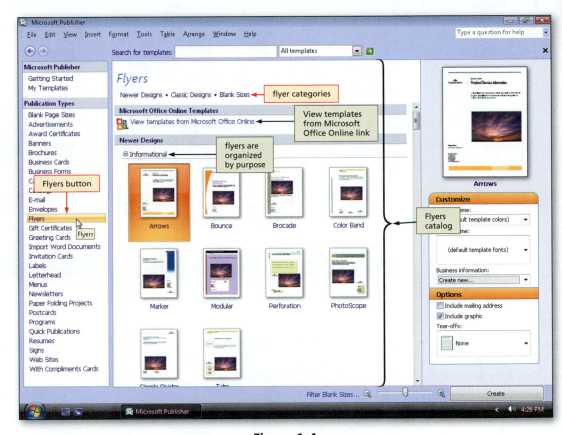

Figure 1–4

2

• Click the Classic Designs link at the top of the catalog to display flyer templates from the Classic Designs.

• Click the down scroll arrow until Special Offer flyers are displayed (Figure 1–5).

Q&A What does the minus sign mean beside Special Offer?

You can click the minus sign to collapse the Special Offer group of templates so that the previews no longer display.

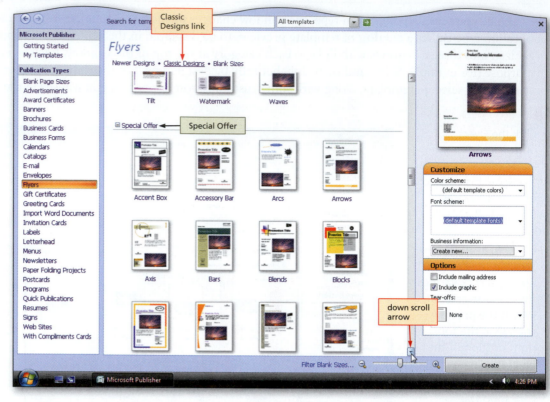

Figure 1–5

3

• Scroll down and then click the Capsules preview to choose the Capsules flyer template (Figure 1–6).

Q&A Can I change the number of templates that display at one time on the screen?

Yes, you can click the Zoom Out or Zoom In button on the status bar to change the way the screen is displayed. If you zoom out to display more templates, the previews are smaller.

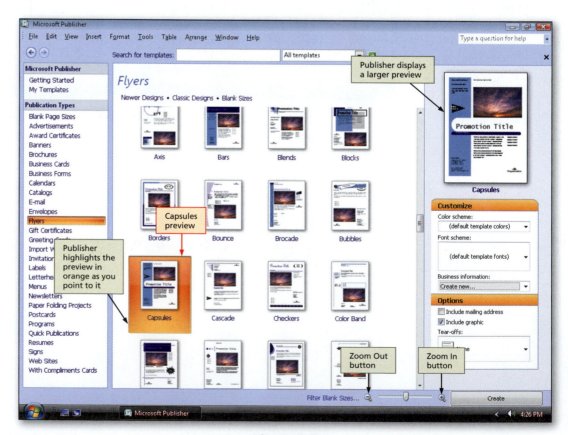

Figure 1–6

Setting Publication Options

Once you choose a publication from the catalog, Publisher will allow you to make choices about the color scheme, font schemes, and other components of the publication.

A **color scheme** is a defined set of colors that complement each other when used in the same publication. Each Publisher color scheme provides a main color and four accent colors. A **font scheme** is a defined set of fonts associated with a publication. A **font**, or typeface, defines the appearance and shape of the letters, numbers, and special characters. For example, a font scheme might be made up of one font for headings and another for body text and captions. Font schemes make it easy to change all the fonts in a publication to give it a new look. Within each font scheme, both a major font and a minor font are specified. Generally, a major font is used for titles and headings, and a minor font is used for body text.

Other options allow you to choose to include business information, a mailing address, a graphic, or tear-offs. As you choose customization options, the catalog and preview will reflect your choices.

Publisher Templates
Many additional templates can be downloaded from Microsoft Office Online. The View templates from Microsoft Office Online link, which can be used to view the online templates, is displayed near the top of the catalog, as shown in Figure 1–4 on page PUB 7.

To Set Publication Options

1
- Click the Color scheme box arrow in the Customize area to display the list of color schemes (Figure 1–7).

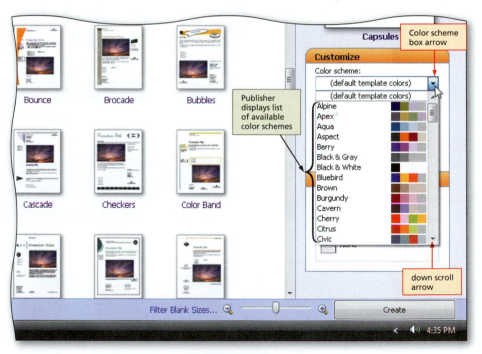

Figure 1–7

2

• Scroll down in the list and then click Sapphire to select the Sapphire color scheme (Figure 1–8).

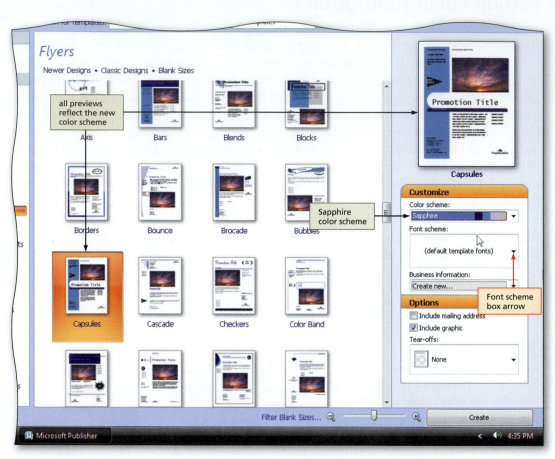

Figure 1–8

3

• Click the Font scheme box arrow in the Customize area to display the list of font schemes (Figure 1–9).

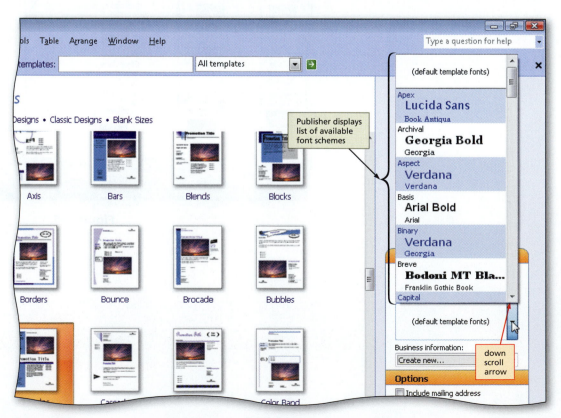

Figure 1–9

4
- Scroll down in the list and then click Civic to select the Civic font scheme (Figure 1–10).

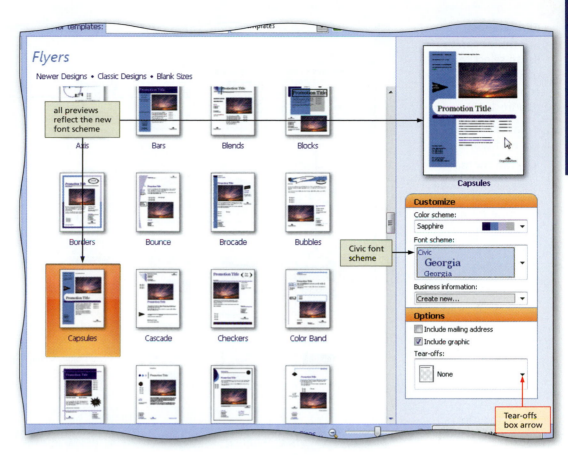

Figure 1–10

5
- Click the Tear-offs box arrow in the Options area to display a list of tear-offs (Figure 1–11).

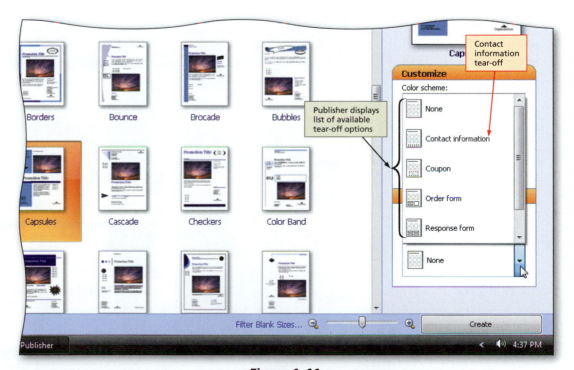

Figure 1–11

6

- Click Contact information in the list to select tear-offs that will display contact information (Figure 1–12).

Q&A

What are the other kinds of tear-offs?

You can choose to display tear-offs for coupons, order forms, response forms, and sign-up forms.

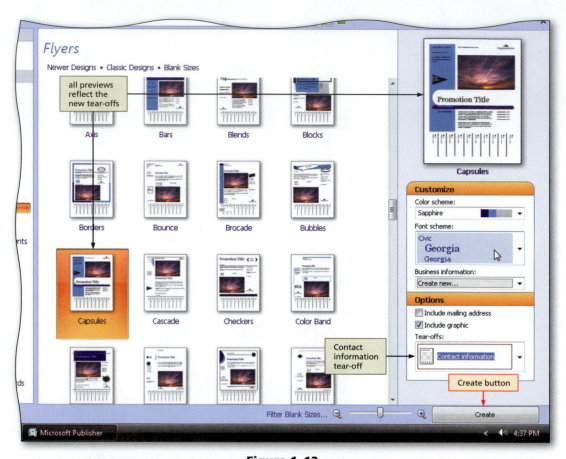

Figure 1–12

7

- Click the Create button on the status bar to create the publication using the selected template and options (Figure 1–13).

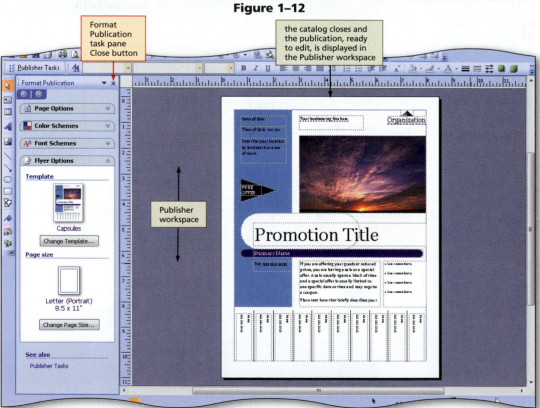

Figure 1–13

The Publisher Window

The Publisher window consists of a variety of components to make your work more efficient and your publication more professional. The following sections discuss these components.

The Workspace

The **workspace** contains several elements similar to the document windows of other applications, as well as some elements unique to Publisher. As you create a publication, the page layout, rulers, scroll bars, guides and boundaries, and status bar are displayed in the gray workspace (Figure 1–14). Objects can display on the page layout or in the gray workspace.

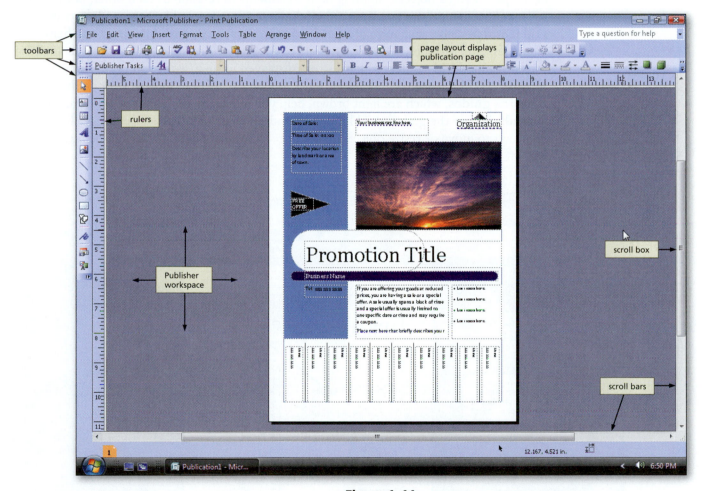

Figure 1–14

Page Layout   The **page layout** contains a view of the publication page, all the objects contained therein, plus the guides and boundaries for the page and its objects. The page layout can be changed to accommodate multipage spreads. You also can use the Special Paper command to view your page layout, as it will be printed on special paper, or see the final copy after preparing your publication for a printing service.

Rulers Two rulers outline the workspace at the top and left. A **ruler** is used to measure and place objects on the page. Although the vertical and horizontal rulers display at the left and top of the workspace, they can be moved and placed anywhere you need them. You use the rulers to measure and align objects on the page, set tab stops, adjust text frames, and change margins. Additionally, the rulers can be hidden to show more of the workspace. You will learn more about rulers in a later chapter.

Scroll Bars By using **scroll bars**, you display different portions of your publication in the workspace. At the right edge of the publication window is a vertical scroll bar. At the bottom of the publication window is a horizontal scroll bar. On both the vertical and horizontal scroll bars, the position of the **scroll box** reflects the location of the portion of the publication that is displayed in the publication window.

Guides and Boundaries Publisher's page layout displays the guides and boundaries of the page and its objects. Aligning design elements in relation to each other, both vertically and horizontally, is a tedious task; therefore, three types of **layout guides** create a grid that repeats on each page of a publication to define sections of the page and help you align elements with precision (Figure 1–15). **Margin guides** are displayed in blue at all four margins. **Grid guides**, which also are displayed in blue, assist you in organizing text pictures and objects into columns and rows to give a consistent look to your publication. **Baseline guides**, which are light brown, help you align text horizontally across text boxes. **Boundaries** are the gray, dotted lines surrounding an object. Boundaries are useful when you want to move or resize objects on the page. Boundaries and guides can be turned on and off using the View menu.

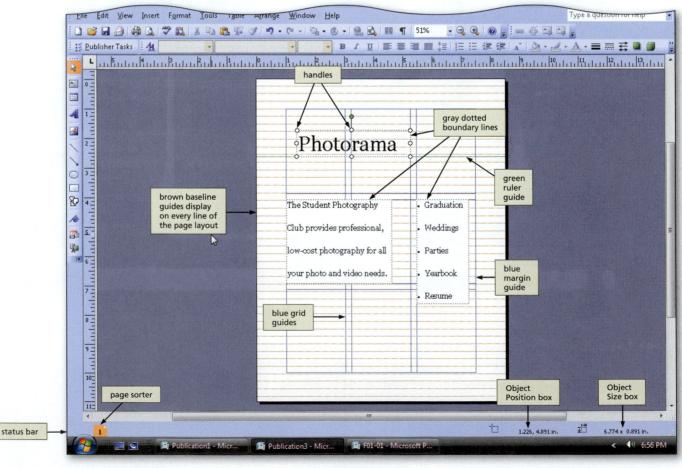

Figure 1–15

Status Bar   Immediately above the Windows taskbar at the bottom of the Publisher window is the status bar. In Publisher, the **status bar** contains the page sorter, the Object Position box, and the Object Size box (Figure 1–15).

The **page sorter** displays a button for each page of your publication. The current page in a multipage document will display selected in orange in the page sorter. You may click any page to display it in the workspace or right-click to display the page sorter shortcut menu.

As an alternative to using the rulers, you can use the **Object Position** and **Object Size boxes** as guidelines for lining up objects from the left and top margins. The exact position and size of a selected object is displayed in inches as you create or move it. You may choose to have the measurement displayed in pica, points, or centimeters. If no object is selected, the Object Position box displays the location of the mouse pointer. Double-clicking the status bar will display the Measurements toolbar. You will learn more about the Measurements toolbar in a future project.

Objects   Objects include anything you want to place in your publication, such as text, WordArt, tear-offs, graphics, pictures, bookmarks, bullets, lines, and Web tools. You click an object to **select** it; selected objects are displayed with **handles** at each corner and middle location of the object boundary. Many objects also display a green rotation handle connected to the top of the object or a yellow adjustment handle used to change the shape of some objects. A selected object can be resized, rotated, moved, deleted, or grouped with other objects. To select an object such as a picture, click the picture. The entire object is selected automatically. If you want to select a text box, however, you must click the boundary of the text box rather than the text inside. You will learn more about object manipulation later in the project.

BTW

Toolbar Rows
The Standard and Connect Frames toolbars are preset to display on one row, immediately below the menu bar. The Publisher Tasks and Formatting toolbar are displayed below that. If the resolution of your display differs from that in the book, some of the buttons that belong on these toolbars may not appear. Use the **Toolbar Options button** to display these hidden buttons.

Menu Bar and Toolbars

Publisher displays the menu bar at the top of the screen just below the title bar. Other toolbars display below the menu bar; another toolbar is displayed down the left side of the Publisher Window (Figure 1–16).

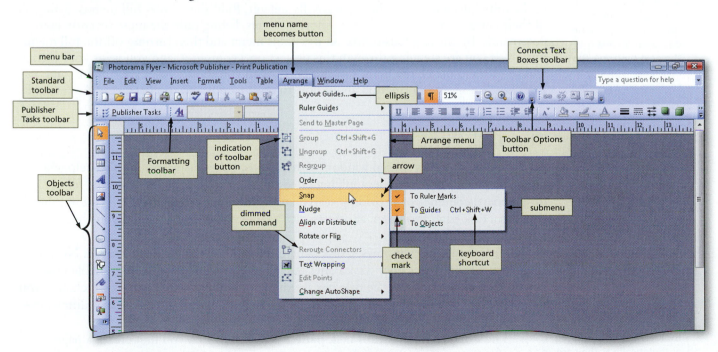

Figure 1–16

Positioning Toolbars

Initially Publisher displays **docked toolbars**, or ones that are attached to the edge of the Publisher window. Additional toolbars may be displayed either stacked below the Formatting toolbar or floating in the Publisher window. A **floating toolbar** is not attached to an edge of the Publisher window. You can rearrange the order of docked toolbars and can move floating toolbars anywhere in the Publisher window by dragging the move handle to the desired location. You will learn about other toolbars in future projects. If you do not see a toolbar in the window, click Toolbars on the View menu and then click the name of the toolbar you want to be displayed.

Toolbar Settings

Each time you start Publisher, the Publisher window is displayed the same way it was the last time you used Publisher. If the toolbar buttons are displayed on one row, then they will be displayed on one row the next time you start Publisher. Typically, four toolbars are displayed on two rows when you first install Publisher: the Standard toolbar, the Connect Frames toolbar, the Publisher Tasks toolbar, and the Formatting toolbar. You can display or hide toolbars by right-clicking any toolbar and clicking the appropriate check boxes, or by clicking Toolbars on the View menu.

As you work through creating a publication, you will find that other toolbars will be displayed automatically as they are needed in order to edit particular types of objects in Publisher.

Menu Bar The **menu bar** is a special toolbar displaying at the top of the window, just below the Publisher title bar. The menu bar lists the menu names. When you point to a **menu name** on the menu bar, the area of the menu bar containing the name displays a button. Publisher shades selected buttons in light orange.

When you click a menu name, Publisher displays a menu. A **menu** contains a list of commands to retrieve, store, print, and manipulate data in the publication (Figure 1–16 on the previous page). In the menu, if you point to a command with an arrow to its right, a **submenu** is displayed. An ellipsis (…) denotes that Publisher will display a dialog box when you click that menu command. **Keyboard shortcuts**, when available, are displayed to the right of menu commands. If a toolbar button exists for the command, it is displayed to the left of the menu command. A check mark displayed left of the menu command indicates the setting currently is being used. A **dimmed command** is displayed gray, or dimmed, instead of black, which indicates it is not available for the current selection.

Toolbars Toolbars contain buttons and boxes that allow you to perform frequent tasks more quickly than when using the menu bar. For example, to print a publication, you can click the Print button on a toolbar instead of navigating through the File menu.

Each button on a toolbar has a picture on its face that helps you remember its function. In addition, when you move the mouse pointer over a button or box, the name of the button or box is displayed below it in a **ScreenTip**. Each button and box is explained in detail as it is used in the projects.

The **Standard toolbar** is displayed just below the menu bar. The **Connect Text Boxes toolbar** is displayed to the right of the Standard toolbar. Immediately below the Standard toolbar, on the second row, the **Publisher Tasks toolbar** provides access to the Publisher Tasks pane; the **Formatting toolbar** is displayed to its right. The **Objects toolbar** is displayed on the left edge of the Publisher window. Additional toolbars, such as the Measurements toolbar, the Picture toolbar, and WordArt toolbar, are object-specific, which means they are displayed only when you use that specific type of object.

Resetting Menus and Toolbars

Each project in this book begins with the menus and toolbars displaying as they did at the initial installation of the software. By default, Publisher shows full menus, listing all of their commands. You can display shorter menus, listing only the most recently used commands, by clicking Customize on the Tools menu and then turning off the full menu option. If you are stepping through this project on a computer, and you want your menus and toolbars to match the figures in this book, then you should reset your menus and toolbars. For more information about how to reset menus and toolbars, read Appendix E.

The Task Pane

A **task pane** is a special window with buttons, boxes, lists, and links to help you perform specific tasks, such as applying publication options or styles, inserting clip art or clipboard contents, or providing search and replace options (Figure 1–17). Publisher displays a task pane at startup, at other times when it is needed, or when you choose Task Pane from the View menu.

Similar to other windows, a task pane has a title bar with a Close button. Next to the Close button is an Other Task Panes button, which displays a list of available task panes when clicked. Below the title bar are the Back and Forward buttons which help you move among recently viewed task panes. Below that, each task pane's content differs; the content will be explained as each task pane is used.

The **Format Publication task pane** is displayed when you first create a page layout. It contains four choices that display options related to page, color, font, and the publication type, to help you format your publication.

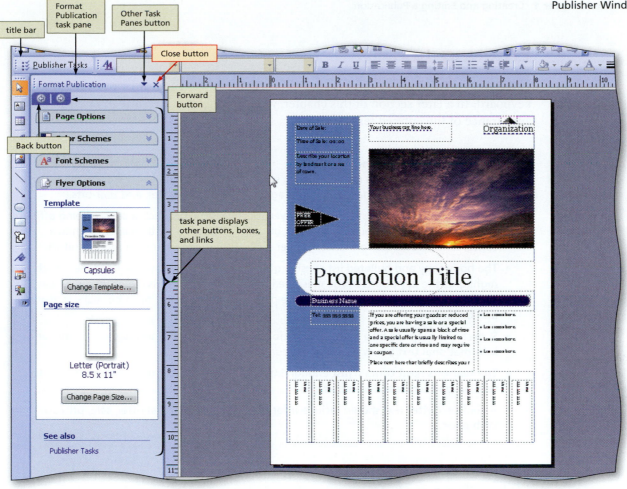

title bar

Format Publication task pane

Other Task Panes button

Close button

Forward button

Back button

task pane displays other buttons, boxes, and links

Figure 1–17

To Close the Task Pane

Because you have already made decisions on the template, font, and color schemes, you can close the task pane as shown in the following step.

1
• Click the Close button on the Format Publication task pane title bar to close the task pane (Figure 1–18).

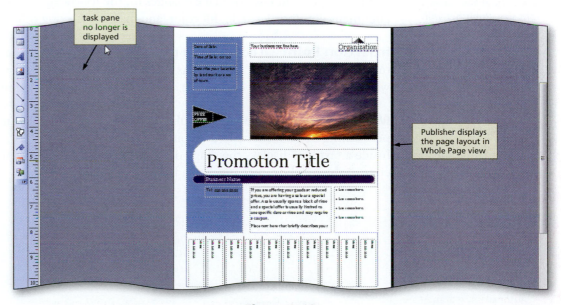

task pane no longer is displayed

Publisher displays the page layout in Whole Page view

Figure 1–18

Entering Text

The first step in editing a publication template is to replace its text by typing on the keyboard. In a later section of this chapter, you will learn how to format, or change the appearance of the entered text.

Plan Ahead

> **Choose the words for the text.**
> The text in a flyer usually is organized into several areas: headline, body copy, bulleted lists, business name, informational text boxes, tag lines, attention getter, and tear-offs.
>
> - The headline is the largest text on the flyer. It conveys the product or service being offered, such as a car for sale or personal lessons, or the benefit that will be gained, such as a convenience, better performance, greater security, higher earnings, or more comfort.
>
> - The body copy and bulleted list consists of descriptive text below the headline, which highlights the key points of the message in as few words as possible. It should be easy to read and follow. While emphasizing the positive, the body text must be realistic, truthful, and believable.
>
> - Sometimes supplied by a database or information set, the business name, tag line, and informational text boxes need to be accurate and easy to read.
>
> - The tear-offs must contain just enough information to contact the flyer's creator or to turn around requested information.
>
> - Attention getter text should include information about a special offer, sale, price, or Web page.

Using Text Boxes

BTW

Flyer Templates
Some flyer templates include a headline text box whose font size is copyfitted, or self-adjusting. If you type too many words in the text box to fit at the current font size, Publisher will autofit the text and reduce the font size to make all the words fit in the box. Clicking AutoFit Text on the Format menu will display a submenu allowing you to change the way text is copyfitted in a text box.

Most of the templates in the design catalog come with text already inserted into text boxes. A **text box** is an object in a publication designed to hold text in a specific shape, size, and style. Text boxes also can be drawn on the page using the Text Box Button on the Objects toolbar. Text boxes can be formatted from the task pane, on the Formatting toolbar, or on the **shortcut menu** displayed by right-clicking the text box. A text box has changeable properties. A **property** is an attribute or characteristic of an object. Within text boxes, you can **edit**, or make changes to, the following properties: font, spacing, alignment, line/border style, fill color, and margins, among others.

Insertion Point   The **insertion point** is a blinking vertical bar that indicates where text will be inserted in a text box. As you type, the insertion point moves to the right, and when you reach the end of a line, it moves downward to the beginning of the next line.

Mouse Pointer   The **mouse pointer** changes shape, depending on the task you are performing in Publisher and the pointer's location on the screen. The mouse pointer inside a text box displays the shape of an I-beam. If the mouse pointer is positioned on the edge of the text box, it changes to a four-headed arrow.

To Enter Text

Flyers typically display a **headline**, or title, using the major font from the font scheme. A headline is designed to identify, with just a few words, the purpose of the flyer and to draw attention to the flyer. Text in the Business Name text box can be entered manually or filled in from information sets of data entered into the software. You will learn about information sets in a later chapter.

Two types of text selection are used in Publisher templates. **Placeholder text**, or text supplied by the template, is selected with a single click, allowing you to begin typing immediately. Other text, such as the business name, address, or tag line, is selected by pressing CTRL+A to select all of the text in the text box before you type. The following steps select and replace template text.

1
- Click the headline text to select it (Figure 1–19).

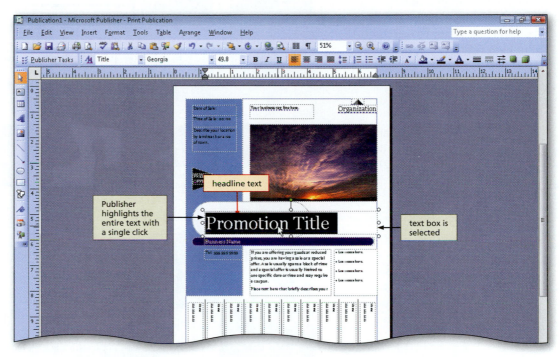

Figure 1–19

2
- Type Photorama as the headline text (Figure 1–20).

Q&A

What if I make an error while typing?

You can press the BACKSPACE key until you have deleted the text in error and then retype the text correctly.

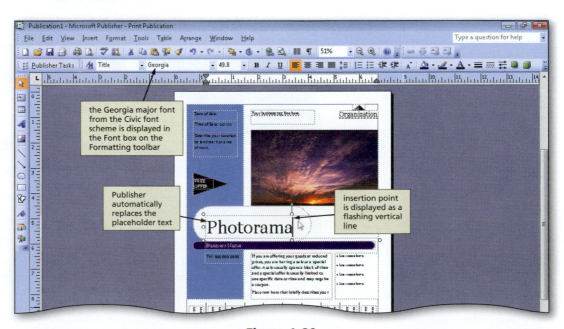

Figure 1–20

3

- Click the text in the Business Name text box to begin editing the text (Figure 1–21).

Q&A

Why does the text have a red, wavy line underneath it?

Publisher is checking for spelling errors. The word, Photorama, is not in Publisher's dictionary. Publisher flags potential errors in the publication with a red wavy underline. Later in the project, you will learn how to use the spell checking features of Publisher to make the red, wavy line disappear.

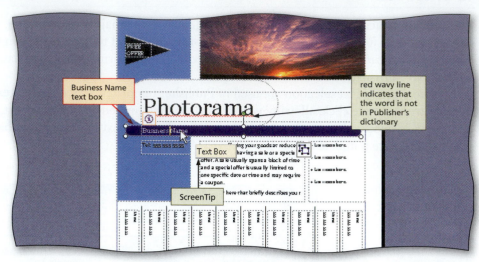

Figure 1–21

4

- Press CTRL+A on the keyboard to select all of the text in the Business Name text box (Figure 1–22).

Q&A

What is the button that is displayed with the i on it?

That is a smart tag button. If you click it, Publisher offers to fill in the text for you with various options. **Smart tag buttons** display when you point to certain text boxes that are part of the business information set or when you click a logo.

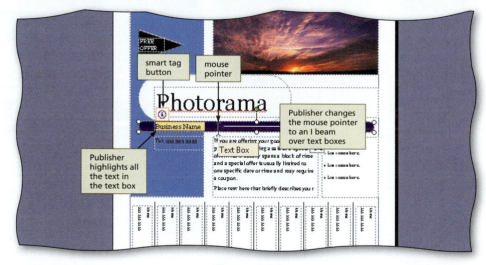

Figure 1–22

5

- Type Student Photography Club to replace the text (Figure 1–23).

Q&A

Why does a blue dotted line display beneath the text?

The blue or purple dotted lines beneath text in your presentation indicate that a smart tag is available for that data.

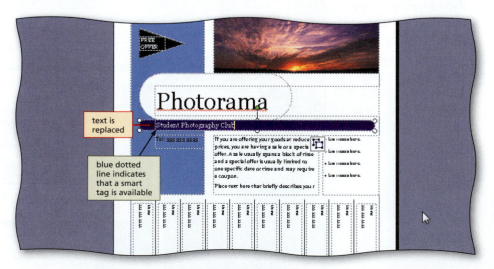

Figure 1–23

To Zoom

Sometimes the size of the text box or other Publisher object is small, and therefore, difficult to edit. Publisher provides several ways to **zoom in**, or increase the magnification of an object to facilitate viewing and editing.

Table 1–1 shows several zoom methods.

Table 1–1 Zoom Methods	
Method	**Result**
Press the F9 key on the keyboard.	Selected object is displayed, centered in the workspace at 100% magnification.
Click the Zoom box arrow on the Standard toolbar. Click the desired magnification.	Objects are displayed at selected magnification.
Click the Zoom In button on the Standard toolbar.	Objects are displayed at a higher magnification.
Right-click object. Point to Zoom on shortcut menu. Click the desired magnification.	Objects are displayed at selected magnification.
On the View menu, point to Zoom. Click the desired magnification.	Objects are displayed at selected magnification.

Editing small areas of text is easier if you use zooming techniques to enlarge the view of the publication. When viewing an entire printed page, 8½-by-11 inches, the magnification is approximately 51 percent, which makes reading the small text difficult. You may press the F9 key to enlarge selected objects to 100 percent magnification. Pressing the F9 key a second time returns the layout to its previous magnification. Publisher also allows you to zoom using the **Zoom box** on the Standard toolbar. Clicking the Zoom box arrow displays a list of magnifications, such as Whole Page, Page Width, and various magnifications. Additionally, the **Zoom In button** on the Standard toolbar allows you to increase magnification. If you click an object before zooming in, Publisher displays the selected object magnified, in the center of the workspace, when you zoom.

To Zoom and Enter Text

The following steps zoom and enter text.

- Click the text in the text box located in the upper-left corner of the template to select it (Figure 1–24).

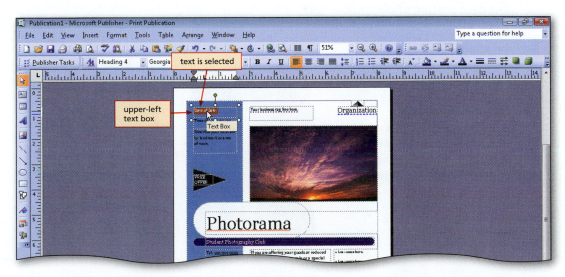

Figure 1–24

2

- Press the F9 key on the keyboard to zoom the text box to 100%. Type `Flexible Times` to replace the text (Figure 1–25).

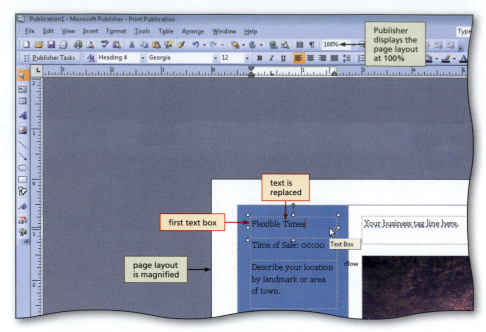

Figure 1–25

3

- Click the text, Time of Sale, to select it.

- Press and hold the SHIFT key while clicking the text, 00.00, to add it to the selection.

- To replace the text, type `Reasonable Rates` (Figure 1–26).

Q&A Why did I have to hold down the SHIFT key while clicking?

Some templates have two sets of placeholder text in individual text boxes. You can press CTRL+A to select all of the text or SHIFT+CLICK to select each portion of placeholder text.

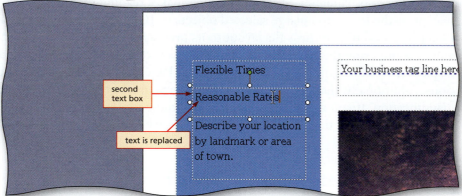

Figure 1–26

4

- To select the placeholder text in the Describe your location text box, click the text.

- Replace the placeholder text with the new text, `Student Photography Club meets every Wednesday at 7pm.` (Figure 1–27).

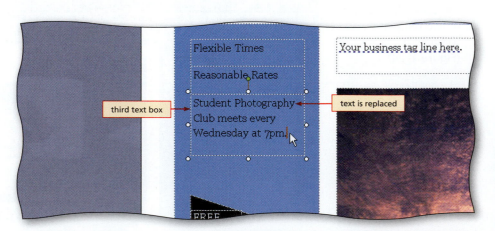

Figure 1–27

- Select the text in the text box that is displayed within the black triangle in order to replace it.
- Type **Student Discount** (Figure 1–28).

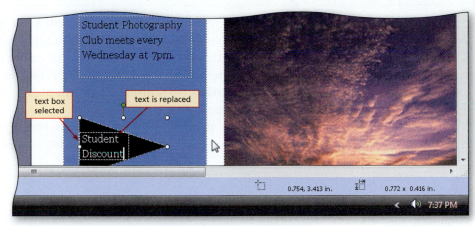

Figure 1–28

- Click the Zoom box arrow on the Standard toolbar (Figure 1–29).

Q&A

What is the best way to zoom to 100%?

If an object on the page is selected, pressing the F9 key toggles between a zoom of 100% and the previous zoom percentage. You also can choose 100% by clicking the Zoom box arrow and then clicking 100% in the list.

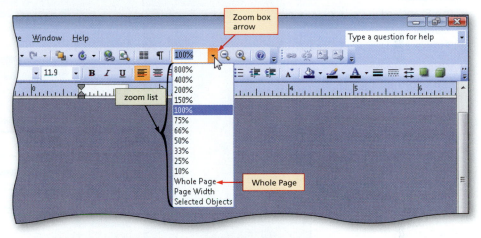

Figure 1–29

- Click Whole Page in the list to zoom to display the whole page (Figure 1–30).

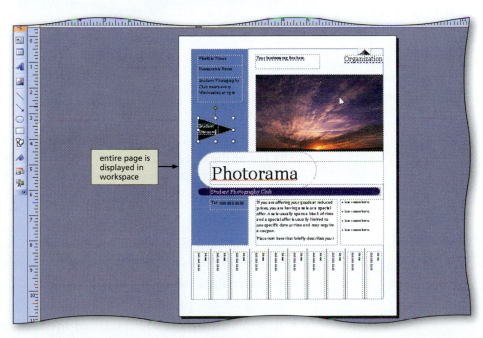

Figure 1–30

To Display Formatting Marks

To view where in a publication you pressed the ENTER key or SPACEBAR, you may find it helpful to display formatting marks. A **formatting mark**, sometimes called a **nonprinting character**, is a special character that Publisher displays on the screen, but one that is not visible on a printed publication. For example, the **paragraph mark** (¶) is a formatting mark that indicates where you pressed the ENTER key. A **raised dot** (·) shows where you pressed the SPACEBAR. An **end of field marker** (¤) is displayed to indicate the end of text in a text box. Other formatting marks are discussed as they appear on the screen.

Depending on settings made during previous Publisher sessions, your Publisher screen already may display formatting marks (Figure 1–31). The following step displays formatting marks, if they do not show already on the screen.

- If it is not selected already, click the Special Characters button on the Standard toolbar (Figure 1–31).

Q&A

What if I do not want formatting marks to show on the screen?

If you feel the formatting marks clutter the screen, you can hide them by clicking the Special Characters button again. The publication windows presented in this book show the formatting marks.

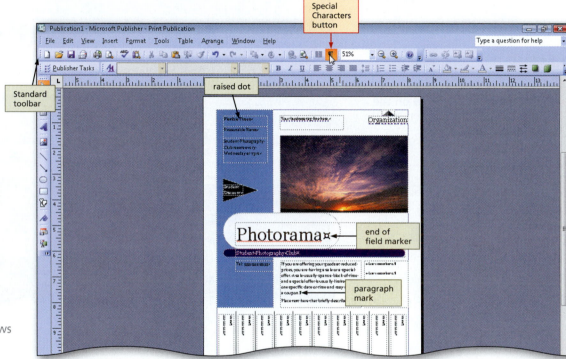

Figure 1–31

Other Ways

1. Press CTRL+SHIFT+Y

Wordwrap

Wordwrap allows you to type words in a text box continually without pressing the ENTER key at the end of each line. When the insertion point reaches the right margin of a text box, Publisher automatically positions the insertion point at the beginning of the next line. As you type, if a word extends beyond the right margin, Publisher also automatically positions that word on the next line along with the insertion point.

Publisher creates a new paragraph or hard return each time you press the ENTER key. Thus, as you type text in a text box, do not press the ENTER key when the insertion point reaches the right margin. Instead, press the ENTER key only in these circumstances:

- To insert blank lines in a text box
- To begin a new paragraph
- To terminate a short line of text and advance to the next line
- To respond to questions or prompts in Publisher dialog boxes, task panes, and other on-screen objects

To Wordwrap Text as You Type

The next step in creating the flyer is to type the body copy. The following step wordwraps the text in the body copy.

1
- Select the text in the center text box below the headline.

- Press the F9 key to zoom to 100%.

- Type The Student Photography Club provides professional, low-cost photography for all your photo and video needs. to replace the text (Figure 1–32).

Q&A

Why does my publication wrap on different words?

Differences in wordwrap relate to your printer. It is possible that the same publication could wordwrap differently if printed on different printers.

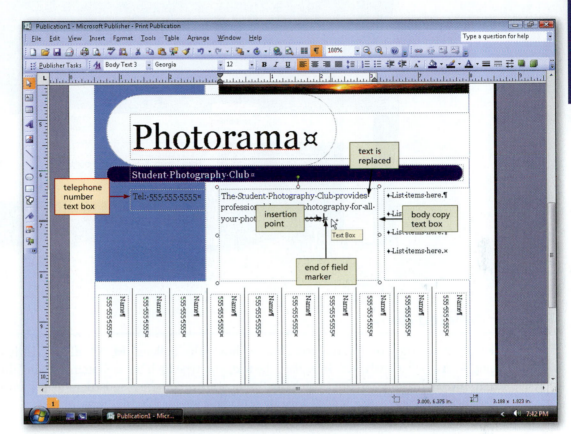

Figure 1–32

To Finish Entering Text

The following steps replace the text in the telephone number text box and the business tag line text box.

1 Select the text in the telephone text box.

2 Type Tel: 317 555 2008 to replace the text.

3 Zoom to Whole Page by pressing the F9 key on the keyboard.

4 Select the tag line text box at the top of the page.

5 Zoom to 100% by pressing the F9 key on the keyboard.

6 Select the text in the business tag line text box by pressing CTRL+A.

7 Type For all your photo and video needs (Figure 1–33 on the next page).

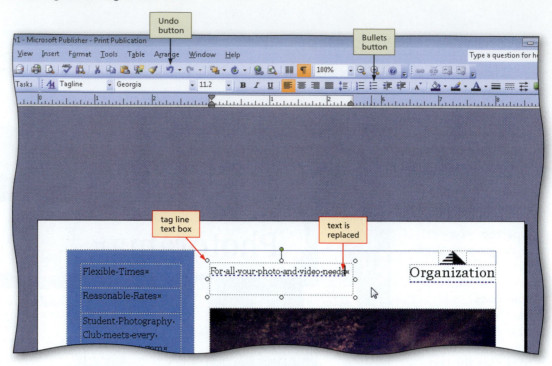

Figure 1–33

To Enter Bulleted Items

In the flyer, to the right of the body copy, is a text box with a bulleted list. A **bulleted list** is a series of paragraphs, each beginning with a bullet character. To replace the text, you type each bulleted item pressing the ENTER key at the end of each line. To turn bullets on or off, you click the **Bullets button** on the Standard toolbar (Figure 1-33).

The following steps create a bulleted list by replacing the placeholder text.

- Click the down scroll arrow until the bulleted list is displayed.

- Select the text in the bulleted list text box (Figure 1–34).

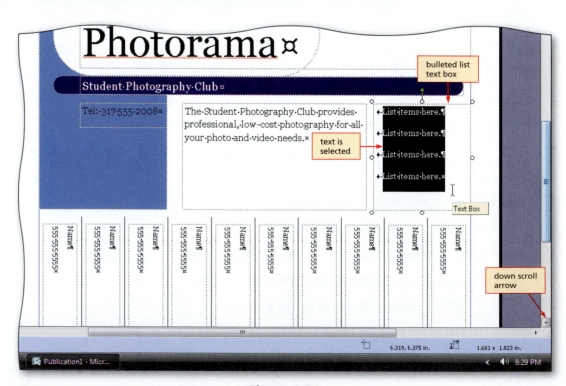

Figure 1–34

2

- Type Graduations and then press the ENTER key.

- Type Weddings and then press the ENTER key.

- Type Passports and then press the ENTER key.

- Type Yearbooks and then press the ENTER key.

- Type Resumes to complete the bullets (Figure 1–35).

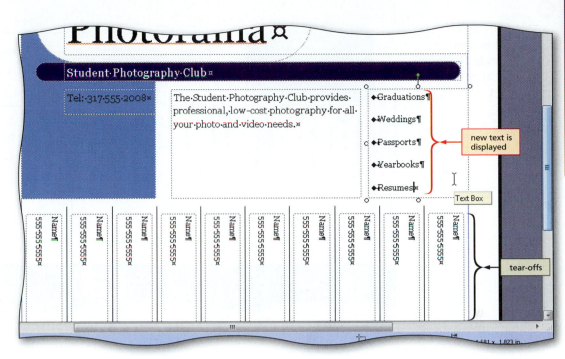

Figure 1–35

To Enter Tear-off Text

Across the lower portion of the flyer are contact information tear-offs. **Tear-offs** are small, ready-to-be scored text boxes with some combination of name, telephone, fax, e-mail, or address. Designed for customer use, tear-offs typically are perforated so a person walking by can tear off a tab to keep, rather than having to stop, find a pen and paper, and write down the name and telephone number. Traditionally, small businesses or individuals wanting to advertise something locally used tear-offs, but more recently, large companies are mass-producing advertising flyers with tear-offs to post at shopping centers, display in offices, and advertise on college campuses.

Publisher tear-offs contain replacement text and are **synchronized**, which means when you finish editing one of the tear-off text boxes, the others change to match it automatically. You may undo synchronization by clicking the **Undo button** on the Standard toolbar (Figure 1–33).

The following steps edit the tear-off text boxes.

1

- Click the text in one of the tear-off text boxes.

- Type E-mail: photorama@univ.edu and then press the ENTER key.

- Type Or call 317 555 2008 to complete the tear-off (Figure 1–36).

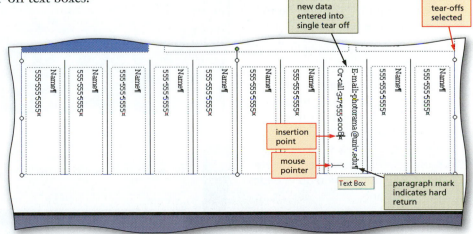

Figure 1–36

• Click outside of the text box to synchronize the other tear-offs (Figure 1–37).

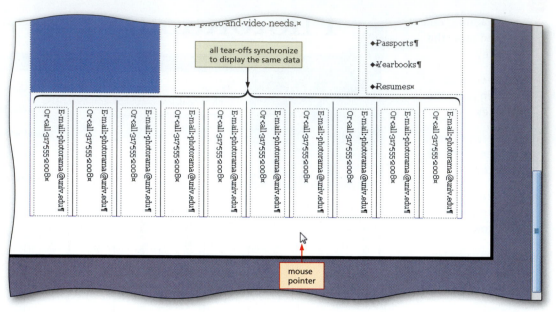

all tear-offs synchronize to display the same data

◆ Passports ¶

◆ Yearbooks ¶

◆ Resumes ¤

mouse pointer

Figure 1–37

Deleting Objects

Templates may display objects in the page layout that you do not wish to use. In those cases, or when you change your mind about including an inserted object, you must **delete objects**.

To Delete an Object

In order to delete an object, it must be selected. To select objects that contain text, you must click the object's boundary; you select other objects by clicking anywhere in the object. In the following steps, the logo is deleted.

• Scroll to the upper portion of the page to display the logo.

• Click the boundary of the logo to select it (Figure 1–38).

Q&A

What if I want to delete only the text?

To delete text inside a text box, click inside the text box rather than on a text box boundary. Then, you can select the text and press the DELETE key. Inside text boxes, you can use other backspace and delete key combinations as you do in basic word processing.

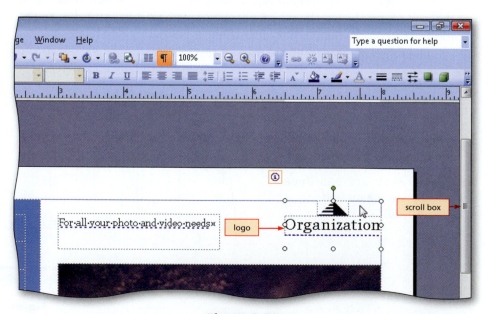

scroll box

logo

For all your photo and video needs ¤   Organization

Figure 1–38

- Press the DELETE key on your keyboard to delete the object (Figure 1–39).

Q&A

My logo was not deleted. Why did only the text disappear?

You clicked the text instead of the boundary of the logo. Logos supplied by the template are a combination of a logo picture and logo text. To delete them, you must select the entire object by clicking its boundary.

Q&A

What if I delete an object by mistake?

If you delete an object by mistake, you can click the Undo button on the Standard toolbar. The object will reappear in the original location.

Figure 1–39

Checking the Spelling

As you type text in a publication, Publisher checks your typing for possible spelling errors. As mentioned earlier, Publisher flags the potential error in the publication window with a red wavy underline. A red wavy underline means the flagged text is not in Publisher's dictionary (because it is a proper name or misspelled). Although you can check the entire publication for spelling errors at once, you also can check these flagged errors as they appear on the screen.

To display a list of corrections for flagged text, right-click the flagged text. When you right-click a flagged word, for example, a list of suggested spelling corrections is displayed in the shortcut menu. A flagged word, however, is not necessarily misspelled. For example, many names, abbreviations, and specialized terms are not in Publisher's main dictionary. In these cases, you tell Publisher to ignore the flagged word. As you type, Publisher also detects duplicate words while checking for spelling errors. For example, if your publication contains the phrase, to the the store, Publisher places a red wavy underline below the second occurrence of the word, the.

To Check Spelling as You Type

In the following steps, the word, Photorama, is not in Publisher's dictionary. You will direct Publisher to ignore the word. If you are doing this project on a computer, your flyer may contain other misspelled words, depending on the accuracy of your typing.

- Scroll to display the headline text.

- Right-click the flagged word, Photorama, in the headline to display a shortcut menu that includes a list of suggested spelling corrections for the flagged word (Figure 1–40).

Q&A What if Publisher does not flag my spelling errors with wavy underlines?

To verify that the Check spelling as you type features are enabled, point to Spelling on the Tools menu and then click Spelling Options. When the Spelling Options dialog box is displayed, ensure the 'Check spelling as you type' check box has a check mark. Also ensure the Hide spelling errors check box does not have a check mark. Click the OK button.

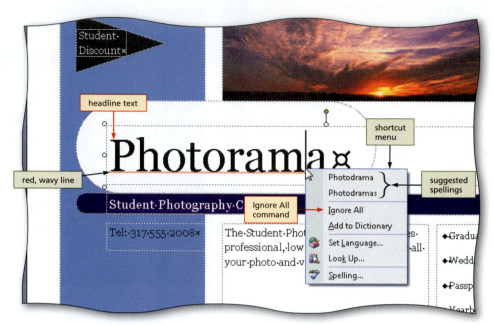

Figure 1–40

- Click Ignore All on the shortcut menu to direct Publisher to ignore the word, Photorama, which is not in its dictionary (Figure 1–41).

- Right-click any other words that display wavy lines to display a shortcut menu that includes a list of suggested spelling corrections for each flagged word.

- Choose the appropriate correct word on the shortcut menu.

Q&A What if, when I right-click the misspelled word, my desired correction is not in the list on the shortcut menu?

You can click outside the shortcut menu to close the menu and then retype the correct word, or you can click Spelling on the shortcut menu to display the Spelling dialog box which will be discussed in a later chapter.

Figure 1–41

Saving the Project

While you are creating a publication, the computer stores it in memory. When you save a publication, the computer places it on a storage medium, such as a USB flash drive, CD, or hard disk. A saved publication is referred to as a **file**. A **file name** is the name assigned to a file when it is saved.

It is important to save a publication frequently for the following reasons:

- The publication in memory will be lost if the computer is turned off, or you lose electrical power while Publisher is open.
- If you run out of time before completing your project, you may finish your publication at a future time without starting over.

BTW

The .pub extension
Some Microsoft Office 2007 applications use a new, four-letter extension on file names; however, Publisher saves print publications in a file format with the three-letter extension, .pub. The **.pub extension** allows Publisher easily to open your formatted file and assign a recognizable icon to the shortcut on your disk.

Plan Ahead

Determine where to save the publication.
When saving a publication, you must decide which storage medium to use.

- If you always work on the same computer and have no need to transport your projects to a different location, then your computer's hard drive will suffice as a storage location. It is a good idea, however, to save a backup copy of your projects on a separate medium in case the file becomes corrupted or the computer's hard disk fails.

- If you plan to work on your projects in various locations or on multiple computers, then you should save your projects on a portable medium, such as a USB flash drive or CD. The projects in this book use a USB flash drive, which saves files quickly and reliably and can be reused. CDs are easily portable and serve as good backups for the final versions of projects because they generally can save files only one time.

To Save a Publication

You have performed many tasks while creating this project and do not want to risk losing the work completed thus far. Accordingly, you should save the publication. The following steps save a publication on a USB flash drive using the file name, Photorama Flyer.

1

- With a USB flash drive connected to one of the computer's USB ports, click the Save button on the Standard Toolbar to display the Save As dialog box (Figure 1–42).

- If the Navigation pane is not displayed in the Save As dialog box, click the Browse Folders button to expand the dialog box.

- If a Folders list is displayed below the Folders button, click the Folders button to remove the Folders list.

Q&A

Do I have to save to a USB flash drive?

No. You can save to any device or folder. A **folder** is a specific location on a storage medium. You can save to the default folder or a different folder. You also can create your own folders, which is explained later in this book.

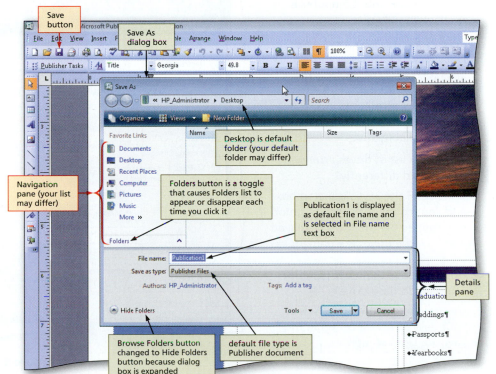

Figure 1–42

2

- Type `Photorama Flyer` in the File name text box to change the file name. Do not press the ENTER key after typing the file name (Figure 1–43).

What characters can I use in a file name?

A file name can have a maximum of 260 characters, including spaces. The only invalid characters are the backslash (\), slash (/), colon (:), asterisk (*), question mark (?), quotation mark ("), less than symbol (<), greater than symbol (>), and vertical bar (|).

What are file properties and tags?

File properties contain information about a file, such as the file name, author name, date the file was modified, size, and tags. A **tag** is a file property that contains a word or phrase about a file. You can organize and locate files based on their file properties.

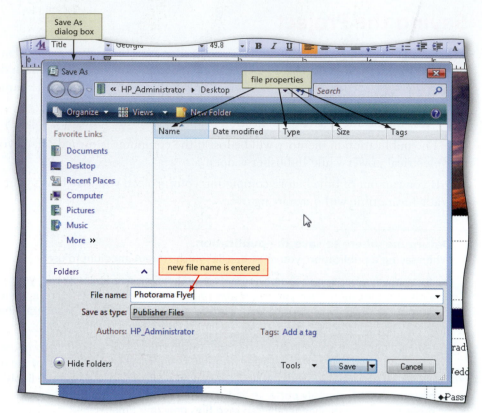

Figure 1–43

3

- If Computer is not displayed in the Favorite Links section, drag the top or bottom edge of the Save As dialog box until Computer is displayed.

- Click Computer in the Favorite Links section to display a list of available drives (Figure 1–44).

- If necessary, scroll until USB (F:) appears in the list of available drives.

Why is my list of drives arranged and named differently?

The size of the Save As dialog box and your computer's configuration determine how the list is displayed and how the drives are named.

How do I save the file if I am not using a USB flash drive?

Use the same process, but select your desired save location in the Favorite Links section.

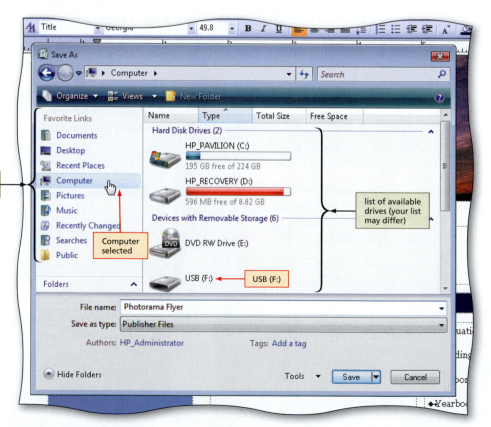

Figure 1–44

4

- Double-click USB (F:) in the Computer list to open the USB flash drive, Drive F in this case, as the new save location (Figure 1–45).

Q&A What if my USB flash drive has a different name or letter?

It is very likely that your USB flash drive will have a different name and drive letter and be connected to a different port.

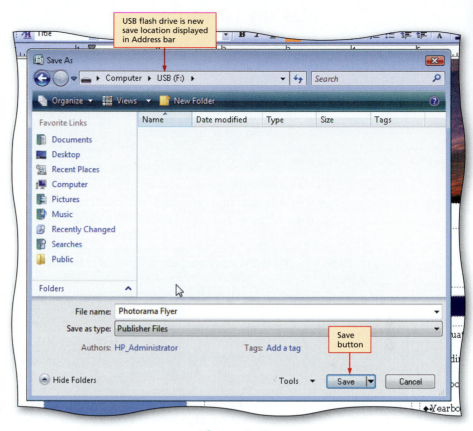

Figure 1–45

5

- Click the Save button in the Save As dialog box to save the publication on the USB flash drive with the file name, Photorama Flyer (Figure 1–46).

Q&A How do I know that the project is saved?

While Publisher is saving your file, Windows briefly displays a busy mouse pointer, while it accesses the storage device. In addition, your USB drive may have a light that flashes during the save process. The title bar and task bar button display the new file name.

Other Ways

1. Click File on the menu bar, click Save As, type file name, click Computer, select drive or folder, click Save button
2. Press CTRL+S, type file name, click Computer, select drive or folder, click Save button

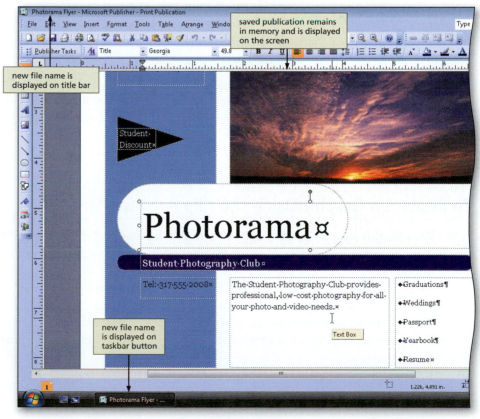

Figure 1–46

Using Graphics

Files containing graphical images, also called **graphics**, are available from a variety of sources. Publisher includes a series of predefined graphics, such as drawings, photographs, sounds, videos, and other media files, called clips. A **clip** is a single media file, including art, sound, animation, or movies, that you can insert and use in print publications, Web publications, and other Microsoft Office documents.

Clip art is an inclusive term given to a variety of predefined graphics, such as images, artwork, and draw-type images, which are created from a set of instructions (also called object-based or vector graphics). You can search for graphics and clip art based on descriptive keywords, file name, file format, or clip collection. The **clip collection** is a hierarchical organization of media clips. You can create your own clip collections; import clip collections; or add, move, or copy clips from one collection to another.

Plan Ahead

Find the appropriate graphical image.
To use graphical images, also called graphics, in a Publisher publication, the image must be stored digitally in a file. Files containing graphical images are available from a variety of sources:

- Publisher includes a collection of predefined graphical images that you can insert in a publication.

- Microsoft has free digital images on the Web for use in a publication. Other Web sites also have images available, some of which are free, while others require a fee.

- You can take a picture with a digital camera and **download** it, which is the process of copying the digital picture from the camera to your computer.

- Appropriate images not only should refer to the context of the publication, but also should represent the reality of that context. If you are trying to sell something or describe a person or place, use a photograph. If you are describing a service or general object, you can use clip art. For example, if you are trying to sell a used car, try to use a real picture of the car. If you're describing cars in general, you can use clip art.

- With a scanner, you can convert a printed picture, drawing, or diagram to a digital file.

If you receive a picture from a source other than yourself, do not use the file until you are certain it does not contain a virus. A **virus** is a computer program that can damage files and programs on your computer. Use an antivirus program to verify that any files you use are virus free.

To Replace a Graphic Using the Clip Art Task Pane

Because this flyer is advertising photographic services, it is more appropriate to choose a graphic related to photography than the picture of the sunset supplied by the template. A graphic should enhance the message of the publication.

In Publisher templates, clip art and pictures commonly are placed within a picture frame. A **picture frame** is an invisible border that helps with placement and text wrapping.

The following steps retrieve an appropriate graphic using the **Clip Art task pane** to replace the supplied graphic. If you cannot access the graphic described, choose a suitable replacement from your system's clip art.

1

- If necessary, zoom to display the Whole Page.

- Click the graphic to select the picture frame.

- Click the graphic again to select the picture within the frame.

- Right-click the graphic to display its shortcut menu.

- Point to Change Picture to display the Change Picture submenu (Figure 1–47).

Why did the sizing handles turn gray with an x inside?

When the frame is selected, the sizing handles are white. When the picture within the frame is selected, Publisher changes the sizing handles so you know you are manipulating the picture rather than the frame.

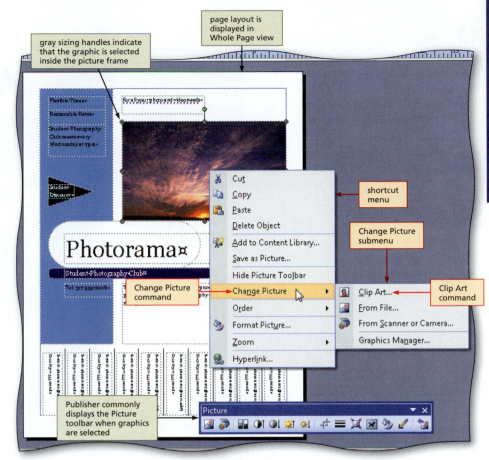

Figure 1–47

2

- Click Clip Art on the Change Picture submenu to display the Clip Art task pane.

- When the Clip Art task pane is displayed, if the Search for text box contains text, drag through the text to select it.

- Type photography in the Search for text box to enter a searchable key word (Figure 1–48).

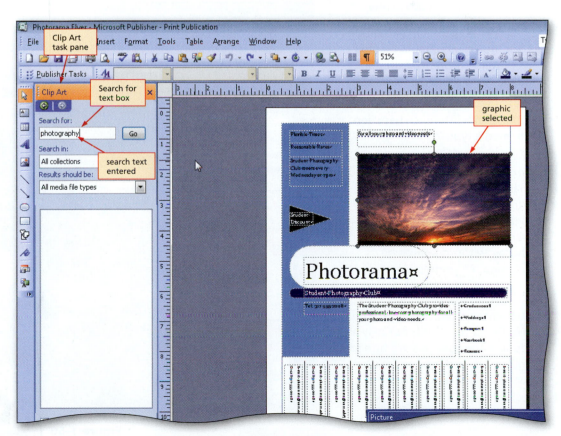

Figure 1–48

3

• Click the Search in box arrow and click the Everywhere check box so that it displays a check mark (Figure 1–49).

Q&A

What if I am not connected to the Web?

If you are not connected to the Web, your Web collections check box will not be checked. Your search then would be limited to the clip art installed locally on your system.

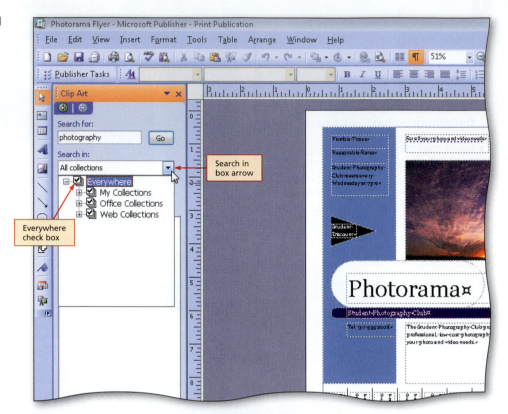

Figure 1–49

4

• Click the Search in box arrow again to close the list.

• Click the Results should be box arrow and ensure that the All media types check box displays a check mark (Figure 1–50).

Q&A

What is the difference between the media types?

The Results should be box arrow displays four types of media to include in the search results: Clip Art, Photographs, Movies, and Sounds. Clip art includes all images that are not real photos, without animation or sound. Photographs are pictures of real objects. Movies include all clips that have any kind of animation or action. Sounds do not display a graphic, but play a sound if the speakers are turned on. Sounds and movies are used for Web publications.

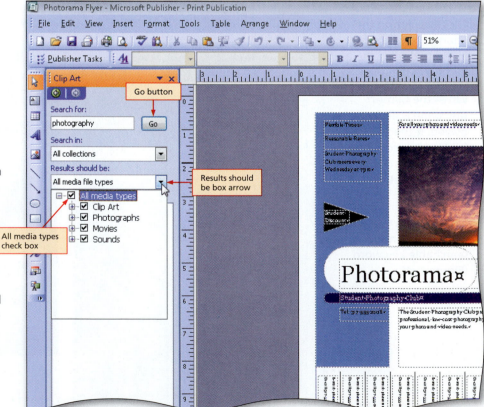

Figure 1–50

5

- Click the Go button to begin the search for clip art (Figure 1–51).

Q&A

What are the links at the bottom of the Clip Art task pane?

You can click the link, Organize clips, to open the Microsoft Clip Organizer. You can use the Clip Organizer to browse through clip collections, add clips, or catalog clips in ways that make sense to you. For example, you can create a collection to group the clips you use most frequently, or let the Clip Organizer automatically add and catalog clips on your hard disk. The second link opens a Web browser and displays content from Microsoft Office Online. The third link offers tips from the Publisher Help system on finding clips.

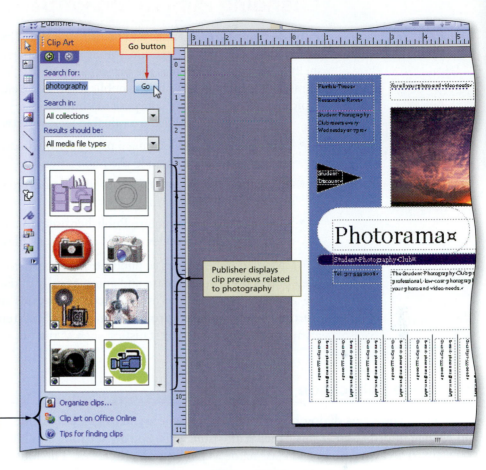

Go button

Publisher displays clip previews related to photography

clip art links

Figure 1–51

6

- When the previews are displayed, click the down scroll arrow until the preview of the photography equipment is displayed.

- Click the preview shown in Figure 1–52 or another one from your clip art collection to replace the current graphic.

7

- Click the close button in the Clip Art task pane title bar to close the task pane.

Other Ways

1. On Insert menu, point to Picture, click Clip Art, enter search criteria, click preview

2. Double-click non-grouped graphic, enter search criteria in Clip Art task pane, click preview

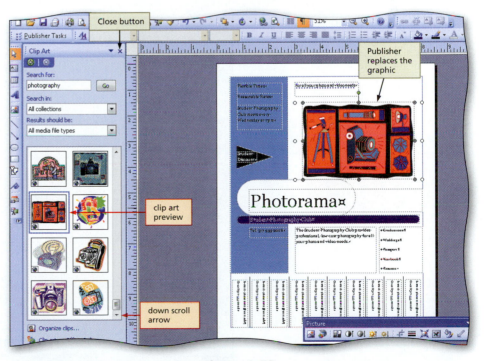

Close button

Publisher replaces the graphic

clip art preview

down scroll arrow

Figure 1–52

Changing Publication Properties and Saving Again

Publisher helps you organize and identify your files by using **publication properties**, which are the details about a file. Publication properties, also known as **metadata**, can include such information as the project author, title, or subject. **Keywords** are words or phrases that further describe the publication. For example, a class name or publication topic can describe the file's purpose or content.

Publication properties are valuable for a variety of reasons:

- Users can save time locating a particular file because they can view a publication's properties without opening the publication.

- By creating consistent properties for files having similar content, users can better organize their publications.

- Some organizations require Publisher users to add publication properties so that other employees can view details about these files.

Many different types of publication properties exist, but the more common ones used in this book are standard and automatically updated properties. **Standard properties** are associated with all Microsoft Office publications and include author, title, and subject. **Automatically updated properties** include file system properties, such as the date you create or change a file, and statistics, such as the file size.

To Change Publication Properties

The **Properties dialog box** contains boxes where you can view and enter publication properties. You can view and change information in this panel at any time while you are creating a publication. Before saving the flyer again, you want to add your name and class name as publication properties. The following steps use the Properties dialog box to change publication properties.

- Click File on the menu bar to display the File menu (Figure 1–53).

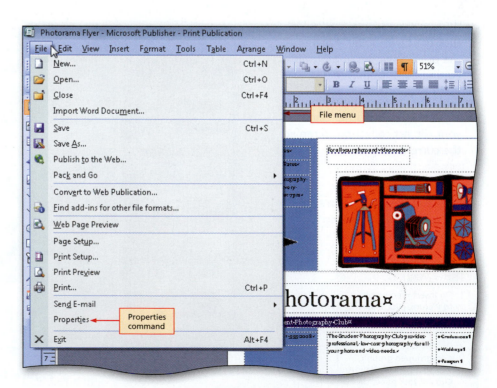

Figure 1–53

2

- Click Properties to access the Properties dialog box (Figure 1–54).

Q&A

Why are some of the publication properties in my Properties dialog box already filled in?

The person who installed Microsoft Office 2007 on your computer or network may have set or customized the properties.

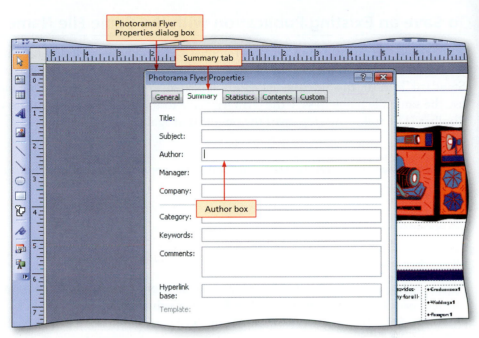

Figure 1–54

3

- Click the Subject text box; if necessary, delete any existing text, and then type your course and section as the Subject property.

- Click the Author text box, if necessary, and then type your name as the Author property. If a name already is displayed in the Author text box, delete it before typing your name.

- Click the Keywords text box; if necessary, delete any existing text, and then type Photography Club as the Keywords property (Figure 1–55).

Q&A

What types of publication properties does Publisher collect automatically?

Publisher records such details as how long you worked at creating your project and how many times you revised the publication.

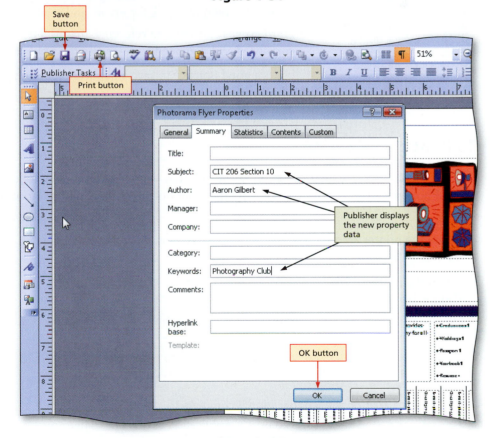

Figure 1–55

4

- Click the OK button in the Properties dialog box so that the dialog box no longer is displayed.

Q&A

What other kinds of things can be done using the Properties dialog box?

You or your instructor can insert comments about the publication in the Comments box. On the Custom tab, you can assign other properties, such as editor, department, language, or publisher, and then enter text, date, yes/no, or a numeric value to these custom properties. For example, your instructor can grade your publication, typing his or her name in the Checked by category, and then assign a letter or numeric grade in the Project or Disposition category.

To Save an Existing Publication with the Same File Name

Saving frequently cannot be overemphasized. You have made several modifications to the publication since you saved it earlier in the chapter. When you first saved the publication, you clicked the Save button on the Standard Toolbar, the Save As dialog box appeared, and you entered the file name, Photorama Flyer. If you want to use the same file name to save the changes made to the publication, you again click the Save button on the Standard Toolbar. The following step saves the publication again.

 1

- Click the Save button on the Standard Toolbar to overwrite the previous Photorama Flyer file on the USB flash drive.

Other Ways
1. Press CTRL+S

BTW

Resaving Files
If you have previously saved a publication, when you click the Save button again, Publisher overwrites the file using the settings specified the first time you saved. To save the file with a different file name or on different media, display the Save As dialog box by clicking Save As on the File menu. Then, fill in the Save As dialog box.

Printing a Publication

After you create a publication, you often want to print it. A printed version of the publication is called a **hard copy** or **printout**.

Printed copies of your publication can be useful for the following reasons:

- Many people prefer proofreading a hard copy of the publication rather than viewing it on the screen to check for errors and readability.
- Hard copies can serve as reference material if your storage medium is lost or becomes corrupted and you need to re-create the publication.

It is a good practice to save a publication before printing it, in the event you experience difficulties with the printer.

To Print a Publication

With the completed publication saved, you may want to print it. The following step prints the contents of the saved Photorama Flyer project by clicking the Print button on the Standard toolbar (Figure 1–55 on the previous page).

 1

- Ready the printer according to the printer instructions. Click the Print button on the Standard toolbar.

- When the printer stops, retrieve the hard copy of the Photorama Flyer (Figure 1–56).

Q&A How can I print multiple copies of my publication other than clicking the Print button twice?

Click File on the menu bar and then click Print on the File menu. Increase the number in the Number of copies box, and then click the OK button.

Q&A Do I have to wait until my publication is complete to print it?

No, you can follow these steps to print a publication at any time while you are creating it.

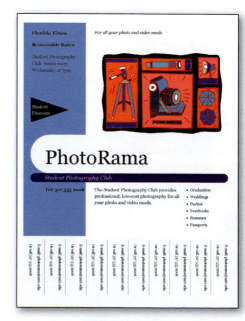

Figure 1–56

Other Ways
1. Press CTRL+P, press ENTER

Quitting Publisher

If you save a publication and then quit Publisher, the Publisher window closes. If you have made changes to a publication since the last time the file was saved, Publisher displays a dialog box asking if you want to save the changes you made to the file before it closes that window. The dialog box contains three buttons with these resulting actions:

- Yes button — Saves the changes and then quits Publisher
- No button — Quits Publisher without saving changes
- Cancel button — Closes the dialog box and redisplays the publication without saving the changes

BTW

Closing vs. quitting
Closing a publication is different from quitting Publisher. Closing a publication, by clicking Close on the File menu, leaves any other Publisher publications open and Publisher running. If no other publication is open, the Close command displays the New Publication task pane.

To Quit Publisher

You saved the publication prior to printing and did not make any changes to the project. The Photorama Flyer project now is complete, and you are ready to quit Publisher. The following steps quit Publisher.

- Point to the Close button on the right side of the Publisher title bar (Figure 1–57).

- Click the Close button to quit Publisher.

Figure 1–57

Other Ways

1. Click File on the menu bar, click Exit
2. Right-click Microsoft Publisher button on Windows taskbar, click Close on shortcut menu
3. Press ALT+F4

Starting Publisher and Opening a Publication

Once you have created and saved a publication, you may need to retrieve it from your storage medium. For example, you might want to revise the publication or reprint it. Opening a publication requires that Publisher is running on your computer.

To Start Publisher

The following steps, which assume Windows Vista is running, start Publisher.

1. Click the Start button on the Windows taskbar to display the Start menu.

2. Click All Programs on the Start menu to display the All Programs submenu.

3. Click Microsoft Office on the All Programs submenu to display the Microsoft Office submenu.

4. Click Microsoft Office Publisher 2007 on the Microsoft Office submenu to start Publisher.

5. If the Publisher window is not maximized, click the Maximize button on its title bar to maximize the window.

To Open a Publication from Publisher

Earlier in this chapter you saved your project on a USB flash drive using the file name, Photorama Flyer. The following steps open the Photorama Flyer file from the USB flash drive.

1

- With your USB flash drive connected to one of the computer's USB ports, click File on the menu bar (Figure 1–58).

Q&A

What files are shown in the Recent Publications list?

Publisher displays, by default, the five most recently opened publication file names in this list. If the file you want to open appears in the Recent Publications list, you could click it to open the file. The recent publications also are displayed at the bottom of the File menu.

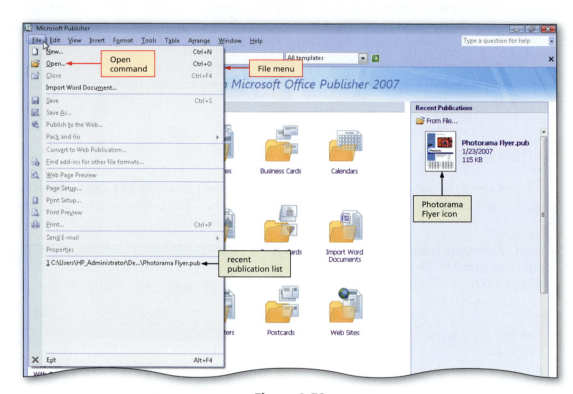

Figure 1–58

2

- Click Open on the File menu to display the Open Publication dialog box.

- If the Folders list is displayed below the Folders button, click the Folders button to remove the Folders list.

- If necessary, click Computer in the Favorite Links section and then scroll until USB (F:) appears in the list of available drives.

- Double-click to select the USB flash drive, Drive F in this case, as the new open location.

- Click Photorama Flyer to select the file name (Figure 1–59).

Q&A

How do I open the file if I am not using a USB flash drive?

Use the same process, but be certain to select your device in the Computer list.

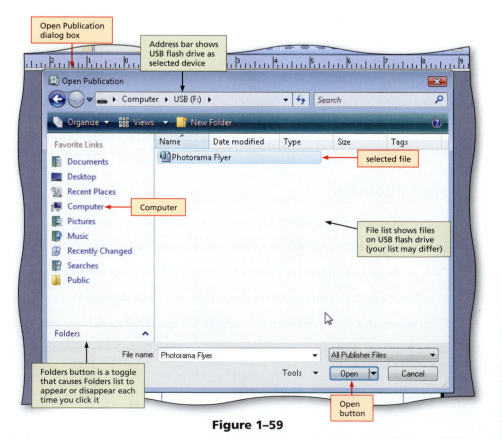

Figure 1–59

3

- Click the Open button to open the selected file and display the Photorama Flyer publication in the Publisher window.

- Click the Close button on the Format Publication task pane title bar (Figure 1–60).

Q&A

Why do I see the Publisher icon and publication name on the Windows taskbar?

When you open a Publisher file, a Publisher program button is displayed on the taskbar. The button in Figure 1–60 contains an ellipsis because some of its contents do not fit in the allotted button space. If you point to a program button, its entire contents appear in a ScreenTip, which in this case would be the file name followed by the program name.

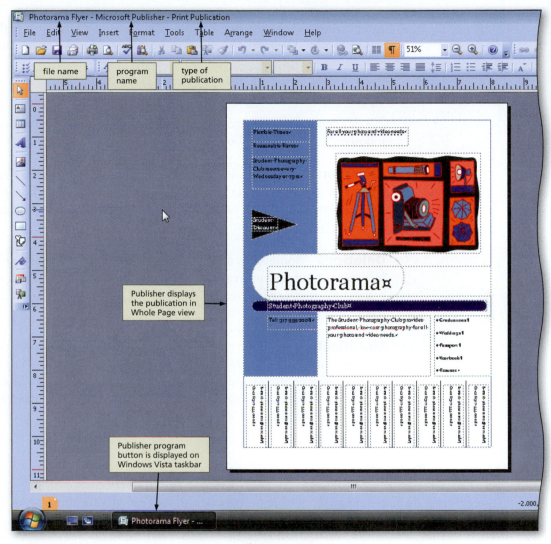

Figure 1–60

Other Ways

1. Click Open button on Standard toolbar, navigate to storage location, double-click file name

2. Press CTRL+O, navigate to storage location, select file name, press ENTER

Correcting Errors

After creating a publication, you often will find that you must make changes to it. Changes can be required because the document contains an error or because of new circumstances.

Types of Changes Made to Publications

The types of changes made to publications normally fall into one of the three following categories: additions, deletions, or modifications.

Additions   Additional text, objects, or formatting may be required in the publication. Additions occur when you are required to add items to a publication. For example, in Project 1 you would like to insert a text box that will display when the flyer is published to the Web.

Deletions   Sometimes deletions are necessary in a publication because objects are incorrect or are no longer needed. For example, to place this advertising flyer on the electronic bulletin board at the school, the tear-offs no longer are needed. In that case, you would delete them from the page layout.

Modifications   If you make an error in a document or want to make other modifications, normal combinations of inserting, deleting, and editing techniques for text and graphics apply. Publisher provides several methods for correcting errors in a document. For each of the text error correction techniques, you first must move the insertion point to the error. For graphic modification, the object first must be selected.

To Delete the Tear-offs

If this flyer is displayed on an electronic bulletin board, the tear-offs are unnecessary and should be deleted. The following steps delete the tear-offs.

1

- Right-click any one of the tear-offs to display the shortcut menu (Figure 1–61).

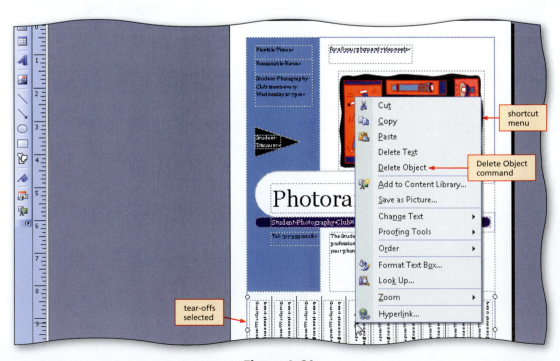

Figure 1–61

2
- Click Delete Object on the shortcut menu to delete the tear-offs (Figure 1–62).

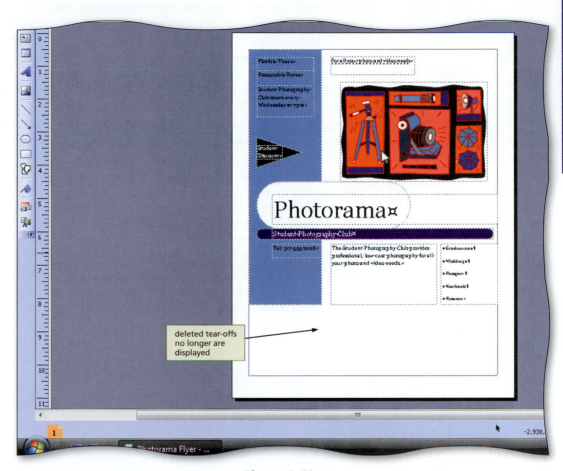

deleted tear-offs no longer are displayed

Figure 1–62

Inserting a Text Box

The next step in modifying the flyer is to create a new text box in preparation for creating a Web version of the publication. Recall that the Objects toolbar contains buttons for many different kinds of objects that you can insert into publications. In the case of a text box, you click the **Text Box button** (Figure 1-63 on the next page) and then drag in the publication to create the text box. Once it is created, you can type in the text box just as you did with those created by the template.

<table>
<tr><td>

Plan Ahead

</td><td>

Identify how to format various elements of the text.
By formatting the characters and paragraphs in a publication, you can improve its overall appearance. In a flyer, consider the following formatting suggestions.

- **Increase the font size of characters.** Flyers usually are posted on a bulletin board or in a window. Thus, the font size should be as large as possible so that passersby easily can read the flyer. To give the headline more impact, its font size should be larger than the font size of the text in the body copy.

- **Change the font of characters.** Use fonts that are easy to read. The font schemes suggest using only two different fonts in a flyer, for example, one for the headline and the other for all other text. Too many fonts can make the flyer visually confusing.

- **Change the alignment and placement.** The default alignment for text in a publication is **left-aligned**, that is, flush at the left margin of the text box with uneven right edges. Consider changing the alignment of some of the text to add interest and variety to the flyer. Overall placement of objects should be done with purpose. Objects usually should be aligned with the margin or with other objects on the page. Objects similar in nature, such as organization information text boxes, should be kept in close proximity of one another.

- **Emphasize important words.** To call attention to certain words or lines, you can underline them, italicize them, or bold them. Use these formats sparingly, however, because overuse will minimize their effect and make the flyer look too busy.

</td></tr>
</table>

To Insert a Text Box in an Existing Publication

In the following step, a new text box is created in the lower portion of the flyer.

- Click the Text Box button on the Objects toolbar to select it and then move the mouse to the position where you want the text box to display (in this case, the lower portion of the flyer where the tear-offs were located).

- Position the mouse pointer in the upper-left corner of the empty area and then drag down and right, forming a rectangle, to create a new text box that fills the area vacated by the tear-offs (Figure 1–63).

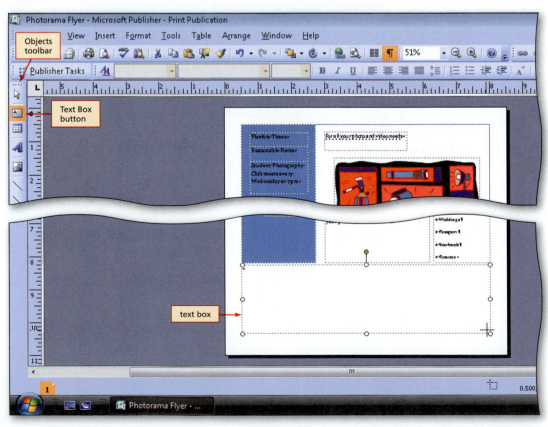

Figure 1–63

To Format Text

To make the text easier to read on an electronic bulletin board, you will change the font size and center the text as shown in the next steps. The **Font Size box** on the Formatting toolbar allows you to type in a font size for text or choose a size from a list. Font sizes are measured in points. A **point** is a measurement of the height of a typed character, approximately 1/72nd of an inch. The **Center button** on the Formatting toolbar centers text within the text box margins.

1

• Click inside the newly created text box to position the insertion point.

• Click the Font Size box arrow on the Formatting toolbar to display the Font Size list (Figure 1–64).

Q&A Is it better to choose the font size before I type or after?

You can do it either way, but if you have already typed the text, you must select it before choosing the new font size. Choosing the font size first eliminates that extra step.

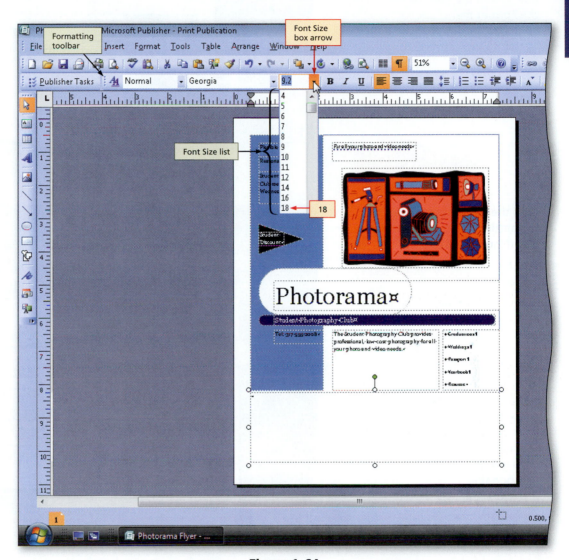

Figure 1–64

2

- Click 18 in the list to change the font size to 18 point (Figure 1–65).

Q&A

Are there other ways to increase the font size?

Yes, in later chapters you will learn how to use the Font command on the Format menu, the Increase Font Size button, and the Best Fit option to increase the font size.

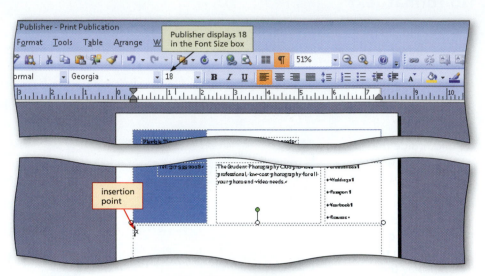

Figure 1–65

3

- Click the Center button on the Formatting toolbar to center the text (Figure 1–66).

Q&A

What are the other alignment buttons?

There are four alignment buttons on the Formatting toolbar when a text box is selected: **Align Text Left**, **Center**, **Align Text Right**, and **Justify**. The default setting for text is to align it on the left side. The Justify button causes Publisher to add extra spaces so that all the lines of a paragraph (except the last line) reach and align with both margins. You will learn about additional alignments in a later project.

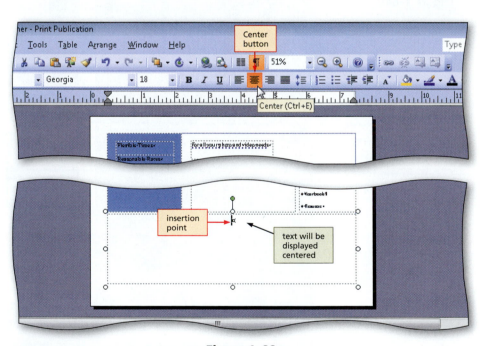

Figure 1–66

4

- Type `E-mail: photorama@univ.edu` to enter the text (Figure 1–67).

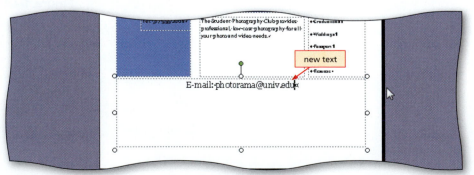

Figure 1–67

Other Ways

1. To center text, press CTRL+E

Inserting a Hyperlink

The final modification in preparation for converting this publication to a Web publication is inserting a hyperlink. A **hyperlink** is colored and underlined text or a graphic that you click to go to a file, a location in a file, a Web page, or an e-mail address. When you insert a hyperlink, you select the text or object and then click the Insert Hyperlink button on the Standard toolbar.

To Insert a Hyperlink

The **Insert Hyperlink dialog box** allows you to select options and enter Web addresses, as shown in the following steps. The TAB key is used to move from one box to another in Publisher dialog boxes.

1

- Drag through the text, photorama@univ.edu, to select it (Figure 1–68).

Q&A Are there other ways to select the text other than dragging?

If the text were a single word, you could double-click to select it. However, because an e-mail address is actually three words separated by the at symbol (@) and a period (.), double-clicking will not select the entire e-mail address. The only other way to select the text would be to click at the beginning and SHIFT+CLICK at the end.

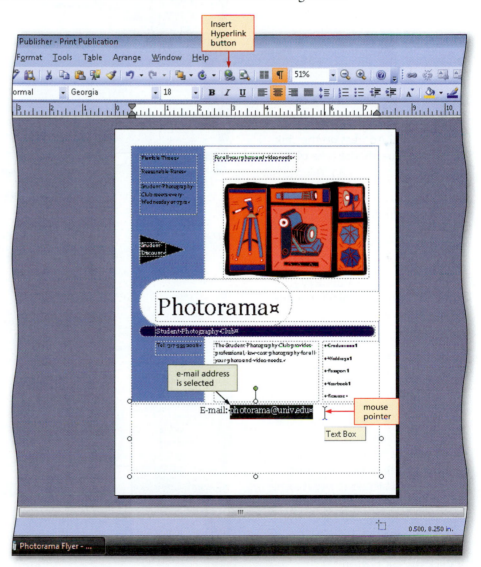

Figure 1–68

• Click the Insert Hyperlink button on the Standard toolbar (Figure 1–69).

Experiment

• When the Insert Hyperlink dialog box is displayed, one at a time, click each kind of hyperlink listed in the Link to bar. Note the different kinds of information requested.

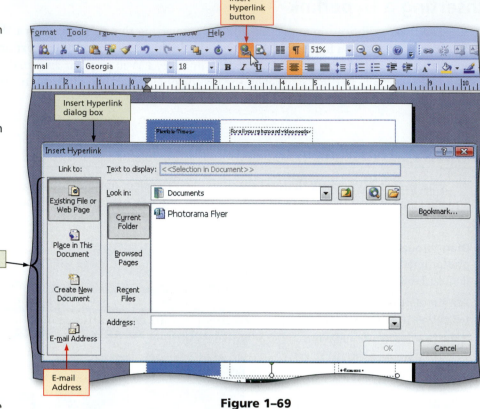

Figure 1–69

• Click E-mail Address on the Link to bar to specify the type of hyperlink.

• Type photorama@univ.edu in the E-mail address text box.

• Press the TAB key to move to the next box.

• Type Photorama Web Flyer Inquiry in the Subject text box (Figure 1–70).

Q&A

What kinds of text should you enter in the Subject text box?

Because this text will become the subject line of the e-mail message when someone clicks the hyperlink on your Web site, you want to include text that identifies the message as coming from your Web flyer, as well as text that identifies from which Web site it came, should you have more than one.

Figure 1–70

4

• Click the OK button.

Other Ways

1. Select text, click Hyperlink on the Insert menu, enter hyperlink information, click OK

2. Select text, press CTRL+K, enter hyperlink information, click OK

Creating a Web Page from a Publication

Publisher can create a Web page from your publication. It is a three-step process. First, Publisher uses a **Design Checker** to look for potential problems if the publication were transferred to the Web. Next, after saving the publication with a new file name, it will be converted to a Web publication, using the Convert to Web Publication command on the File menu. Finally, Publisher allows you to publish the Web page.

Determine whether the flyer will be more effective as a print publication, Web publication, or both.

- **Print publications** – When creating a print publication, you must consider the kind of paper you are going to use, the color options, the number of copies, and the plan for publishing. Ask yourself if the publication has to be in print to reach the target audience. How will readers find the printed publication? The included objects in the layout should be designed keeping the limitations of print and reading in mind.

- **Web publications** – Will the publication be accessible and reasonable on the Web? Is the target audience a common Web user? If so, determine whether an e-mail, Web page, or Web site would be the most efficient means of communication. How will readers find the Web page? When converting to a Web publication, determine which objects will work effectively on the Web and which ones will not. Modify the publication as necessary.

Plan Ahead

To Run the Design Checker

If your publication contains a layout that may not be appropriate, such as one with overlapping text boxes, or one with objects that extend beyond the margin, the Design Checker will alert you. If you use links or hot spots to other Web pages within your publication, Design Checker will verify the addresses if you are connected to the Web. The following steps run the Design Checker.

- Click Tools on the menu bar to display the Tools menu (Figure 1–71).

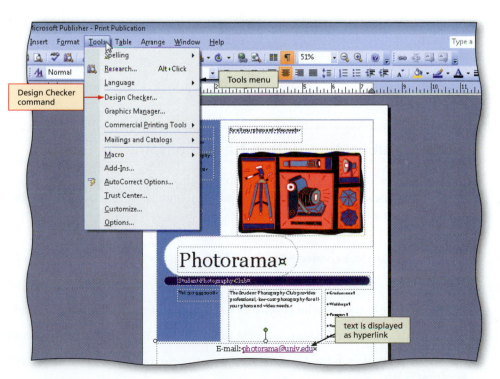

Figure 1–71

2

- Click the Design Checker command to display the Design Checker task pane. Publisher displays a message, indicating there are no problems in the publication (Figure 1–72).

Q&A

What happens if I have some design errors?

If your publication has a problem or contains a design error, the problem is displayed in the 'Select an item to fix' text box. You can click the problem's box arrow to display options to go to the error, ignore, continue, or obtain more information about the problem.

3

- Click the Close button on the Design Checker task pane title bar to close the task pane.

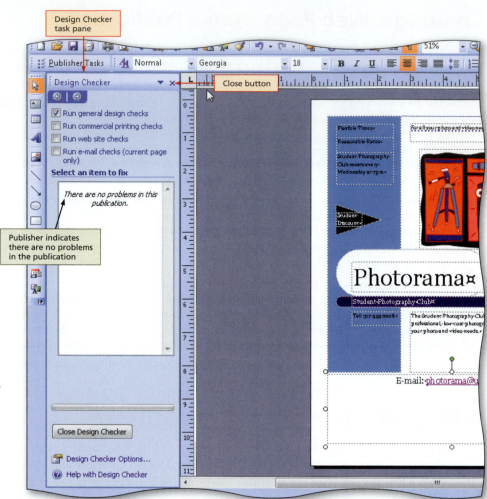

Figure 1–72

Other Ways
1. On View menu, click Task Pane, click Other Task Panes button, click Design Checker   2. Press CTRL+F1, click Other Task Panes button, click Design Checker

To Save a Publication with a New File Name

The following step illustrates how to save the publication with a new file name in preparation for converting it to a Web publication. It is important to save the publication before converting it to a Web publication so you can make changes at a later time, if necessary.

1

- With a USB flash drive connected to one of the computer's USB ports, click Save As on the File menu.

- When the Save As dialog box is displayed, type `Photorama Web Flyer` in the File name text box. Do not press the ENTER key.

- Click Computer in the Favorite Links area to display a list of available drives and folders.

- Double-click USB (F:) in the Computer list to open the USB flash drive, Drive F in this case, as the new save location.

- Click the Save button in the Save As dialog box to save the publication on the USB flash drive with the file name, Photorama Web Flyer.

Converting a Print Publication to a Web Publication

You can create two types of publications with Microsoft Publisher: print publications and Web publications. A **Web publication** is one suitable for publishing to the Web with certain objects, formatting options, hyperlinks, and other features specific to Web pages.

A command on Publisher's File menu converts publications from one type to another. Up to now, you have worked on a print publication, as noted on the title bar (Figure 1–60 on page PUB 43). Once you convert the file, you work in **Web mode**. The options available to you in Web mode are tailored specifically to Web publications so that you can create a publication that is optimized for display in a Web browser. A **browser** is a piece of software that interprets and formats files into Web pages and displays them. A Web browser, such as Microsoft Internet Explorer, can follow hyperlinks, transfer files, and play sound or video files that are embedded in Web pages. You always can determine which publication mode you are in by looking at the title bar of your open publication, which will display either Print Publication or Web Publication, depending on the publication type.

When you convert a publication from one type to the other, Publisher copies the text and graphics from your original publication into the new publication type. Because certain print features are not available in Web mode, and certain Web features are not available in Print mode, your publication may undergo formatting changes when you convert it from one publication type to the other.

BTW

Design Checker
The Design Checker looks for appropriate layouts. If text overlaps an object, the Design Checker offers to convert the text box to a graphic so it will display properly. The Design Checker looks at all graphics and may display suggestions on those that load slowly. More about the Design Checker and information on types of graphics will be covered in future projects.

To Convert a Print Publication to a Web Publication

The following steps convert a print publication to a Web publication. Two dialog boxes help you through the conversion process. Each dialog box lists the purpose of the step at the top, and then lists questions to help you make choices, and formats the publication based on your responses.

1
- Click Convert to Web Publication on the File menu to begin the process of converting a print publication to a Web publication.

- When Publisher displays the 'Save Your Current Print Publication' step, click the 'No, do not save my print publication before converting it to a Web publication' button to select it (Figure 1–73).

Q&A

Why didn't I choose to save it?

Because you previously saved the file with a new name, you do not have to save the file again.

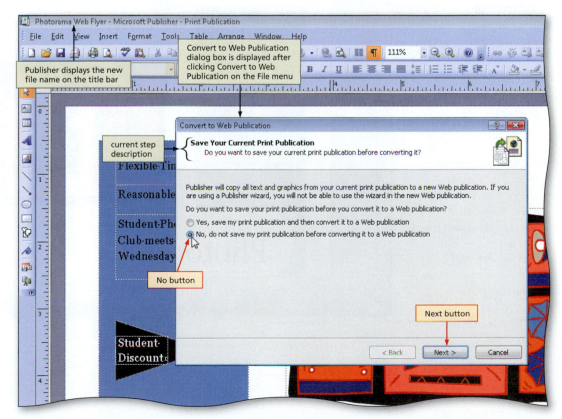

Figure 1–73

2

• Click the Next button to proceed to the second step of the conversion process.

• When the 'Add a Navigation Bar' step is displayed, click the 'No, do not add a navigation bar' button (Figure 1–74).

Q&A

Why didn't I choose to add a navigation bar?

It is a single Web page rather than a Web site, so navigation is not needed. Additionally, there are no links to other Web pages in your publication.

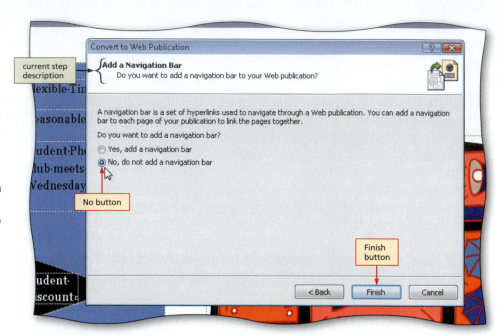

Figure 1–74

3

• Click the Finish Button to complete the process (Figure 1–75).

• Click the Close button in the Format Publication task pane.

Q&A

Why did my title bar change?

Your publication is now a Web publication, so the words, Print Publication, change to the words, Web Publication. The Web publication has not been saved in its current format, so a temporary name has been applied, labeled as Publication2 in this case.

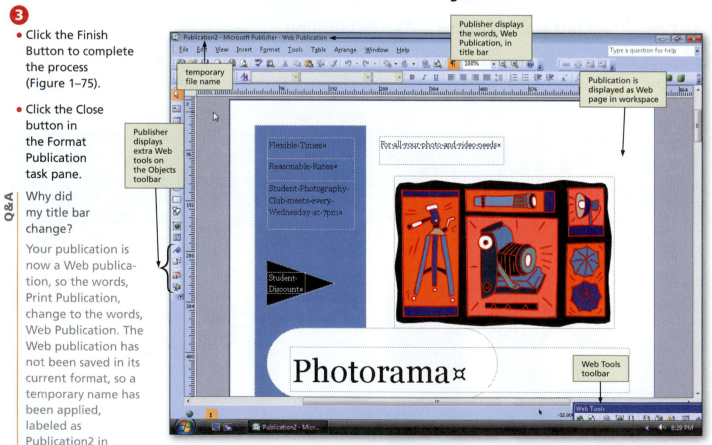

Figure 1–75

Publishing to the Web

The final step in preparing the Web flyer is to publish it to the Web. **Publishing to the Web** is the process of making Web pages available to others, for example, on the World Wide Web or on a company's intranet. Files intended for use on the Web, however, need a different format. A **Hypertext Markup Language (HTML)** file is a file capable of being stored and transferred electronically on a file server in order to display on the Web. When you publish, Publisher saves your file in a **filtered HTML format** that is smaller than regular HTML files. It can be published to and downloaded from the Internet quickly.

In Publisher, you can publish to the Web using a wizard accessed through the File menu, which creates a filtered HTML file, or you can save a publication as a Web page to a Web folder, which creates a traditional HTML file. Either way, Publisher creates an accompanying folder for each separate publication intended for the Web. A **folder** is a logical portion of a disk created to group and store similar documents. Inside this folder, Publisher will include copies of the associated graphics. Once created and uploaded, your publication can be viewed by a Web browser, such as Microsoft Internet Explorer.

BTW

Web folders

The concept of a Web folder facilitates integration of Publisher with other members of the Microsoft Office 2007 Suite and Windows Vista. With Windows Vista, you can choose to use Web style folders on your desktop, which means that the desktop is interactive, and all your folders look like Web pages. Publisher also will take care of uploading, or transferring, your files to the Web, if you are connected to an Internet service provider or host. See Appendix D for more information on Web folders.

To Publish to the Web

The following steps use the Publish to the Web command on the File menu to create a Web site from your publication. Because not all systems are connected to the Internet, and not all users subscribe to a Web hosting service, the following steps store the resulting Web files on a USB flash drive.

1
- Click Publish to the Web on the File menu.

- If a Microsoft Publisher dialog box is displayed, reminding you about Web hosting services, click its OK button.

- When the Publish to the Web dialog box is displayed, navigate if necessary, to the USB flash drive or other location on your computer (Figure 1–76).

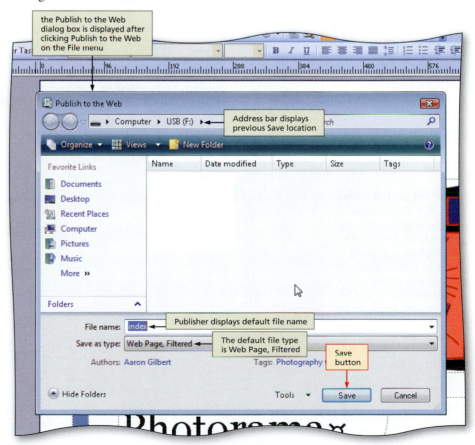

Figure 1–76

2

- Click the Save button in the Publish to the Web dialog box, to save the Web publication.

- When Publisher displays a Microsoft Office Publisher dialog box describing filtered HTML files, read the description and then click the OK button to close the dialog box (Figure 1–77).

Q&A

Why did Publisher supply the name, index?

A single- file Web page or the first page in a multipage Web site is commonly called index. Browsers will display a page named index automatically when users navigate to the site.

Q&A

Is my Web publication now on the Web?

No, the Web publication file is stored on your flash drive or the location to which you saved the print publication. See your instructor for ways to upload your files.

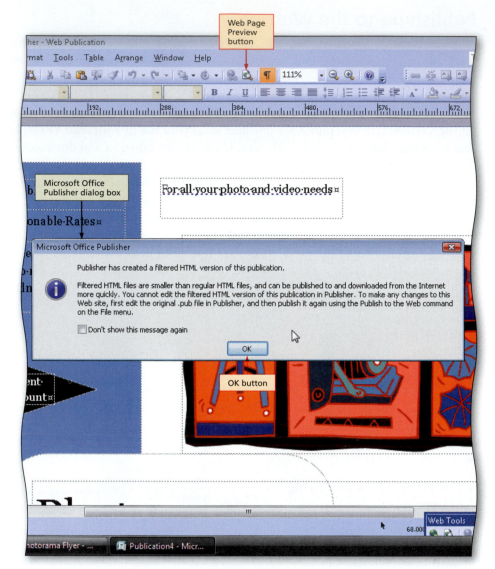

Figure 1–77

BTW

Web Folder Locations
If a Web folder is one of the locations listed in the Publish to the Web dialog box, you could save to that location; then, with proper authentication, your publication would be on the Web. If you do not have a Web folder, you will have to upload the published file to a Web server location. For more information on Web folders, see Appendix D.

To Preview the Web Publication in a Browser

To preview what the Web publication will look like on the Web, click the **Web Page Preview button** on the Standard toolbar, as shown in the following steps.

1

- Click the Web Page Preview button on the Standard toolbar, to preview the Web publication.

- When the browser window opens, if necessary, maximize the window (Figure 1–78).

Q&A Why does my display look different?

Each brand and version of Web browser software displays information in a slightly different manner. Additionally, your browser settings, such as Text Size and Zoom level, may differ.

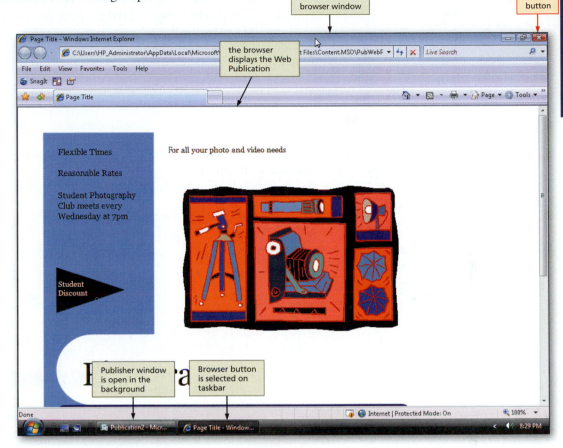

Figure 1–78

2

- Click the Close button on the browser window title bar.

Closing the Entire Publication

Sometimes, everything goes wrong. If this happens, you may want to close the publication entirely and start over with a new publication. You also may want to close a publication when you are finished with it so you can begin your next publication. If you wanted to close a publication, you would use the following steps.

To Close the Entire Publication

1 Click Close on the File menu.

2 If Publisher displays a dialog box, click the No button to ignore the changes since the last time you saved the publication.

BTW

Online Versus Offline Searches
You can determine where Help is searching by looking at the Connection Status button on the status bar. Clicking the Connection Status button provides a menu with commands for selecting online or offline searches .

Publisher Help

At any time while using Publisher, you can find answers to questions and display information about various topics through **Publisher Help**. Used properly, this form of assistance can increase your productivity and reduce your frustrations by minimizing the time you spend learning how to use Publisher.

This section introduces you to Publisher Help. Additional information about using Publisher Help is available in Appendix C.

To Search for Publisher Help

Using Publisher Help, you can search for information based on phrases, such as save a publication or format text, or key terms, such as copy, save, or format. Publisher Help responds with a list of search results displayed as links to a variety of resources. The following steps, which use Publisher Help to search for information about text boxes, assume you are connected to the Internet.

1

- Press the F1 key to access Publisher Help. In the Publisher Help toolbar, click the Home key.

- Type text box in the 'Type words to search for' text box at the top of the Publisher Help window to enter the search term (Figure 1–79).

Figure 1–79

• Press the ENTER key to display the search results.

• Maximize the Publisher Help window (Figure 1–80).

Q&A

Where is the Publisher window with the Photorama flyer publication?

Publisher is open in the background, but the Publisher Help window is overlaid on top of the Microsoft Publisher window. When the Publisher Help window is closed, the publication will reappear.

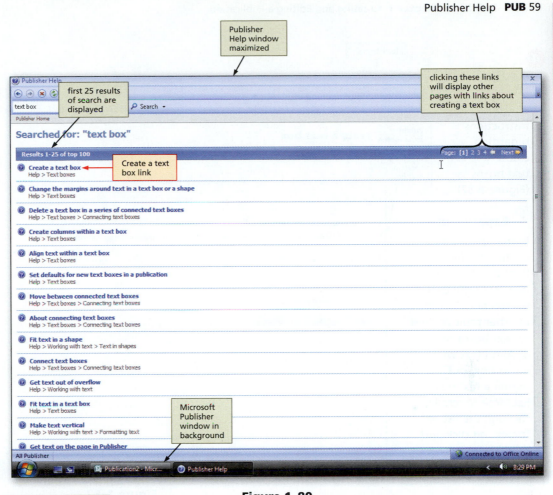

Figure 1–80

• Click the Create a text box link to display information regarding creating text boxes (Figure 1–81).

Q&A

What is the purpose of the buttons at the top of the Publisher Help window?

Use the buttons in the upper-left corner of the Publisher Help window to navigate through the Help system, change the display, show the Publisher Help table of contents, and print the contents of the window.

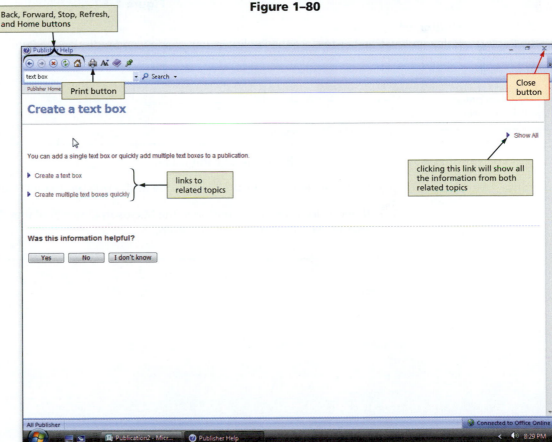

Figure 1–81

4

• Click the Create a text box link to display detailed instructions regarding creating text boxes (Figure 1–82).

Experiment

• In the upper-left portion of the Publisher Help window, click the Back button and choose another topic related to text boxes, such as Align text within a text box, or Fit text within a text box. Feel free to scroll through the list of topics and click and read any topics of interest to you.

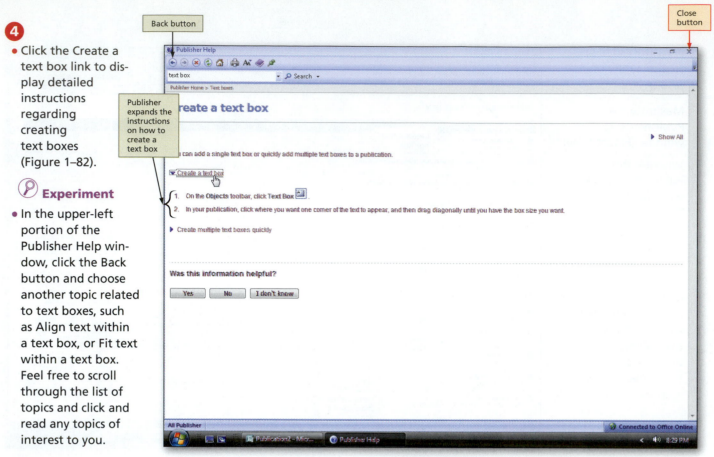

Figure 1–82

5

• Click the Close button on the Publisher Help window title bar to close the Publisher Help window and redisplay the Publisher window.

Other Ways

1. On Help menu, click Microsoft Office Publisher Help

To Quit Publisher

The following steps quit Publisher.

1 Click the Close button on the right side of the title bar to quit Publisher.

2 If necessary, click the No button in the Microsoft Office Publisher dialog box so that any changes you have made are not saved.

Chapter Summary

In this chapter you have learned how to choose a publication template, set font and color schemes, enter text in a publication, delete objects in a publication, replace a graphic, print a publication, and convert a print publication to a Web publication. The items listed below include all the new Publisher skills you have learned in this chapter.

1. Start Publisher (PUB 5)
2. Select a Template (PUB 7)
3. Set Publication Options (PUB 9)
4. Close the Task Pane (PUB 17)
5. Enter Text (PUB 19)
6. Zoom and Enter Text (PUB 21)
7. Display Formatting Marks (PUB 24)
8. Wordwrap Text as You Type (PUB 25)
9. Enter Bulleted Items (PUB 26)
10. Enter Tear-off Text (PUB 27)
11. Delete an Object (PUB 28)
12. Check Spelling as You Type (PUB 30)
13. Save a Publication (PUB 31)
14. Replace a Graphic Using the Clip Art Task Pane (PUB 34)
15. Change Publication Properties (PUB 38)
16. Save an Existing Publication with the Same File Name (PUB 40)
17. Print a Publication (PUB 40)
18. Quit Publisher (PUB 41)
19. Open a Publication from Publisher (PUB 42)
20. Delete the Tear-offs (PUB 44)
21. Insert a Text Box in an Existing Publication (PUB 46)
22. Format Text (PUB 47)
23. Insert a Hyperlink (PUB 49)
24. Run the Design Checker (PUB 51)
25. Save a Publication with a New File Name (PUB 52)
26. Convert a Print Publication to a Web Publication (PUB 53)
27. Publish to the Web (PUB 55)
28. Preview the Web Publication in a Browser (PUB 57)
29. Close the Entire Publication (PUB 57)
30. Search for Publisher Help (PUB 58)

Learn It Online

Test your knowledge of chapter content and key terms.

Instructions: To complete the Learn It Online exercises, start your browser, click the Address bar, and then enter the Web address scsite.com/pub2007/learn. When the Office 2007 Learn It Online page is displayed, click the link for the exercise you want to complete and then read the instructions.

Chapter Reinforcement TF, MC, and SA
A series of true/false, multiple choice, and short answer questions that test your knowledge of the chapter content.

Flash Cards
An interactive learning environment where you identify chapter key terms associated with displayed definitions.

Practice Test
A series of multiple choice questions that test your knowledge of chapter content and key terms.

Who Wants To Be a Computer Genius?
An interactive game that challenges your knowledge of chapter content in the style of a television quiz show.

Wheel of Terms
An interactive game that challenges your knowledge of chapter key terms in the style of the television show *Wheel of Fortune*.

Crossword Puzzle Challenge
A crossword puzzle that challenges your knowledge of key terms presented in the chapter.

Apply Your Knowledge

Reinforce the skills and apply the concepts you learned in this chapter.

Modifying Text and Formatting a Publication
Instructions: Start Publisher. Open the publication, Apply 1-1 University Bookstore Flyer, from the Data Files for Students. See the inside back cover of this book for instructions on downloading the Data Files for Students, or contact your instructor for more information about accessing the required files.

The publication you open is a flyer in which you modify the color and font schemes, replace text, delete objects, and convert the publication from print to the Web so that it looks like Figure 1–83.

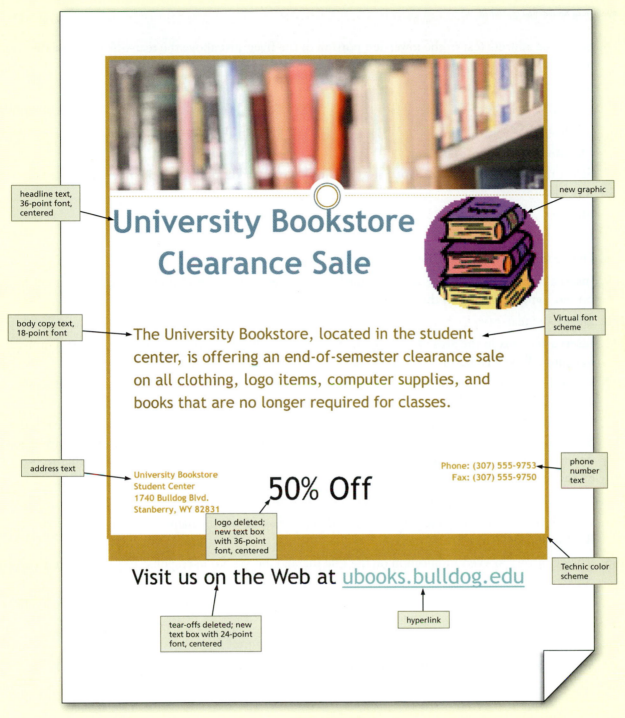

Figure 1–83

Perform the following tasks:

1. Change the color scheme to Technic.

2. Change the font scheme to Virtual.

3. Select the headline text and center it.

4. Change the font size of the headline to 36.

5. Select the body copy text and replace it with the text shown in Figure 1–83. Change the font size of the body copy to 18 point.

Continued >

Apply Your Knowledge *continued*

6. Select the address text in the lower-left portion of the flyer, just above the tear-offs. Replace the text with:

   ```
   University Bookstore
   Student Center
   1740 Bulldog Blvd.
   Stanberry, WY 82831
   ```

7. Select the text in the phone number text box in the lower-right portion of the flyer. Replace the text with:

   ```
   Phone: (307) 555-9753
   Fax: (307) 555-9750
   ```

8. Delete the logo centered above the tear-offs.

9. Insert a text box in the area vacated by the logo. Set the font size to 36 point. Set the alignment to center. Type 50% Off in the text box.

10. Delete the tear-offs.

11. Insert a text box in the area vacated by the tear-offs. Set the font size to 24 point. Set the alignment to center. Type Visit us on the Web at ubooks.bulldog.edu in the text box.

12. Select the Web address and then click the Insert Hyperlink button. Type ubooks.bulldog.edu in the Address box and then click OK in the Insert Hyperlink dialog box.

13. Double-click the book graphic to display the Clip Art task pane. Type book to replace any text in the Search for box. Click the Results should be box arrow and ensure that Movies is the only choice that displays a check mark. Click the Go button. Select a graphic similar to the one shown in Figure 1–83 on the previous page.

14. Change the publication properties, as specified by your instructor.

15. Click Save As on the File menu. Save the publication using the file name, Apply 1-1 University Bookstore Web Flyer Formatted.

16. Click Convert to Web Publication on the File menu. Choose No in response to each step in the conversion process.

17. Click Publish to the Web. When asked for a file name, type Apply 1-1 University Bookstore Web Flyer Index to replace the default text.

18. Preview the Web publication using the Web Preview button.

19. Submit the revised publications, as specified by your instructor.

Extend Your Knowledge

Extend the skills you learned in this chapter and experiment with new skills. You may need to use Help to complete the assignment.

Modifying Text and Graphics Formats

Instructions: Start Publisher. Open the publication, Extend 1-1 Strawberry Jam Flyer, from the Data Files for Students. See the inside back cover of this book for instructions on downloading the Data Files for Students, or contact your instructor for more information about accessing the required files.
    You will enhance the look of the flyer shown in Figure 1–84.

change headline to be Best Fit

change attention getter to italicized

change date to be underlined

Figure 1–84

Perform the following tasks:

1. Use Help to learn about copyfitting text, and the use of bold, underline, and italic formatting.

2. Select inside the headline text box. Click Format on the menu bar, point to AutoFit Text, and then click Best Fit.

3. Change several other text boxes to Best Fit.

4. Select the words, Free Admission, in the attention getter and then click the Italic button on the Formatting toolbar.

5. Select the words, best-tasting, in the body copy and then click the Bold button on the Formatting toolbar.

6. Select the date and then click the Underline button on the Formatting toolbar.

7. Change the publication properties, as specified by your instructor. Save the revised publication and then submit it in the format specified by your instructor.

Make It Right

Analyze a publication and correct all errors and/or improve the design.

Correcting Replacement Text and Spelling Errors

Instructions: Start Publisher. Open the publication, Make It Right 1-1 Violin Recital Flyer, from the Data Files for Students. See the inside back cover of this book for instructions on downloading the Data Files for Students, or contact your instructor for more information about accessing the required files.

The publication is a flyer that contains text boxes that have yet to be replaced and spelling errors, as shown in Figure 1–85. You are to replace the placeholder text in the Business Name text box by selecting it and then typing the new text, Senior Music Majors. Then, when Publisher displays the red wavy underlines, you are to correct each spelling error by right-clicking the flagged text and then clicking the appropriate correction on the shortcut menu. If your screen does not display the wavy underlines, click Tools on the menu bar and then point to Spelling to display the spelling submenu. Click Spelling Options. In the Spelling Options dialog box, click to remove the check mark in the Hide spelling errors check box.

Change the publication properties, as specified by your instructor. Save the revised publication and then submit it in the format specified by your instructor.

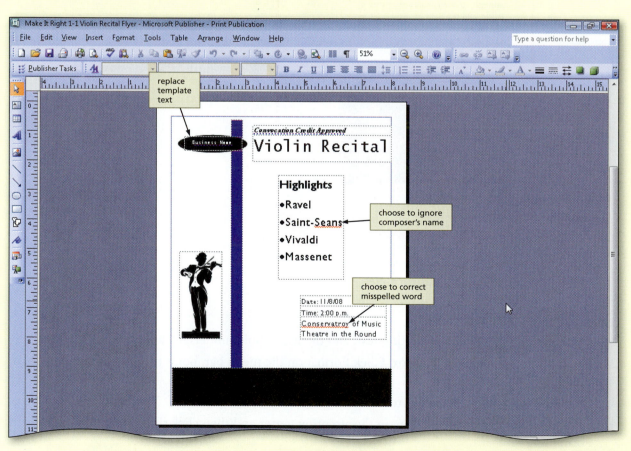

Figure 1–85

In the Lab

Design and/or create a publication using the guidelines, concepts, and skills presented in this chapter. Labs are listed in order of increasing difficulty.

Lab 1: Creating a Flyer with a Picture

Problem: You work part-time for the Alumni Association at the local college. Your supervisor has asked you to prepare a flyer that advertises a travel package for away football games. You prepare the flyer shown in Figure 1–86, using the instructions on the next page.

Figure 1–86

Continued >

In the Lab *continued*

Instructions: Perform the following tasks:

1. Start Publisher.
2. Choose Flyers in the catalog and then scroll down to Announcements flyers.
3. Choose the Lost Pet/Item flyer template.
4. Choose the Iris color scheme.
5. Choose the Casual font scheme.
6. Do not include tear-offs.
7. Create the publication and display formatting marks on the screen.
8. Save the publication on a USB flash drive using the file name, Lab 1-1 Follow the Team Flyer.
9. Replace the headline text, as shown in Figure 1–86 on the previous page.
10. Change the graphic to a football photograph from your system's clip art.
11. Change the template text in the bulleted list to include:
    - Three Away Games
    - Game Tickets
    - Charter Bus
    - Tailgate Party
    - Souvenir Program
    - Preferred Seating
    - Post Game Dinner
    - Event Coordinator on Each Bus
12. Zoom as necessary to edit the body copy text under the blue line. Select the text and then type: The Alumni Association has put together this travel package for the three October away games. This is a special offer provided to Alumni Association members.
13. Change the template text in the contact information text box to match Figure 1–86.
14. Change the template text in the attention getter to $200 per person.
15. Zoom to Whole Page view.
16. Insert a new text box above the graphic, near the bulleted list. Set the font size to 26 point. Type Package includes: as the text.
17. Change the publication properties, as specified by your instructor.
18. Save the flyer again with the same file name.
19. Submit the publication in the format specified by your instructor.

In the Lab

Lab 2: Creating an Award Certificate

Problem: Your boss is in charge of the Marion County IT Fair, a showcase event that displays student IT projects. She has asked you to create an award certificate for each of the participants. You decide to explore some of Publisher's other single-page templates besides flyers. You prepare the certificate shown in Figure 1–87.

Figure 1–87

Instructions: Perform the following tasks:

1. Start Publisher. When the catalog is displayed, click the Award Certificates button in the Publication Types area.

2. In the catalog, choose the Appreciate 8 template.

3. Choose the Mountain Color scheme.

4. Choose the Foundry font scheme.

5. Click the headline text and type `Certificate of Participation`. Press the ENTER key and then type `Marion County IT Fair`.

6. Change the vertical text to read, `I.T. Showcase Competition in Marion County`.

7. Select the text, Name of Recipient text box and delete it.

8. Insert a text box below the headline. Set the font size to 28 point. Enter the text, `Fall 2009` in the new text box as shown in Figure 1–87.

9. Correct any spelling errors.

10. Run the Design Checker and correct any problems that it finds.

11. Change the document properties as specified by your instructor.

12. Save the flyer with the name, Lab 1-2 Participation Certificate.

13. Submit the publication, shown in Figure 1–87, in the format specified by your instructor.

In the Lab

Lab 3: Creating a Newspaper Advertisement

Problem: Your sorority has asked you to prepare an advertisement that promotes the spring break ski trip. The advertisement will run in the school newspaper, which prints in black and white. You prepare the advertisement as shown in Figure 1–88.

Figure 1–88

Instructions: Start Publisher. Select Advertisements from the list of Publication Types, and then choose The Works template. Accept the default customization options. Replace all the text boxes, using the text shown in Figure 1–88. Delete the logo. Use the Clip Art task pane to search for a clip art related to skiing. Chose a black-and-white graphic. Change the publication properties, as specified by your instructor. Save the publication on a USB flash drive, using the file name, Lab 1-3 Spring Break Trip Advertisement. Submit the publication, shown in Figure 1–88, in the format specified by your instructor.

Cases and Places

Apply your creative thinking and problem-solving skills to design and implement a solution.

● Easier   ●● More Difficult

● 1: Design and Create a Play Annoucement Flyer

You are in charge of creating a flyer for a local dramatic production, presented by The Oak Leaf Troupe. Use the Play Flyer template in the Announcement group, with a Burgundy color scheme and the Breve font scheme. Do not include any tear-offs. Use the techniques in Chapter 1 to edit the text boxes. The name of the play is *The Taming of the Shrew*. The author is William Shakespeare. The dates are November 9, 10, and 11. The time is 7:30 p.m. at the Performing Arts Center. The phone number at the center is 555-1217. The ticket price is $11.50. The production is sponsored by the Knights of Columbus, the Junior Business Association, and the Fine Arts Council. Choose an appropriate graphic, using the Clip Art task pane, with the search term, drama. You may delete the sponsor logos or edit them as desired. Use the concepts and techniques presented in this chapter to create and format this flyer. Be sure to check spelling and then run the Design Checker.

● 2: Design and Create an Advertising Flyer with Tear-Offs

You decide to make some spare money typing term papers and research reports for other students. Prepare a flyer with tear-offs advertising your services. Using the Perforation flyer template in the Special Offer group, choose the Ocean color scheme, Foundry font scheme, and Contact Information tear-offs. The headline should read: Professional Desktop Publishing. The tag line should read: Fast Accurate Solutions! The body copy should read as follows: Need something typed? I offer a wide variety of professional desktop publishing services using Microsoft Office Publisher 2007. Overnight service is available on most projects. Samples and references upon request. Press the ENTER key after the first sentence and before the last sentence to create three paragraphs. The bulleted list should include the following items: Letters, Memos, Reports, Term Papers, Flyers, and Brochures. The tear-offs should read: Contact Sheila at 555-8059 or sheila@college.net. The location description text box should read: Services are located close to campus. Select the graphic within its frame and then double-click it to access the Clip Art task pane. Use the search term, printer, to locate a colorful printer that matches the color scheme. Delete the Business Name text box, the organization logo, the Date of Sale text box, and the Time of Sale text box.

●●3: Design and Create a Flyer for the Sale of a Business

After 30 years, your Uncle J.R. has decided to sell his bait shop. He wants you to help him create a sales flyer. The shop is in a choice location on Smithville Lake and has an established customer base. He wants to sell the store and all its contents, including the equipment, counter, tanks, and refrigeration unit. The 900-square-foot shop recently was appraised at $200,000, and your uncle is willing to sell for cash or on contract. Use the concepts and techniques presented in this chapter to create and format a sales flyer using a template. Include a headline, descriptive body copy, a tear-off, an appropriate photograph or clip art image, and bulleted list. Be sure to check spelling in the flyer. Then, delete the tear-offs and create a text box with your uncle's e-mail address. Run the Design Checker, convert the flyer to a Web publication, and then use the Publish to the Web command to generate the Web page.

Cases and Places *continued*

••4: Design and Create a Flyer for Your Community

Make It Personal

Many communities offer free Web page hosting for religious organizations. Using a flyer template, create a Web page for a local house of worship. Include the name, address, telephone, worship and education hours, as well as the name of a contact person. If possible, include a photo or line drawing of the building. If specific colors or fonts are associated with the organization, try to find a close match among the Publisher schemes. Use the Design Checker, the Convert to Web publication command, and the Publish to the Web command to prepare your publication.

••5: Redesign and Enhance a Poorly Designed Flyer

Working Together

Public locations, such as stores, schools, and libraries, have bulletin boards or windows for people to post flyers. Often, these bulletin boards or windows have so many flyers that some go unnoticed. Locate a posted flyer on a bulletin board or window that you think might be overlooked. Copy the text from the flyer and distribute it to each team member. Each member then independently should use this text, together with the techniques presented in this chapter, to create a flyer that would be more likely to catch the attention of passersby. Be sure to check the spelling. As a group, critique each flyer and have team members redesign their flyer based on the group's recommendations. Hand in each team member's original and final flyers.

2 | Designing a Newsletter

Objectives

You will have mastered the material in this chapter when you can:

- Describe the advantages of using a newsletter medium and identify the steps in its design process

- Edit a newsletter template

- Insert, delete, and navigate pages in a newsletter

- Edit a masthead

- Import text files and graphics, and continue stories across pages

- Use color scheme colors

- Insert page numbers in headers and footers

- Resize objects

- Edit captions, sidebars, and pull quotes

- Employ correct cut, copy, and paste techniques

- Check a newsletter for spelling and design errors

- Print a two-sided page

2 | Designing a Newsletter

Introduction

Desktop publishing is becoming the most popular way for businesses of all sizes to produce their printed publications. The desktop aspects of design and production make it easy and inexpensive to produce high-quality publications in a short time. **Desktop Publishing** implies doing everything from a desk, including the planning, designing, writing, and layout, as well as printing, collating, and distributing. With a personal computer and a software program, such as Publisher, you can create a professional publication from your computer without the cost and time of sending it to a professional publisher.

Project — Newsletter

Newsletters are a popular way for offices, businesses, schools, and other organizations to distribute information to their clientele. A **newsletter** usually is a double-sided multipage publication with newspaper features, such as columns and a masthead, and the added eye appeal of sidebars, pictures, and other graphics.

Newsletters have several advantages over other publication media. Typically, they are cheaper to produce than brochures. Brochures, designed to be in circulation longer as a type of advertising, usually are published in greater quantities and on more expensive paper than newsletters and are, therefore, more costly. Newsletters also differ from brochures in that newsletters commonly have a shorter shelf life, making newsletters a perfect forum for information that rapidly might become dated. Newsletters are narrower and more focused in scope than newspapers; their eye appeal is more distinctive. Many companies commonly distribute newsletters to interested audiences; however, newsletters also are becoming an integral part of many marketing plans to wider audiences because they offer a legitimate medium by which to communicate services, successes, and issues.

The project in this chapter uses a Publisher newsletter template to produce Communiquarium, the newsletter shown in Figures 2–1a and 2–1b. This monthly publication informs the community about events sponsored by the Riverside Aquarium. The institution's two-page newsletter contains a masthead, headings, articles, sidebars, pull quotes, and graphics.

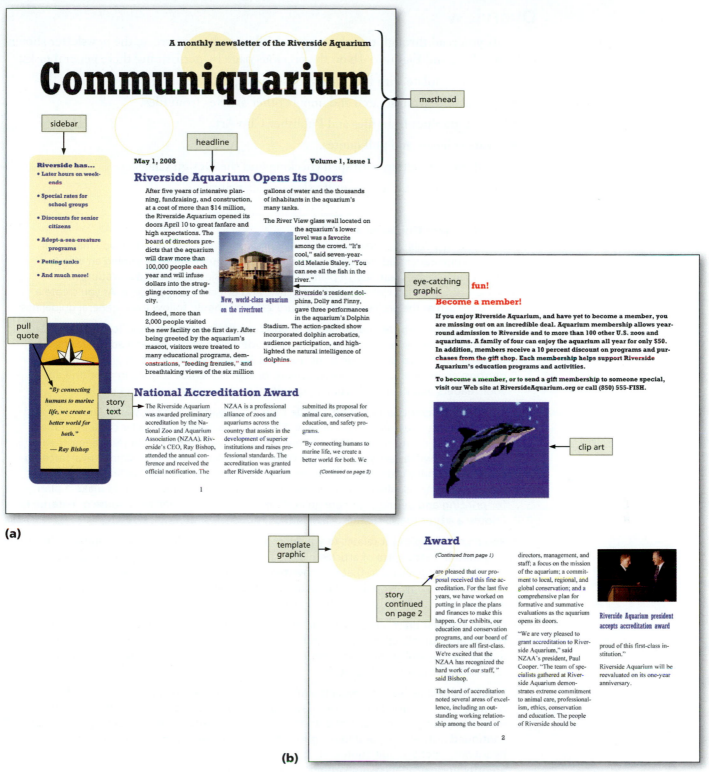

A monthly newsletter of the Riverside Aquarium

Communiquarium

masthead

sidebar

headline

Riverside has...
- Later hours on week-ends
- Special rates for school groups
- Discounts for senior citizens
- Adopt-a-sea-creature programs
- Petting tanks
- And much more!

May 1, 2008   Volume 1, Issue 1

Riverside Aquarium Opens Its Doors

After five years of intensive planning, fundraising, and construction, at a cost of more than $14 million, the Riverside Aquarium opened its doors April 10 to great fanfare and high expectations. The board of directors predicts that the aquarium will draw more than 100,000 people each year and will infuse dollars into the struggling economy of the city.

Indeed, more than 2,000 people visited the new facility on the first day. After being greeted by the aquarium's mascot, visitors were treated to many educational programs, demonstrations, "feeding frenzies," and breathtaking views of the six million

New, world-class aquarium on the riverfront

gallons of water and the thousands of inhabitants in the aquarium's many tanks.

The River View glass wall located on the aquarium's lower level was a favorite among the crowd. "It's cool," said seven-year-old Melanie Staley. "You can see all the fish in the river."

Riverside's resident dolphins, Dolly and Finny, gave three performances in the aquarium's Dolphin Stadium. The action-packed show incorporated dolphin acrobatics, audience participation, and highlighted the natural intelligence of dolphins.

pull quote

"*By connecting humans to marine life, we create a better world for both.*"

— Ray Bishop

story text

National Accreditation Award

The Riverside Aquarium was awarded preliminary accreditation by the National Zoo and Aquarium Association (NZAA). Riverside's CEO, Ray Bishop, attended the annual conference and received the official notification. The

NZAA is a professional alliance of zoos and aquariums across the country that assists in the development of superior institutions and raises professional standards. The accreditation was granted after Riverside Aquarium

submitted its proposal for animal care, conservation, education, and safety programs.

"By connecting humans to marine life, we create a better world for both. We

(Continued on page 2)

1

(a)

eye-catching graphic

fun!

Become a member!

If you enjoy Riverside Aquarium, and have yet to become a member, you are missing out on an incredible deal. Aquarium membership allows year-round admission to Riverside and to more than 100 other U.S. zoos and aquariums. A family of four can enjoy the aquarium all year for only $50. In addition, members receive a 10 percent discount on programs and purchases from the gift shop. Each membership helps support Riverside Aquarium's education programs and activities.

To become a member, or to send a gift membership to someone special, visit our Web site at RiversideAquarium.org or call (850) 555-FISH.

clip art

template graphic

Award

(Continued from page 1)

are pleased that our proposal received this fine accreditation. For the last five years, we have worked on putting in place the plans and finances to make this happen. Our exhibits, our education and conservation programs, and our board of directors are all first-class. We're excited that the NZAA has recognized the hard work of our staff, " said Bishop.

The board of accreditation noted several areas of excellence, including an outstanding working relationship among the board of

story continued on page 2

directors, management, and staff; a focus on the mission of the aquarium; a commitment to local, regional, and global conservation; and a comprehensive plan for formative and summative evaluations as the aquarium opens its doors.

"We are very pleased to grant accreditation to Riverside Aquarium," said NZAA's president, Paul Cooper. "The team of specialists gathered at Riverside Aquarium demonstrates extreme commitment to animal care, professionalism, ethics, conservation and education. The people of Riverside should be

Riverside Aquarium president accepts accreditation award

proud of this first-class institution."

Riverside Aquarium will be reevaluated on its one-year anniversary.

2

(b)

Figure 2–1

Overview

As you read through this chapter, you will learn how to create the newsletter shown in Figure 2–1a and Figure 2–1b on the previous page by performing these general tasks:

- Select a template with font and color schemes, and specify the page layout.
- Type articles from scratch and import other articles from files.
- Import graphics from files and Publisher Clip Art.
- Create sidebars and pull quotes.
- Proof the newsletter, with spell checking and the Design Checker.
- Save the newsletter and print it using duplex printing.

Plan Ahead

General Project Guidelines

When creating a Publisher newsletter, the actions you perform and decisions you make will affect the appearance and characteristics of the finished publication. Designing an effective newsletter involves a great deal of planning. A good newsletter, or any publication, must deliver a message in the clearest, most attractive, and effective way possible. As you create a newsletter, such as the project shown in Figure 2–1, you should follow these general guidelines:

1. **Decide on the purpose and audience.** Spend time brainstorming ideas for the newsletter. Think about why you want to create one. Decide on one purpose and adjust your plans to match that purpose. Decide if the audience is composed of local, interested clientele, patrons, employees, prospective customers, or family members. Keep in mind the age of your readers and their backgrounds, including both present and future readers.

2. **Plan for the layout and printing.** Decide how many pages your newsletter should be and how often you are going to produce it. Base your decisions on regular content that will continue into future newsletters. Choose the paper size and how columns, a masthead, and graphics will affect your layout. A consistent look and feel with simple, eye-catching graphics normally is the best choice for the design set. Plan to include one other graphic with each story. Usually mass-produced, collated, and stapled, you should make a plan for printing and decide if you are going to publish your newsletter in-house or externally. Choose a paper that is going to last until the next newsletter.

3. **Research the topic as it relates to your purpose and gather data.** Gather credible, relevant information in the form of articles, pictures, dates, figures, tables, and discussion threads. Plan far enough ahead so that you have time to take pictures or gather graphics for each story — even if you do not end up using them. Stay organized. Keep folders of information. Store pictures and stories together.

4. **Create the first draft.** Create a layout and masthead and receive approval if necessary. Follow any guidelines or required publication style. Reference all sources of information. Import stories and graphics as necessary. Determine the best layout for eye appeal and reliable dissemination of content.

5. **Proofread and revise the newsletter.** If possible, proofread the paper with a fresh set of eyes, that is, at least one to two days after completing the first draft. Proofreading involves reading the newsletter with the intent of identifying errors (spelling, grammar, continued notices, etc.) and looking for ways to improve it (purposeful graphics, catchy headlines, sidebars, pull quotes, etc.). Try reading the newsletter out loud, which helps to identify unclear or awkward wording. Ask someone else to proofread the paper and give you suggestions for improvements. Revise as necessary and then use the spelling and design checking features of the software.

When necessary, more specific details concerning the above guidelines are presented at appropriate points in the chapter. The chapter also will identify the actions performed and decisions made regarding these guidelines during the creation of the newsletter shown in Figure 2–1a and Figure 2–1b.

Benefits and Advantages of Newsletters

Table 2–1 lists some benefits and advantages of using the newsletter medium.

Table 2–1 Benefits and Advantages of Using a Newsletter Medium	
Purpose	**Benefits and Advantages**
Exposure	An easily distributed publication — office mail, bulk mail, electronically
	A pass-along publication for other interested parties
	A coffee table reading item in reception areas
Education	An opportunity to inform in a nonrestrictive environment
	A directed education forum for clientele
	An increased, focused feedback — unavailable in most advertising
Contacts	A form of legitimized contact
	A source of free information to build credibility
	An easier way to expand a contact database than other marketing tools
Communication	An effective medium to highlight the inner workings of a company
	A way to create a discussion forum
	A method to disseminate more information than a brochure
Cost	An easily designed medium using desktop publishing software
	An inexpensive method of mass production
	A reusable design

Using a Newsletter Template

The Publisher newsletter templates include a four-page layout with stories, graphics, sidebars, and other elements typical of newsletters using a rich collection of intuitive design, layout, typography, and graphics tools. Because Publisher takes care of many of the design issues, using a template to begin a newsletter gives you the advantage of proven layouts with fewer chances of publication errors.

Plan Ahead

Decide on the purpose and audience.
As you consult with all parties involved in the decision to create a newsletter, make sure you have a clear purpose. Remember that newsletters both communicate and educate. Ask yourself why you want to create a newsletter in the first place.

- **Decide on the audience.** As you decide on your audience, ask yourself these questions:
  - Who will be reading the articles?
  - What are the demographics of the population? That is, what are the characteristics such as gender, age, educational background, and heritage?
  - Why do you want those people to read your newsletter?
- **Finally choose your general topic.** As you make final decisions on the topic, ask yourself these questions:
  - Will the newsletter be about the company or only about one aspect of the company?
  - Will the newsletter cover a narrow topic or be more of a general information newsletter?
  - Use the phrase, "I want to tell *<audience>* about *<topic>* because *<purpose>*."

After starting Publisher, the following pages choose a template and select font and color schemes.

To Start Publisher

If you are using a computer to step through the project in this chapter, and you want your screens to match the figures in this book, you should change your computer's resolution to 1024 × 768. For information about how to change a computer's resolution, read Appendix D.

The following steps, which assume Windows is running, start Publisher based on a typical installation. You may need to ask your instructor how to start Publisher for your computer.

Note: If you are using Windows XP, see Appendix F for alternate To Start Publisher steps.

1 Click the Start button on the Windows Vista taskbar to display the Start menu, and then click All Programs at the bottom of the left pane on the Start menu to display the All Programs list.

2 Click Microsoft Office in the All Programs list to display the Microsoft Office list, and then click Microsoft Office Publisher 2007 to start Publisher and display the Getting Started with Microsoft Office Publisher 2007 catalog.

3 If the Publisher window is not maximized, click the Maximize button next to the Close button on its title bar to maximize the window.

Newsletter Design Choices

Many design planning features are built into Publisher, including 65 different newsletter templates from which you may choose, each with its own set of design, color, font, and layout schemes.

Plan Ahead

Plan for the layout and printing.
Choosing a layout and printing options before you even write the articles is a daunting but extremely important task. The kind of printing process and paper you will be using will affect the cost and, therefore, the length of the newsletter. Based on what you can afford to produce and distribute, the layout may need more or fewer articles, graphics, columns, and sidebars. Decide on a consistent theme with repeated elements on each page. Make conscious decisions about the kind of alignment you plan to use with the masthead, graphics, and text. Decide what kinds of features in the newsletter should be close to other features.

To Choose a Newsletter Template and Change Options

The following steps choose a newsletter template and make design choices. The Watermark template goes along with the theme of the aquarium, as does the Tropics color scheme.

1

- Click the Newsletters button in the list of publication types to display the catalog of newsletter templates.

- Scroll to display the Watermark preview and then click the Watermark preview to select it (Figure 2–2).

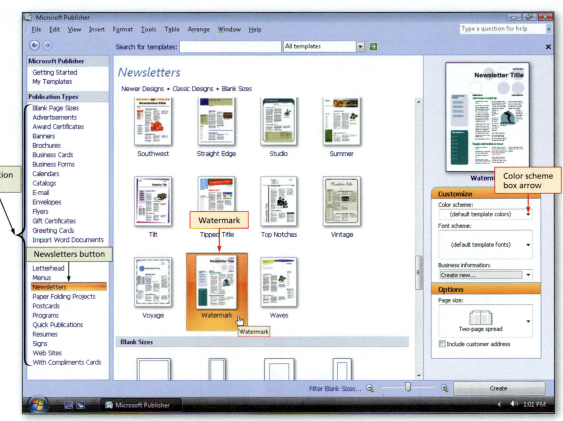

Figure 2–2

2

- In the Customize area, click the Color scheme box arrow to display the list of color schemes.

Experiment

- Scroll in the list of color schemes and click various schemes to see the preview change in the right portion of the window.

- Click Tropics in the list to change the color scheme for the publication (Figure 2–3).

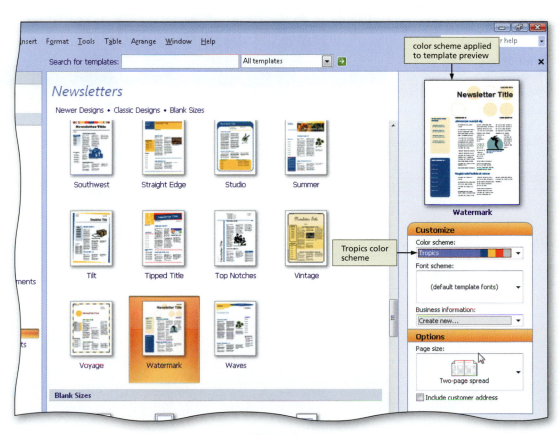

Figure 2–3

3

• Click the Font scheme box arrow and then scroll as necessary to view and click Foundry in the list to select the font scheme (Figure 2–4).

Q&A

How do the newsletter templates differ?

Each newsletter template produces four pages of stories, graphics, and other objects in the same way. The difference is the location and style of the shapes and graphics, as well as the specific kind of decorations unique to each publication set. A **publication set** is a predefined group of shapes, designed in patterns to create a template style. A publication set is constant across publication types; for example, the Watermark newsletter template has the same shapes and style of objects as does the Watermark brochure template. A publication set helps in branding a company across publication types.

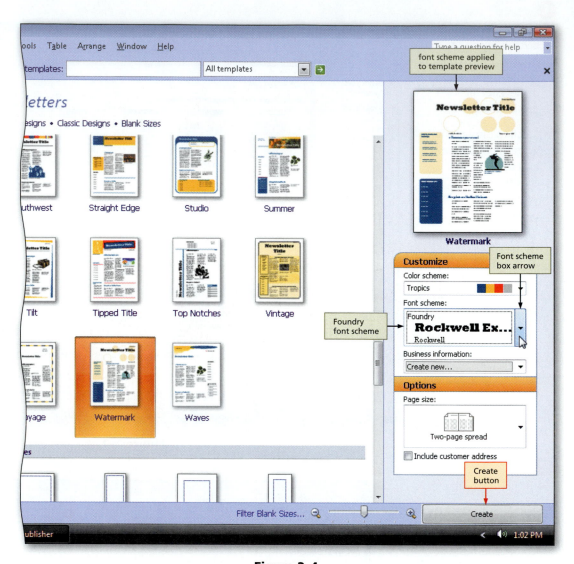

Figure 2–4

4

- Click the Create button in the lower-right corner of the window to create the publication based on the template settings (Figure 2–5).

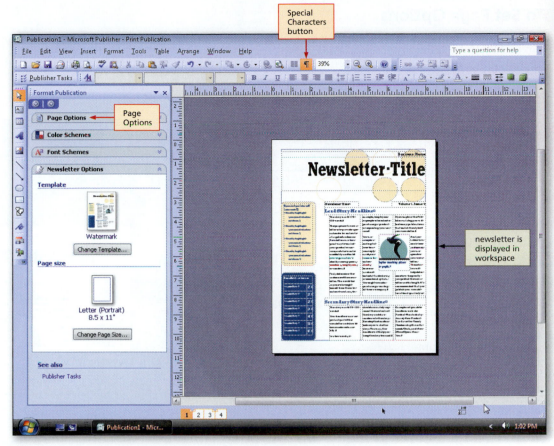

Figure 2–5

To Display Formatting Marks

As discussed in Chapter 1, it is helpful to display formatting marks, which indicate where in the publication you pressed the ENTER key, SPACEBAR, and other keys. The following step displays formatting marks.

1 If the Special Characters button on the Standard toolbar is not selected already, click it to display formatting marks on the screen.

To Set Page Options

The next steps set one final page option. Publisher newsletters typically display story text in 1, 2, or 3 columns or in a mixed format. The aquarium newsletter will use the mixed format. The choice to mix the number of columns complements the variety of articles that will be presented each month in the newsletter.

1

- Click Page Options in the Format Publication task pane to display the various options.

Experiment

- Click 1, 2, and 3 in the Columns area to view the effect on the newsletter template.

- Click Mixed in the Columns area to choose a mixed number of columns for the various stories in the newsletter (Figure 2–6).

 Q&A

What is the Suggested objects area?

The Suggested objects area is a list of graphical objects, including logos, table of contents, sidebars, and pull quotes typically used in newsletters.

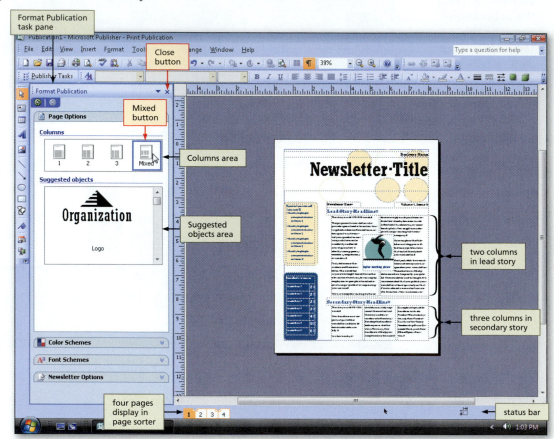

Figure 2–6

2

- To close the task pane, click the Close button in the Format Publication task pane.

Editing the Newsletter Template

The purpose of a newsletter is to communicate and educate its readers. Publisher places the lead story in a prominent position on the page and uses a discussion of purpose and audience as the default text.

The following pages discuss how to edit various articles and objects in the newsletter.

Pagination

Each Publisher newsletter template creates four pages of text and graphics. This template is appropriate for some applications, but the aquarium staff wants to print a single-sheet, two-sided newsletter. Page 4 of the newsletter template contains objects typically used on the back page, so you will delete pages 2 and 3 to create a two-page newsletter.

Recall that the page sorter is located on the status bar. Its paged-shaped controls represent each page of the publication and can be used to go to, rearrange, or work with publication pages. You can click the page sorter to move to new pages or right-click it to display a shortcut menu.

To Change and Delete Pages in a Newsletter

The following steps change and delete pages.

1

• Click the Page 2 icon on the page sorter to display page 2 (Figure 2–7).

Q&A How do I know what page is being displayed?

The page sorter displays the selected page or pages in orange.

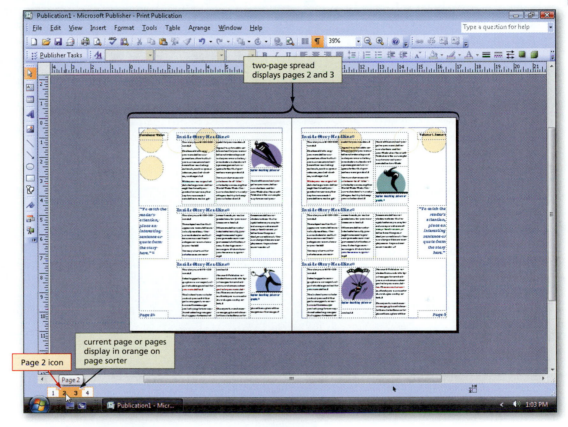

Figure 2–7

2

• Right-click the Page 2 icon to display the shortcut menu (Figure 2–8).

Q&A What does the Rename command do?

The Rename command allows you to change the name of the page. The name of the page displays only when you point to the page icon in the status bar. It does not print or display in the page layout.

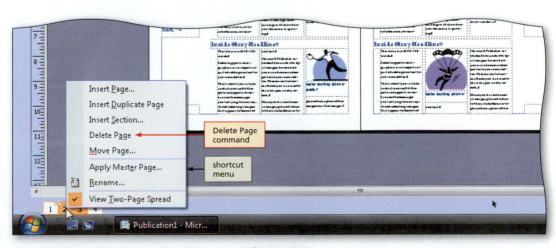

Figure 2–8

3

- Click Delete Page to display the Delete Page dialog box.

- If necessary, click the Both pages option button to select it (Figure 2–9).

Q&A

What would happen if I delete only one of the two pages?

If you delete only one of the two pages, your newsletter will have an odd number of pages, which might cause problems when you print or cause a blank page to print at the end of your newsletter.

Figure 2–9

4

- Click the OK button in the Delete Page dialog box.

- If a Microsoft Publisher dialog box is displayed to confirm the deletion, click the OK button to delete the pages (Figure 2–10).

Q&A

What if I delete a page by accident?

Simply click the Undo button on the Standard toolbar.

Other Ways

1. To change pages, on Edit menu, click Go to Page
2. To change pages, press CTRL+G
3. To change pages, press F5
4. To delete page, on Edit menu, click Delete Page

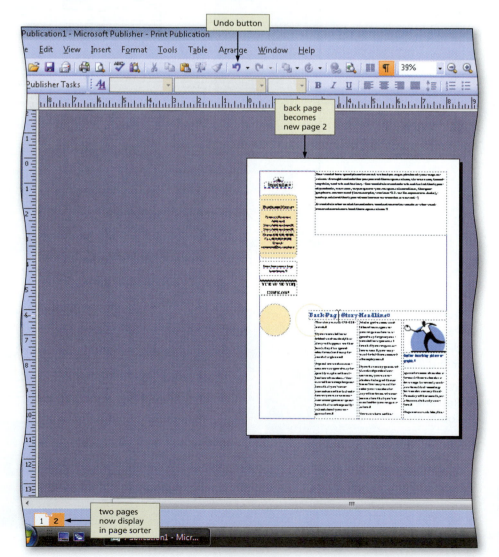

Figure 2–10

Editing the Masthead

Most newsletters and brochures contain a masthead similar to those used in newspapers. A **masthead** is a box or section printed in each issue that lists information, such as the name, publisher, location, volume, and date. The Publisher-designed masthead, included in the Watermark newsletter design set, contains several text boxes and color-filled shapes that create an attractive, eye-catching graphic that complements the set. You need to edit the text boxes, however, to convey appropriate messages.

Publisher incorporates four text boxes in the Watermark newsletter masthead (Figure 2–11). The newsletter title is displayed in a text box layered on top of the template graphics. A text box above the title displays the default text, Business Name. Two text boxes display in the lower portion of the masthead for the date and volume/issue.

BTW

Inserting Pages
Inserting pages in a newsletter is just as easy as deleting them. The Page command on the Insert menu provides the option of inserting a left- or right-hand page, as well as choices in the types of objects to display on the page. When you choose to insert or delete when working on the first or last page, Publisher will warn you of pagination problems and will offer you a confirmation button.

Editing Techniques

Recall that Publisher uses text-editing techniques similar to most word processing programs. To insert text, position the insertion point and type the new text. Publisher always inserts the text to the left of the insertion point. The text to the right of the insertion point moves to the right and downward to accommodate the new text.

The BACKSPACE key deletes text to the left of the insertion point. To delete or change more than a few characters, however, you first should select the text. Publisher handles selecting text in a slightly different manner from word processing programs. In Publisher, you select unedited default text, such as placeholder titles and articles in the newsletters, with a single click. To select large amounts of text, click the text and then press CTRL+A, or drag through the text. To select individual words, double-click the word, as you would in word processing.

To Edit the Masthead

The following steps edit text in the masthead.

1
- Click the Page 1 icon on the page sorter to change the display to page 1.

- Click the text, Newsletter Title, to select it.

- Press the F9 key to view the masthead at actual size (Figure 2–11).

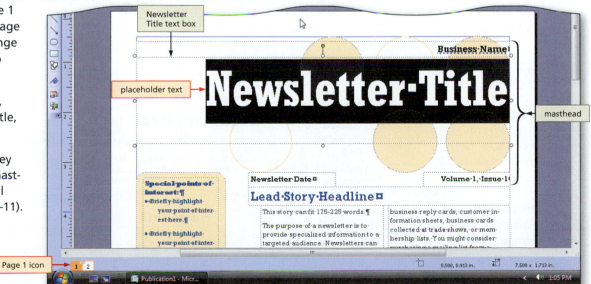

Figure 2–11

2

- Type
  Communiquarium
  to replace the text
  (Figure 2–12).

Q&A Why does my
font look
different?

Publisher
replaces the selected
text using the font
from the design set.
Because fonts some-
times are printer-
dependent, your
font may differ from
the one shown.

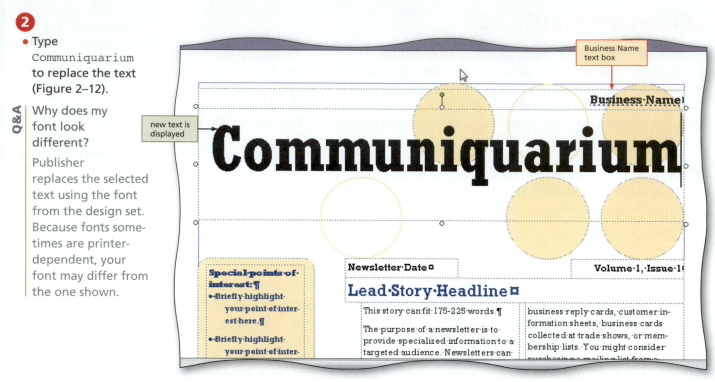

Figure 2–12

3

- To select the
  placeholder text in
  the Business Name
  text box, click the
  text and then press
  CTRL+A to select
  all of the text
  (Figure 2–13).

Q&A Why does my
Business Name text
box have different
words?

The Business Name
text sometimes
is taken from the
Publisher installation
process. The name of
your school or busi-
ness may be displayed
in the text box.

Q&A Should I fix the red
wavy line below the
word Communiquarium?

No, you will fix it later in the chapter.

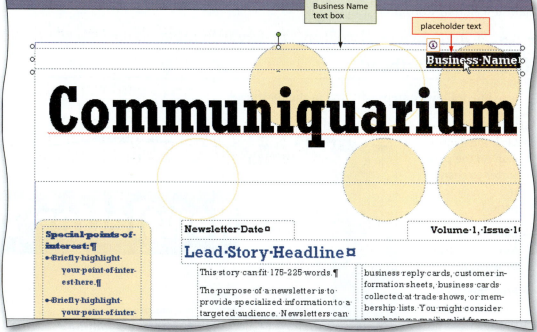

Figure 2–13

4

• Type A monthly newsletter of the Riverside Aquarium to replace the text (Figure 2–14).

What do the blue dots mean below the text?

The blue dots are a smart tag notation. Recall that certain template text boxes are designed to hold business informa- tion, tag lines, and address data. Each of these special text boxes will display this kind of smart tag notation under the text. The dots will not print.

Figure 2–14

5

• Click the text in the Newsletter Date text box (Figure 2–15).

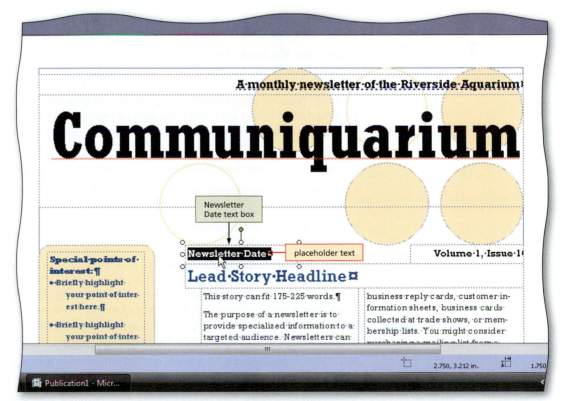

Figure 2–15

6
- **Type** May 1, 2008 to replace the text (Figure 2–16).

Q&A

Should I enter new information in the volume and issue box?

This is the first issue of the aquarium's newsletter. Only subsequent issues would require a change in that box.

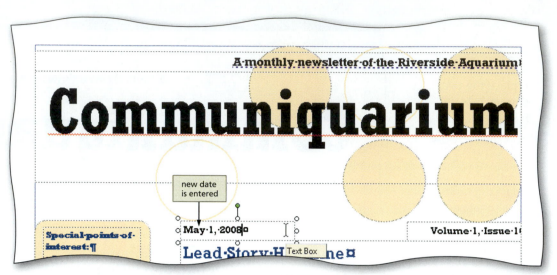

Figure 2–16

Newsletter Text

You will import some stories for the newsletter; others you will type yourself.

Plan Ahead

Research the topic as it relates to your purpose and gather data.

- **Researching the topic.** If you have to write a story from scratch, gather your data, do your research, and have an informed reader go over your content. The same principles of audience, purpose, and topic apply to individual stories, just as they did for the newsletter as a whole. Evaluate your sources for authority, currency, and accuracy. Be especially wary of information obtained from the Web. Any person, company, or organization can publish a Web page on the Internet. Ask yourself these questions about the source:

  - Authority: Does a reputable institution or group support the source? Is the information presented without bias? Are the author's credentials listed and verifiable?

  - Currency: Is the information up to date? Are dates of sources listed? What is the last date revised or updated?

  - Accuracy: Is the information free of errors? Is it verifiable? Are the sources clearly identified?

- **Gather the data.** Identify the sources for your text and graphics. Notify all writers of important dates and allow time for gathering the data. Make a list of each story; include the author's name, the approximate length of the story, the electronic format, and associated graphics. Ask the author for suggestions for headlines. Consult with colleagues about other graphics, features, sidebars, and the masthead.

- **Acknowledge all sources of information; do not plagiarize.** Not only is plagiarism unethical, but it also is considered an academic crime that can have severe punishments, such as failing a course or being expelled from school.

  When you summarize, paraphrase (rewrite information in your own words), present facts, give statistics, quote exact words, or show a map, chart, or other graphical image, you must acknowledge the source. Information that commonly is known or accessible to the audience constitutes common knowledge and does not need to be acknowledged. If, however, you question whether certain information is common knowledge, you should document it — just to be safe.

Publisher allows users to import text and graphics from many sources, from a variety of different programs, and in many different file formats. Publisher uses the term **importing** to describe inserting text or objects from any other source into the Publisher workspace. The stories for the newsletter are included in the Data Files for Students. See the inside back cover of this book for instructions on downloading the Data Files for Students, or contact your instructor for more information about accessing the required files.

Publisher uses the term, **story**, to mean text that is contained within a single text box or a chain of linked text boxes. Each newsletter template provides **linked text boxes**, or text boxes whose text flows from one to another. In the templates, two or three text boxes may be linked automatically; however, if a story is too long to fit in the linked text boxes, Publisher will offer to link even more text boxes for easy reading.

Replacing Placeholder Text Using an Imported File

Publisher suggests that 175 to 225 words will fit in the space allocated for the lead story. The story displays in a two-column text box format that **connects,** or wraps, the running text from one linked text box to the next.

This edition of Communiquarium has three stories, two of which have been typed previously and stored using Microsoft Word. The stories, stored on the Data Disk that accompanies this text, are ready to be used in the newsletter. The third story you will type yourself. Each story will include a headline, which is a short phrase printed at the top of a story, usually in a bigger font than the story. A headline summarizes the story that follows it.

BTW

Zooming
Recall that the F9 key toggles between the current page view and 100% magnification, or actual size. **Toggle** means the same key will alternate views, or turn a feature on and off. Editing text is easier if you view the text at 100% magnification or even larger. Page editing techniques, such as moving graphics, inserting new objects, and aligning objects, are performed more easily in Whole Page view. Toggling back and forth with the F9 key works well. You also may choose different magnifications and views in the Zoom list on the Standard toolbar.

To Edit a Headline and Import a Text File

The following steps first edit the Lead Story Headline placeholder text and then import a text file to replace the Publisher-supplied default text. The text file is included in the Data Files for Students. See the inside back cover of this book for instructions on downloading the Data Files for Students, or contact your instructor for more information about accessing the required files.

1

- Click the text, Lead Story Headline, to select it.

- If necessary, zoom to 100% by clicking the Zoom In button on the Standard toolbar.

- Type Riverside Aquarium Opens Its Doors to replace the text (Figure 2–17).

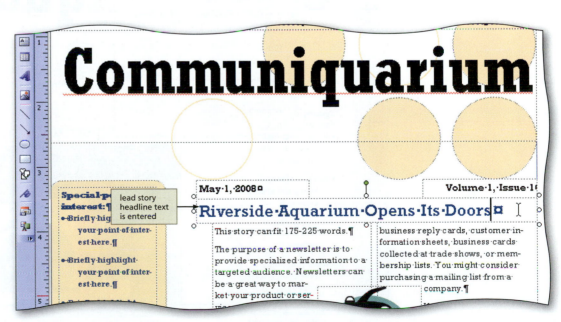

Figure 2–17

2
- Click the story below the headline (Figure 2–18).

🔍 **Experiment**
- Scroll as necessary to read the story to learn about design suggestions related to newsletter publications.

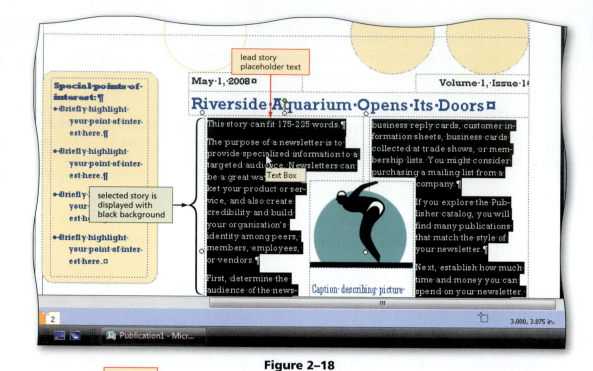

Figure 2–18

3
- Click Insert on the menu bar to display the Insert menu (Figure 2–19).

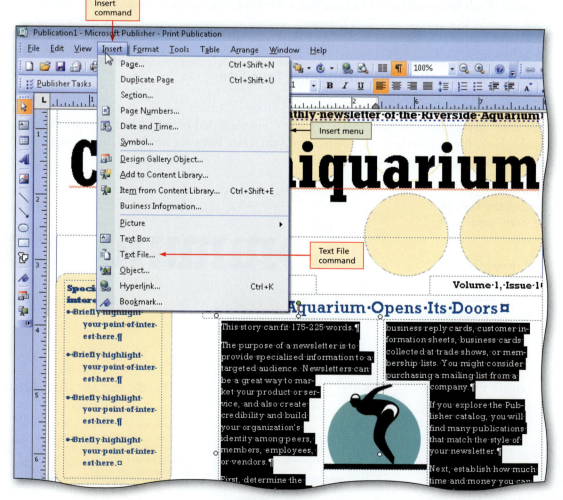

Figure 2–19

4

- Click Text File to display the Insert Text dialog box.

- If Computer is not displayed in the Favorite Links section, drag the top or bottom edge of the Insert Text dialog box until Computer is displayed.

- Click Computer in the Favorite Links section to display a list of available drives.

- If necessary, scroll until UDISK 2.0 (F:) appears in the list of available drives.

- Double-click UDISK 2.0 (F:) in the Computer list to open the USB flash drive (Figure 2–20).

Q&A I do not have UDISK 2.0 (F:) drive. What do I do?

The name of your USB flash drive may differ. If you did not download the Data Files, see the inside back cover of this book for instructions on downloading the Data Files for Students, or contact your instructor for more information about accessing the required files.

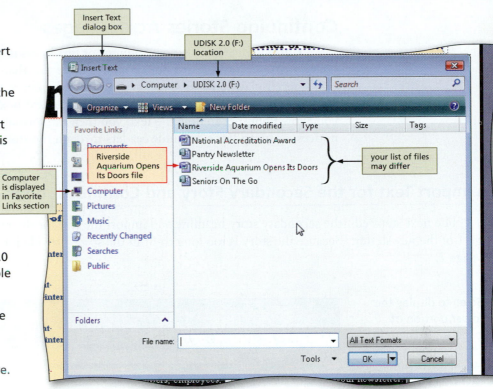

Insert Text dialog box

UDISK 2.0 (F:) location

Computer is displayed in Favorite Links section

Riverside Aquarium Opens Its Doors file

your list of files may differ

Figure 2–20

5

- Double-click the file, Riverside Aquarium Opens Its Doors, to insert the text into the newsletter (Figure 2–21).

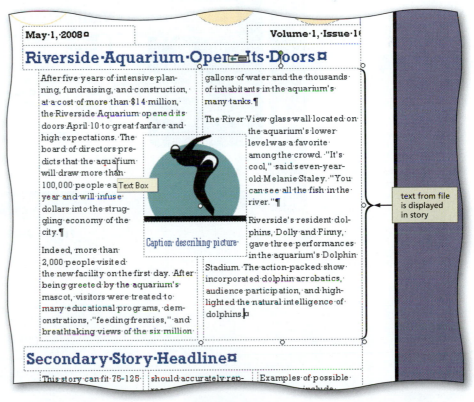

text from file is displayed in story

Figure 2–21

Other Ways

1. Right-click article, point to Change Text, click Text File

Continuing Stories Across Pages

Continuing a story across columns or text boxes is one of the features that Publisher helps you to perform. If the story contains more text than will fit in the default text box, Publisher displays a message to warn you. You then have the option to allow Publisher to connect or **autoflow** the text to another available text box, or to flow the text yourself. If you allow Publisher to flow the text, you then can format the text boxes with continued notices, or **jump lines**, to guide readers through the story.

To Import Text for the Secondary Story and Continue It on Page 2

The next steps edit the secondary story headline and import the text for the article in the lower portion of page 1 of the newsletter. Because the story is too long to fit in the space provided, you will continue the story on page 2.

- Scroll to display the lower portion of page 1 and then click the Secondary Story Headline placeholder text to select it.

- Type National Accreditation Award to replace the selected headline (Figure 2–22).

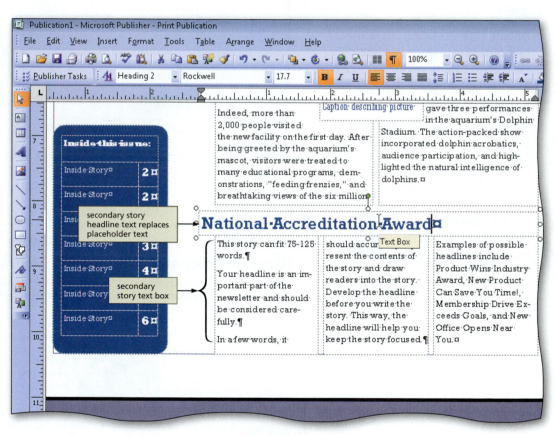

Figure 2–22

2

- Click the text in the secondary story text box to select it.

- Click Insert on the menu bar and then click Text File to open the Insert Text dialog box.

- Navigate to the UDISK 2.0 (F:) drive, if necessary (Figure 2–23).

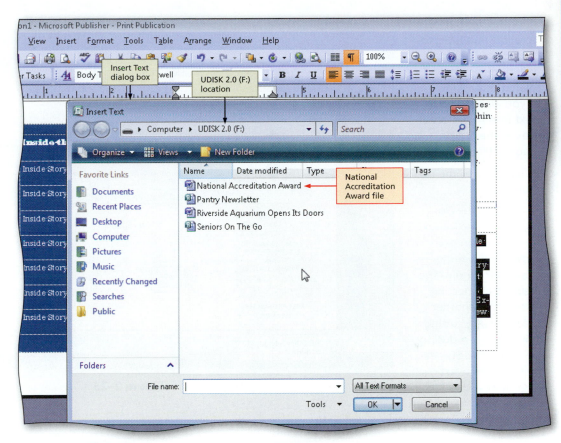

Figure 2–23

3

- Double-click the file, National Accreditation Award, to insert it in the publication. Publisher will display a dialog box asking if you want to use autoflow (Figure 2–24).

Q&A

Where is the rest of the story?

As much text as possible was added to the secondary story text boxes. Because the story did not fit, a dialog box helps you make decisions about the rest of the story.

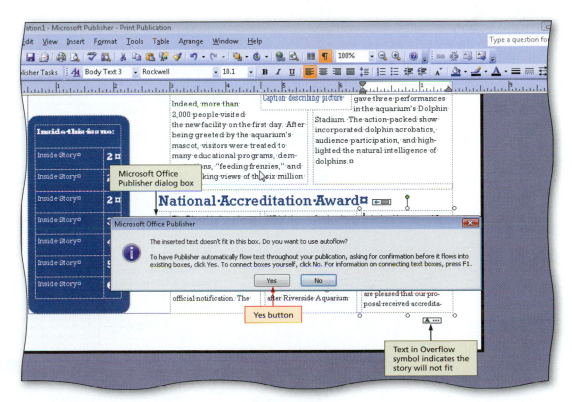

Figure 2–24

4

- Click the Yes button to allow Publisher to flow text. Publisher will display a second dialog box asking if you want to flow text into the selected box at the top of page 2. (Figure 2–25).

What if I click the No button?

If you click the No button, the extra text is stored in an overflow area, waiting for you to resolve the issue by connecting the text to another box yourself, cutting the story, or reducing the font size. Stories with **text in overflow** will cause a Design Checker error.

5

- Click the No button to cause Publisher to move to the back page story and display another dialog box about autoflowing. (Figure 2–26).

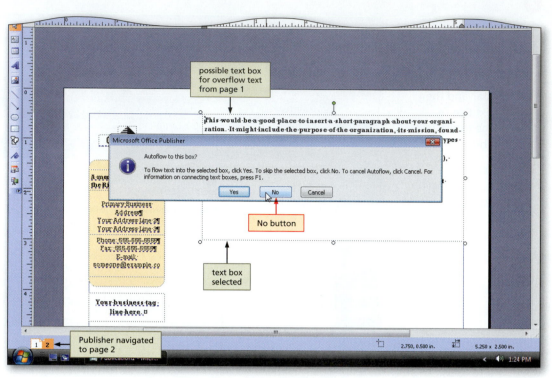

Figure 2–25

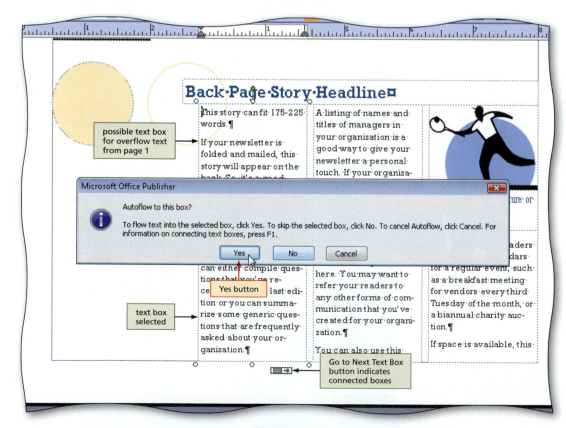

Figure 2–26

6

- Click the Yes button to autoflow into the back page story (Figure 2–27).

Q&A

What if I have no spare text boxes to flow into?

Publisher will ask if you want new text boxes created. If you answer yes, Publisher will automatically create text boxes on a new page.

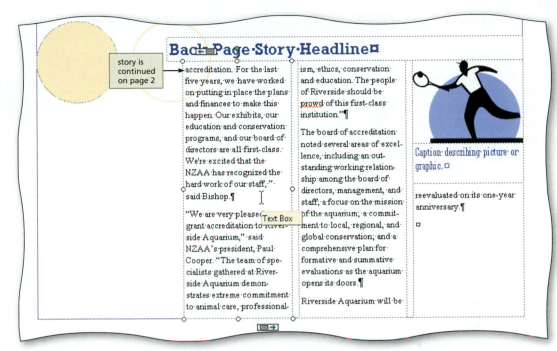

Figure 2–27

story is continued on page 2

BTW

The Text Overflow Symbol
Below the text box in Figure 2–24 on page PUB 93 is a **Text in Overflow symbol**, which means that there is more text than can fit in the current text box. The **overflow area** is an invisible storage location within your publication to hold extra text — similar to a clipboard, but saved with the publication. The overflow area is not electricity-dependent, like the system or Office clipboard. It is saved with the document. You can move your text out of overflow and back into your publication by one of several means: flowing text into a new text box, autofitting text, enlarging the text box, changing the text size, changing the margins within the text box, or deleting some of the text in the text box.

To Format with Continued Notices

In the story that flows from page 1 to page 2, the steps on the next page format the last box on page 1 with a **continued on notice**. Then, on page 2, the first text box is formatted with a **continued from notice**. To access the formatting options for text boxes, double-click the border of the text box. The Text Box tab in the Format dialog box displays options to flow stories from one page to another. The placement of the notices and the page numbering is automatic.

1

- To move to page 1, click the Page 1 icon.

- Double-click the border of the lower-right text box. When Publisher displays the Format Text Box dialog box, click the Text Box tab.

- Click to display a check mark in the Include "Continued on page …" check box (Figure 2–28).

Q&A

What do I do if my dialog box is covering up the text box?

The setting changes will take place when you click the OK button. If you want to see both the dialog box and the text box, you can drag the title bar of the dialog box to the left, as shown in Figure 2–28.

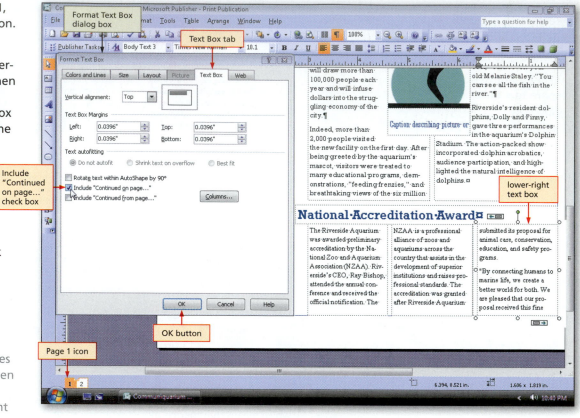

Figure 2–28

2

- Click the OK button.

- To move to page 2, click the Page 2 icon.

- Double-click the border of the lower-left text box. When Publisher displays the Format Text Box dialog box, click the Text Box tab.

- Click to display a check mark in the Include "Continued from page …" check box (Figure 2–29).

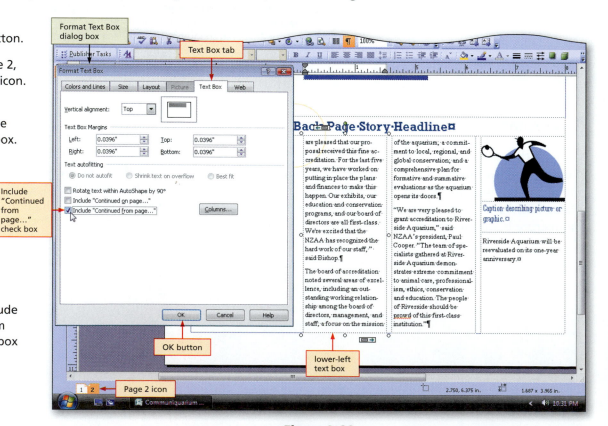

Figure 2–29

3

• Click the OK button (Figure 2–30).

 Experiment

• Move between pages 1 and 2 and look at the jump lines with the supplied page numbers.

Other Ways

1. Select text box, click Format on menu bar, click Text Box, click Text Box tab, click continued notice check box

2. Right-click selected text box, click Format Text Box, click Text Box tab, click continued notice check box

continued notice

Back Page Story Headline¤

(Continued from page 1)¤

Are pleased that our proposal received this fine accreditation. For the last five years, we have worked on putting in place the plans and finances to make this happen. Our exhibits, our education and conservation programs, and our board of directors are all first-class. We're excited that the NZAA has recognized the hard work of our staff," said Bishop. ¶

The board of accreditation noted several areas of excellence, including an outstanding working relationship among the board of

directors, management, and staff, a focus on the mission of the aquarium; a commitment to local, regional, and global conservation; and a comprehensive plan for formative and summative evaluations as the aquarium opens its doors. ¶

"We are very pleased to grant accreditation to Riverside Aquarium," said NZAA's president, Paul Cooper. "The team of specialists gathered at Riverside Aquarium demonstrates extreme commitment to animal care, professionalism, ethics, conservation and education. The people of Riverside should be

Caption describing picture or graphic. ¤

proud of this first-class institution." ¶

Riverside Aquarium will be reevaluated on its one-year anniversary. ¤

Figure 2–30

To Replace the Back Page Story Headline

The following steps replace the Back Page Story Headline.

1 Select the text, Back Page Story Headline.

2 Type `Award` to replace the text (Figure 2–31).

BTW

Importing Text
Importing the articles instead of typing them saves time and adds the convenience of using word processing. Publisher accepts most file formats from popular word processing programs and text editors.

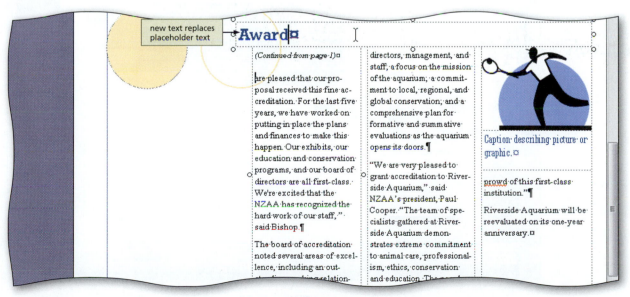

new text replaces placeholder text

Award¤

(Continued from page 1)¤

Are pleased that our proposal received this fine accreditation. For the last five years, we have worked on putting in place the plans and finances to make this happen. Our exhibits, our education and conservation programs, and our board of directors are all first-class. We're excited that the NZAA has recognized the hard work of our staff," said Bishop. ¶

The board of accreditation noted several areas of excellence, including an out-

directors, management, and staff, a focus on the mission of the aquarium; a commitment to local, regional, and global conservation; and a comprehensive plan for formative and summative evaluations as the aquarium opens its doors. ¶

"We are very pleased to grant accreditation to Riverside Aquarium," said NZAA's president, Paul Cooper. "The team of specialists gathered at Riverside Aquarium demonstrates extreme commitment to animal care, professionalism, ethics, conservation and education. The

Caption describing picture or graphic. ¤

proud of this first-class institution." ¶

Riverside Aquarium will be reevaluated on its one-year anniversary. ¤

Figure 2–31

Editing Stories in Microsoft Word

You have seen that you can edit text directly in Microsoft Publisher or import text from a previously stored file. A third way to edit text is to use Microsoft Word as your editor. Publisher provides an easy link between the two applications.

If you need to edit only a few words, it is faster to stay in Publisher. If you need to edit a longer story that appears on different pages in a publication or one that has not been previously stored, it might be easier to edit the story in Word. Many users are accustomed to working in Word and want to take advantage of available Word features, such as grammar checking and revision tracking. It sometimes is easier to drag and drop paragraphs in a Word window rather than performing the same task in a Publisher window, especially when it involves moving across pages in a larger Publisher publication.

Occasionally, if you have many applications running, such as virus protection and other memory-taxing programs, Publisher may warn you that you are low on computer memory. In that case, close the other applications and try editing the story in Word again.

While you are working on a story in Word, you cannot edit the corresponding text box in Publisher. Editing your stories in Word allows you to manipulate the text using the full capabilities of a word processing program.

To Edit a Story Using Word

In the Communiquarium newsletter, the back page contains a text box to display more information or articles about the organization. The aquarium's informational text has not been previously stored in a file for importing, so it must be typed. The following steps use Microsoft Word in conjunction with Publisher to create the text. Microsoft Word version 6.0 or later must be installed on your computer for this procedure to work.

- Scroll to display the text box in the upper-right portion of page 2.

- Select the placeholder text.

- Click Edit on the menu bar to display the Edit menu (Figure 2–32).

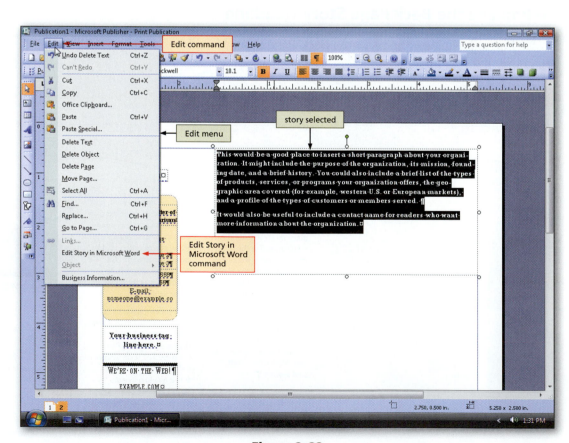

Figure 2–32

2

- Click the Edit Story in Microsoft Word command to launch the application.

- When Microsoft Word starts in a new window, maximize the window if necessary, by double-clicking the title bar.

- Press CTRL+A to select all of the text (Figure 2–33).

Q&A Why are my fonts different?

Usually, the text displays the same formatting as the previous text in Publisher. Your display may differ depending on available fonts.

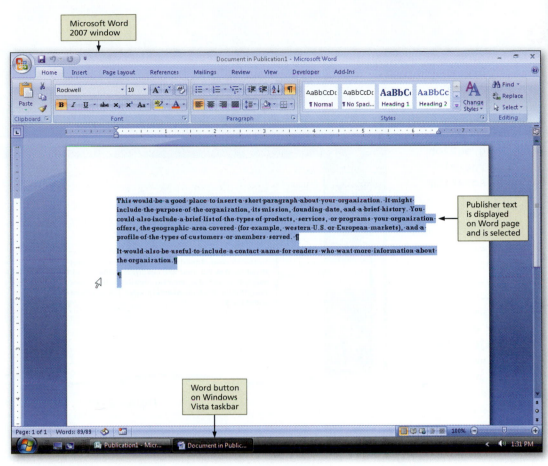

Figure 2–33

3

- Type Join the fun! and then press the ENTER key.

- Type Become a member! and then press the ENTER key (Figure 2–34).

Q&A Why are my formatting marks not showing in Microsoft Word?

It is possible that someone has turned off formatting marks. Click the Show/Hide ¶ button to turn them on and off.

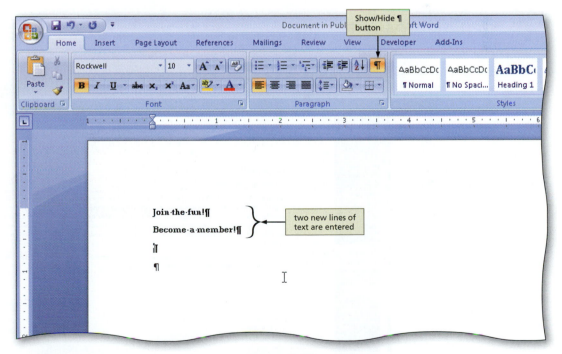

Figure 2–34

4

- **Type** If you
  enjoy Riverside
  Aquarium, and
  have yet to
  become a
  member, you are
  missing out on
  an incredible
  deal. Aquarium
  membership
  allows year-
  round admission
  to Riverside
  and to more
  than 100 other
  U.S. zoos and
  aquariums. A
  family of four
  can enjoy the
  aquarium all
  year for only
  $50. In
  addition,
  members receive a
10 percent discount on programs and purchases from the gift shop. Each membership helps support Riverside Aquarium's education programs and activities. and then press the ENTER key (Figure 2–35).

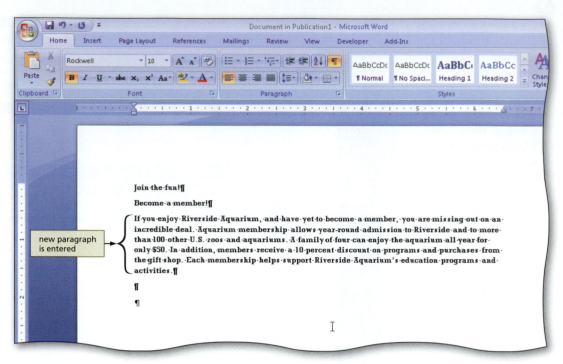

Figure 2–35

5

- **Type** To become a
  member, or to
  send a gift
  membership
  to someone
  special, visit
  our Web site at
  RiversideAquarium.
  org or call (850)
  555-FISH. to finish
  the text (Figure 2–36).

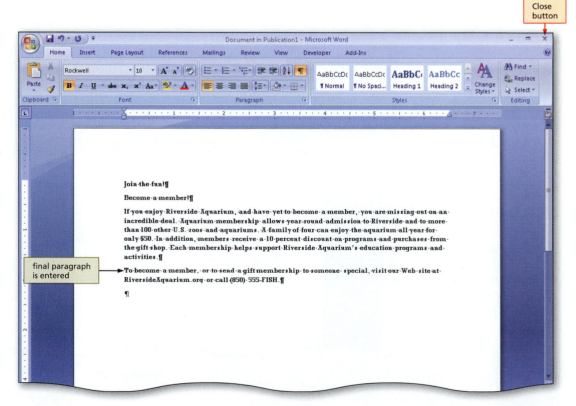

Figure 2–36

6
- Click the Close button on the title bar of the Document in Publication1 – Microsoft Word window to close it (Figure 2–37).

Q&A
Why do I see only gray lines instead of the text?

Launching Microsoft Word from within Microsoft Publisher is a drain on your system's memory and on the refresh rate of your screen. Try going to page 1 and then back to page 2 to refresh the screen.

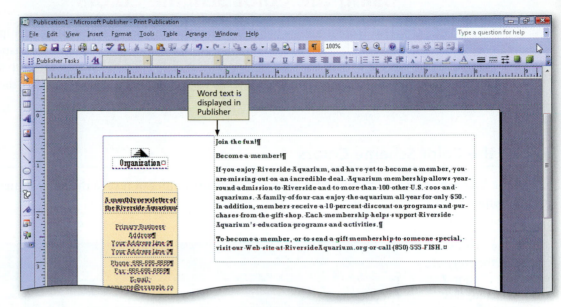

Figure 2–37

To Change the Font Size

The following steps change the font size of the first two paragraphs of the newly imported story.

1 Drag to select the first two paragraphs of text.

2 On the Formatting toolbar, click the text in the Font Size box to select it.

3 Type 14 and then press the ENTER key. Do not deselect the first two paragraphs of text (Figure 2–38).

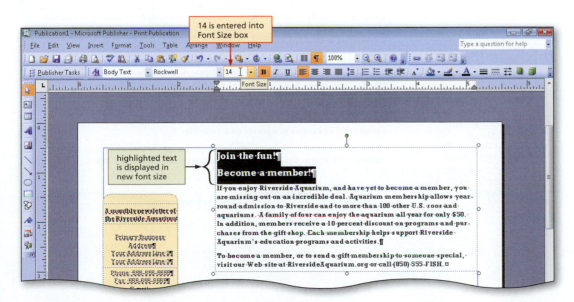

Figure 2–38

Using the Color Scheme Colors

The Tropics color scheme chosen earlier in this chapter contains complementary colors that can be used for text, graphics, or backgrounds. Publisher automatically displays the color scheme colors at the top of each dialog box and button menu that has to do with color, allowing you to choose the correct tint or shade that matches the other colors in your publication.

To Use the Color Scheme Colors

The following steps change the font color of the first two lines of text in the story to match the color in the color scheme.

- With the first two lines of the story at the top of page 2 still selected, click the Font Color button arrow on the Formatting toolbar to display the button menu (Figure 2–39).

Q&A

How many colors are in the color scheme?

Publisher provides a main color, which is usually black for standard text; five accent colors, the first of which is used for headlines in newsletters, for example; a hyperlink color; and a color for hyperlinks that have been previously clicked.

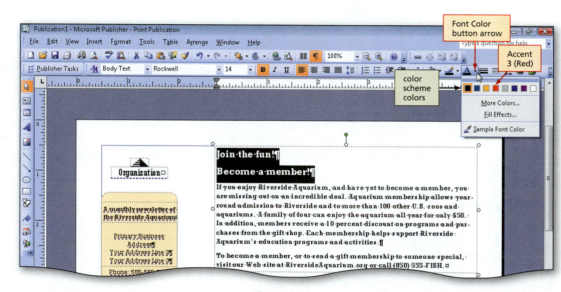

Figure 2–39

- Click the Accent 3 (Red) color to change the font color of the selected text.

- Click outside the text box to deselect the text (Figure 2–40).

Q&A

What if I change my mind about the color scheme?

Any text or object color chosen from the color scheme or top row of the Font Color button menu automatically will convert when you choose the new scheme. If you choose a color scheme that is not in the five basic colors of the color scheme, the color will not change when converting to a new scheme.

Figure 2–40

To Delete the Logo and Edit Other Text Boxes on Page 2

The following steps delete the logo and edit other text boxes on page 2.

1 In the upper-left portion of page 2, right-click the logo, and then click Delete Object on the shortcut menu.

2 Click the text in the Primary Business Address text box. Press CTRL+A to select all of the text. Type `Riverside Aquarium` and press the ENTER key.

3 Type `1400 River Drive` and then press the ENTER key.

4 Type `Pensacola, FL 32503` to finish the address.

5 Click the text in the Phone text box. Press CTRL+A to select all of the text. Type `Phone: (850) 555-FISH` and press the ENTER key.

6 Type `Fax: (850) 555-3470` and then press the ENTER key.

7 Type `E-mail: riverside@nzaa.com` to finish the phone and e-mail information.

8 Click the text in the business tag line text box. Press CTRL+A to select all of the text. Type `More than just fish!` to replace the default tag line text.

9 Right-click the text in the 'We're on the Web' attention getter text box and then click Delete Object on the shortcut menu to delete the text box (Figure 2–41).

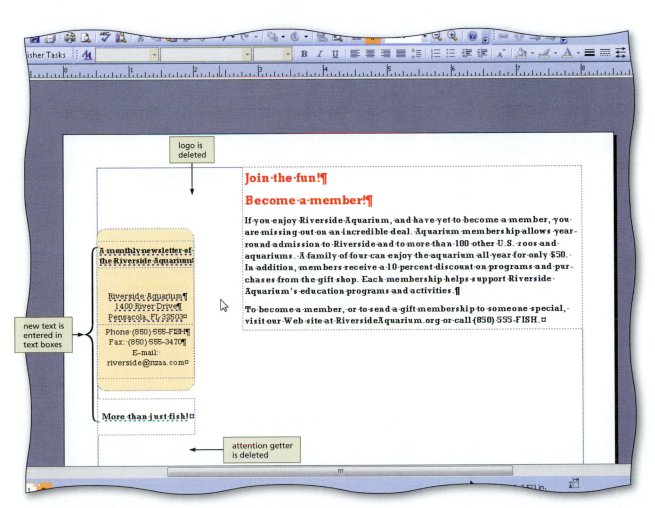

Figure 2–41

Selecting Text and Objects

In the previous steps and throughout Chapters 1 and 2, you have selected text and graphics. Table 2–2 lists some editing techniques used to select various items using the mouse.

Table 2–2 Techniques for Selecting Text and Objects with the Mouse	
Item to Select	**Mouse Action**
Block of text or sentence	Click at beginning of selection, scroll to end of selection, position mouse pointer at end of selection, hold down SHIFT key, and then click; or drag through the text
Character(s)	Drag through character(s)
Graphic	Click the graphic
Picture with caption	Click the picture, and then click the picture again
Line	Move mouse to left of line until mouse pointer changes to a right-pointing block arrow and then click
Lines	Move mouse to left of text until mouse pointer changes to a right-pointing block arrow, and then drag up or down; or triple-click
Paragraph	Triple-click paragraph
Word	Double-click the word
Words	Drag through the words

To Save an Intermediate Copy of the Newsletter

A good practice is to save intermediate copies of your work. That way, if your computer loses power or you make a serious mistake, you always can retrieve the latest copy from disk. With the masthead and story headlines edited, and the text files imported, it now is a good time to save the entire newsletter before continuing. For a detailed example of the procedure summarized below, refer to pages PUB 31 through PUB 33 in Chapter 1.

1 With a USB flash drive connected to one of the computer's USB ports, click the Save button on the Standard toolbar.

2 Type `Communiquarium Newsletter` in the File name text box to change the file name. Do not press the ENTER key.

3 Navigate to your USB flash drive (Figure 2–42).

4 Click the Save button in the Save As dialog box to save the publication on the USB flash drive with the file name, Communiquarium Newsletter.

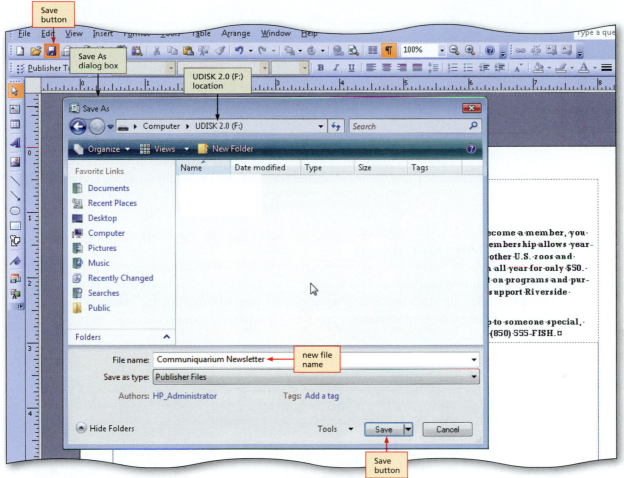

Figure 2–42

Using Graphics in a Newsletter

Saving
Click the Save button on the Standard toolbar often. When you do, the stored copy on your system is updated with the current changes. The file name remains the same. You then can retrieve the publication later, if the unexpected happens.

Most graphic designers employ an easy technique for deciding how many graphics are too many. They hold the publication at arm's length and glance at it. Then, closing their eyes, they count the number of things they remember. Remembering more than five graphics indicates too many; two or fewer indicates too few. Without question, graphics can make or break a publication. The world has come to expect them. Used correctly, graphics enhance the text, attract the eye, and brighten the look of the publication.

You can use Publisher's clip art images in any publication you create, including newsletters. Publisher also accepts graphics and pictures created by other programs, as well as scanned photographs and digital photos. You can import and replace graphics into publications in the same way that you imported stories and replaced template text. Once inserted, graphics can be resized and moved to appropriate locations. In newsletters, you should use photographs as true-to-life representations, such as pictures of employees and products. Drawings, on the other hand, can explain, instruct, entertain, or represent images for which you have no picture. The careful use of graphics can add flair and distinction to your publication.

Graphics do not have to be images and pictures. They also can include tables, charts, shapes, lines, boxes, borders, pull quotes, and sidebars. A **sidebar** is a small piece of text, set off with a box or graphic, and placed beside an article. It contains text that is not vital to understanding the main text, but usually adds interest or additional information. Tables of contents, art boxes, and bulleted points of interest are examples of sidebars. A **pull quote** is an excerpt from the main article to highlight the ideas or to attract readers. As with other graphics, it adds interest to the page. Pull quotes, like sidebars, can be set off with a box or graphic.

<table>
<tr><td>**Plan**
Ahead</td><td>**Create the first draft.**
As you insert graphics and arrange stories, follow any guidelines from the authors or from the company for which you are creating the newsletter. Together, determine the best layout for eye appeal and reliable dissemination of content. Make any required changes. Print a copy and mark the places where sidebars and pull quotes would make sense. Verify that all photographs have captions.</td></tr>
</table>

The following sections import graphics from the Data Files for Students, edit the captions and sidebar text, delete a sidebar (but not the graphic behind it), and insert a pull quote.

To Replace a Graphic and Edit the Caption

Graphics can be imported from previously stored files, just as stories can. The following steps show how to import graphics from the Data Files for Students. See the inside back cover of this book for instructions on downloading the Data Files for Students, or contact your instructor for more information about accessing the required files.

- To display the first page of the newsletter, click the Page 1 icon on the page sorter.

- Right-click the workspace, which is the gray area behind the newsletter, and point to Zoom (Figure 2–43).

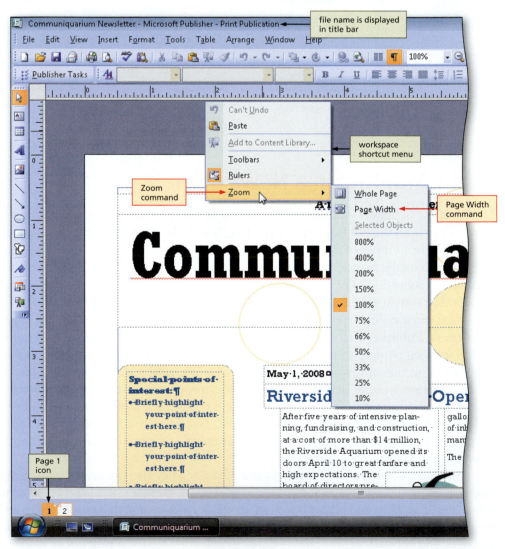

Figure 2–43

2

- Click Page Width to zoom to page width.

- Click the graphic in the lead story to select the grouped graphic and caption object.

- Click the graphic again to select only the picture.

- Right-click the graphic to display the shortcut menu.

- Point to Change Picture to display its submenu (Figure 2–44).

Q&A

What is the toolbar that appeared on the screen?

When a picture is selected, Publisher offers you its Picture toolbar in case you want to make changes to the picture.

Figure 2–44

3

- Click the From File command to open the Insert Picture dialog box.

- Navigate to the UDISK 2.0 (F:) drive (Figure 2–45).

Q&A

What do the other choices on the Change Picture submenu do?

The **Clip Art command** opens the Clip Art task pane to allow you to search for an appropriate graphic. The **From Scanner or Camera command** allows you to import directly from a digital camera or flatbed scanner

Figure 2–45

without intermediary software. The **Graphics Manager command** opens the Graphics Manager task pane to allow you to choose from among graphics already used in the publication.

4

- To insert the picture, double-click the file, aquarium (Figure 2–46).

Q&A What if I choose a bigger or smaller picture?

If necessary, imported graphics may be resized to better complement the stories. Publisher automatically wraps the text around the graphic regardless of its size.

Figure 2–46

5

- Select the text in the caption.

- Zoom to 100%.

- Type New, world-class aquarium on the riverfront to replace the selected placeholder text (Figure 2–47).

Q&A What if I do not want a caption?

If you do not want a caption, you can ungroup the object by clicking the **Ungroup Objects button** and then deleting the text box. Deleting the text only, will cause an error when running the Design Checker because it will leave an empty box in the publication.

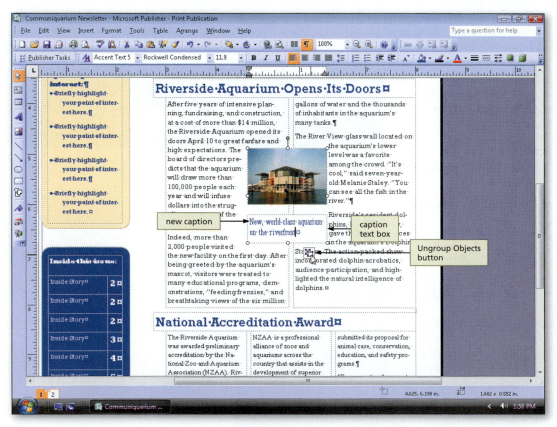

Figure 2–47

To Replace a Graphic on Page 2 and Edit the Caption

1 Go to page 2 of the newsletter.

2 Select only the picture in the Award story to prepare to replace it.

3 Right-click the picture to display the shortcut menu. Point to Change Picture and then click From File on the Change Picture submenu to display the Insert Picture dialog box.

4 If necessary, navigate to the USB flash drive to view the pictures stored there.

5 Double-click the picture, handshake, to place it in the publication.

6 Select the text in the Caption text box. Type `Riverside Aquarium president accepts accreditation award` to replace the placeholder text (Figure 2–48).

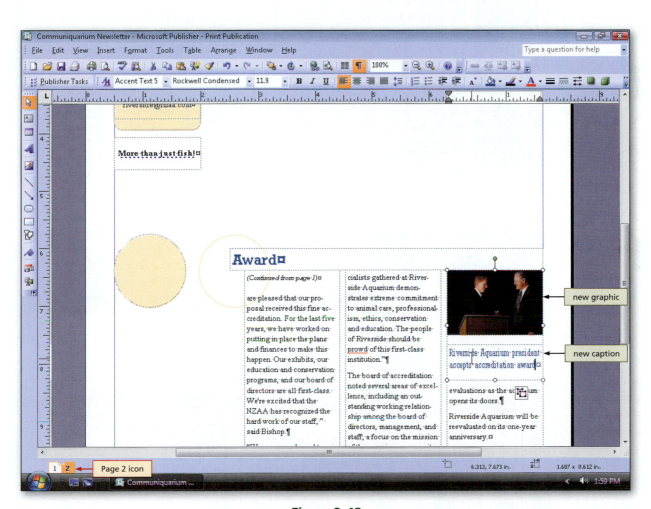

Figure 2–48

Resizing Clip Art

If you choose to include Publisher-supplied graphics, remember that Clip Art graphics are not all the same size. Some of the images and clip art will be displayed in **portrait orientation**, which means they are taller than they are wide. The opposite graphic orientation is **landscape orientation**. When you change graphics, your choice may alter both the way the columns look and where the columns break. Experiment with dragging the picture in small increments to make the columns symmetrical. Text automatically wraps around graphics in newsletter templates. Clip Art graphics are proportional, which means the height and width have been set in relation to each other, so as not to distort the picture. If you resize a graphic, be sure to hold down the SHIFT key while dragging a corner handle. Shift-dragging maintains the graphic's proportional height and width.

To Insert a New Picture from Clip Art

Recall that you have used the Clip Art task pane to replace template graphics. You also have replaced template graphics with imported files. The final graphic in the newsletter will not replace a previous graphic. The next steps insert a new picture from Clip Art, using the menu.

- Click the workspace to deselect the picture.

- Scroll as necessary to display the upper half of page 2 in the newsletter.

- Click Insert on the menu bar and then point to Picture (Figure 2–49).

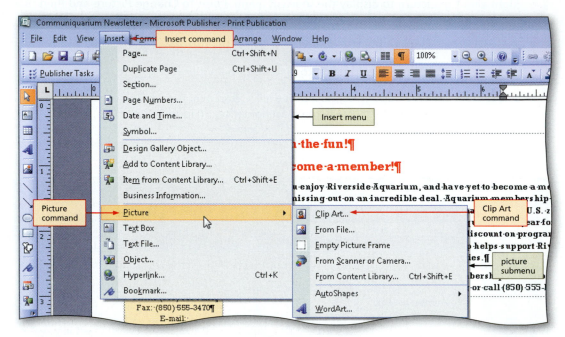

Figure 2–49

- Click Clip Art to display the Clip Art task pane.

- Type dolphin in the Search for box.

- If necessary, click the Search in box arrow and then click Everywhere in the list.

- If Necessary, click the Results should be box arrow and then click All media types in the list.

- Click the Go button to search for clip art related to the term, dolphin (Figure 2–50).

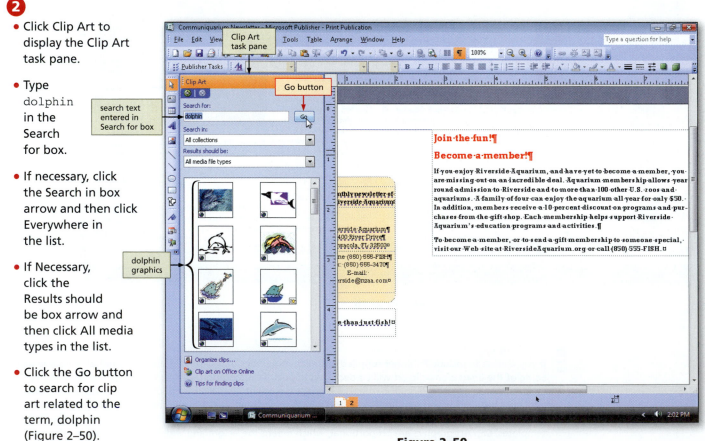

Figure 2–50

3
- Scroll to find a picture of a dolphin similar to the one shown in Figure 2–51.

- To insert the picture into the newsletter, click the picture.

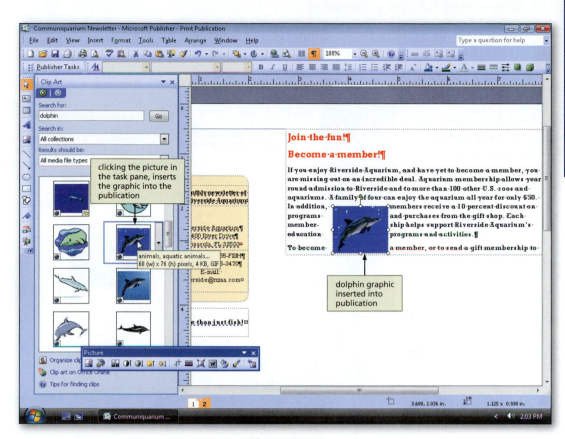

Figure 2–51

Moving and Resizing Objects

Sometimes objects are not in the right place. In those cases you have to select the object and then move the object by dragging its gray, dotted-line border.

Sometimes pictures and graphics are not the right size. In that case you need to resize the object. To resize any object in Publisher, select the object, and then drag a handle. A handle is one of several small shapes displayed around an object when the object is selected. To resize by dragging, position the mouse pointer over one of the handles and then drag the mouse. Pressing the CTRL key while dragging keeps the center of the graphic in the same place while resizing. Pressing the SHIFT key while dragging maintains the graphic's proportions while resizing. Finally, pressing the CTRL+SHIFT keys while dragging maintains the proportions and keeps the center in the same place. You will learn about more ways to resize and position graphics in a later chapter.

To Move and Resize a Graphic

The following steps move the dolphin graphic and resize it.

 1

- If necessary, close the Clip Art task pane.

- With the graphic still selected, drag it to a location below the text box, as shown in Figure 2–52.

- Point to the lower-right handle.

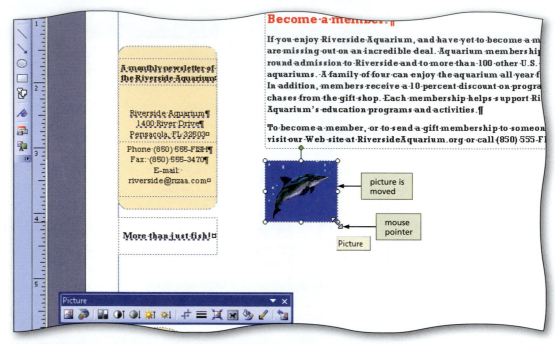

Figure 2–52

2

- SHIFT+drag the handle until the graphic is approximately 2.5 inches wide, as measured by the horizontal ruler (Figure 2–53).

Q&A

How can I tell if it is 2.5 inches wide?

The size does not have to be exact in this newsletter. Zooming until the graphic is closer to the rulers is one way to measure more precisely. You also can see the size change on the right side of the status bar as you drag.

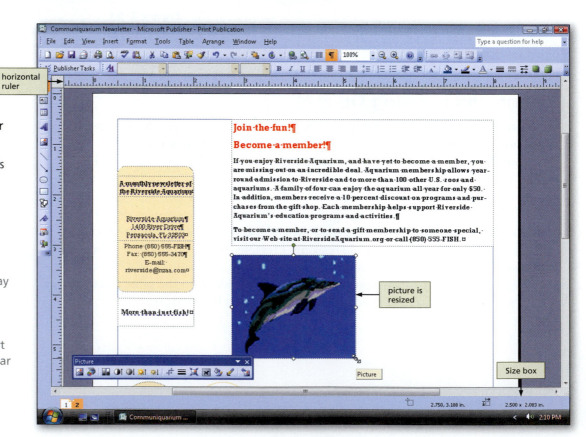

Figure 2–53

To Edit a Sidebar

The Watermark newsletter template includes two sidebars on page 1. The first is a bulleted list of special points of interest. The following steps edit that bulleted list.

1

- Go to page 1 of the newsletter.

- Right-click the gray, dotted border of the Special points of interest sidebar in the upper-left part of page 1.

- Point to Zoom on the shortcut menu to display its submenu (Figure 2–54).

Figure 2–54

2

- Click the Selected Objects command to center the sidebar and display it at the largest possible magnification that still fits in the workspace.

- Select the text, Special points of interest:.

- Type Riverside has... to replace the text (Figure 2–55).

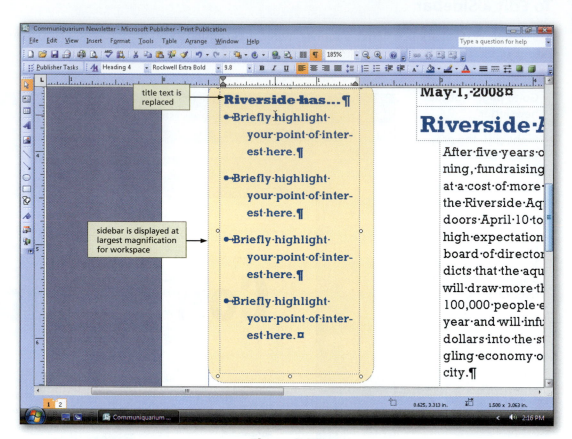

Figure 2–55

3

- Select the bulleted list.

- Type Later hours on weekends and then press the ENTER key.

- Type Special rates for school groups and then press the ENTER key.

- Type Discounts for senior citizens and then press the ENTER key.

- Type Adopt-a-sea-creature programs and then press the ENTER key.

- Type Petting tanks and then press the ENTER key.

- Type And much more! to complete the list (Figure 2–56).

 Q&A

How do I turn off or change the bullets?

Recall that you can turn off bullets by clicking the Bullets button on the Formatting toolbar. You also can change the format of bullets by clicking Bullets and Numbering on the Format menu.

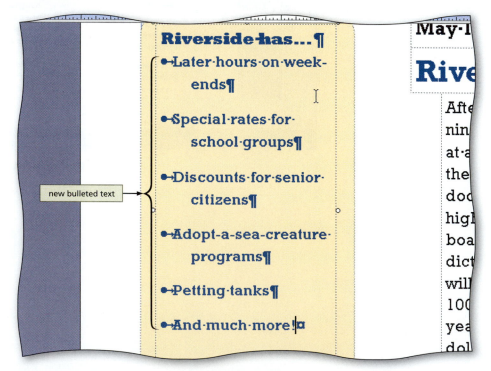

Figure 2–56

To Delete the Sidebar

The other sidebar in the Watermark newsletter template is a table of contents. Because the newsletter now has only two pages, a table of contents is not necessary. The following steps delete the sidebar.

1 Press the F9 key to return to 100% magnification.

2 Scroll to display the Inside this issue sidebar.

3 Right-click the text in the sidebar, and then click Delete Object on the shortcut menu (Figure 2–57).

BTW

A sidebar table many times is used as an index to locate articles in longer newsletters. Many newsletters have a table of contents, not only to reference and locate, but also to break up a long text page and attract readers to inside pages. Tables can be used for purposes other than displaying contents and page numbers. You will learn more about tables in a later project.

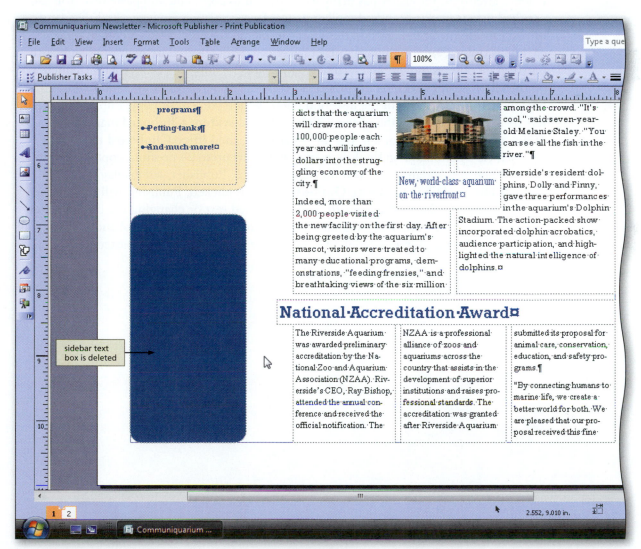

Figure 2–57

Inserting a Pull Quote

People often make reading decisions based on the size of the story. Using a pull quote brings a small portion of the text to their attention and invites readership. Pull quotes especially are useful for breaking the monotony of long columns of text. Desktop publishers also use pull quotes to add visual interest. Finally, pull quotes and sidebars are good multiple entry devices, offering readers many ways to digest information. Layout specialists say article titles and pull quotes should summarize the intended message.

The final step to complete page 1 of the newsletter is to create a pull quote using Publisher's Design Gallery. The **Design Gallery** is a group of objects that you can place in your publications, including sidebars, pull quotes, mastheads, and other individual objects. To access the Design Gallery, you click the **Design Gallery Object button** on the Objects toolbar.

The pull quote in this newsletter will contain a quote from the National Accreditation Award story and should be placed appropriately on the page to grab the reader's attention. Publisher has many ways for you to copy, cut, and paste text. You can use the buttons on the Standard toolbar, you can use the commands on the Edit menu, or you can use the commands on the short-cut menu, which display when you right click selections. **Copying** involves placing a copy of the selected item on the Clipboard. **Cutting** involves removing the selected item from the publication and then placing it on the Clipboard. **Pasting** is the process of copying an item from the Clipboard into the document at the location of the insertion point. When you cut or copy, Publisher transfers the text or objects to the system Clipboard. The **system Clipboard** maintains a copy of the most current copy or cut. On the other hand, the **Office Clipboard task pane**, accessed via a command on the Edit menu, maintains up to 24 previous copies and cuts.

When you cut and paste text for the pull quote, Publisher will display a Paste Options button. When the **Paste Options button** is clicked, Publisher will display the choice of keeping the source formatting of the copied text or changing the text to match the new formatting. The Paste Options button gives you greater control and flexibility in choosing the format for a pasted item. The button appears just below pasted text.

To Insert a Pull Quote

The following steps insert a pull quote from the Design Gallery and use the Standard toolbar and Paste Options button as text is copied and pasted.

1

- With the lower-left portion of page 1 still displayed, click the Design Gallery Object button on the Objects toolbar.

 Experiment

- When the Design Gallery window is displayed, one at a time click the buttons down the left side of the window and take note of the various kinds of available objects.

- Click the Pull Quotes button in the list (Figure 2–58).

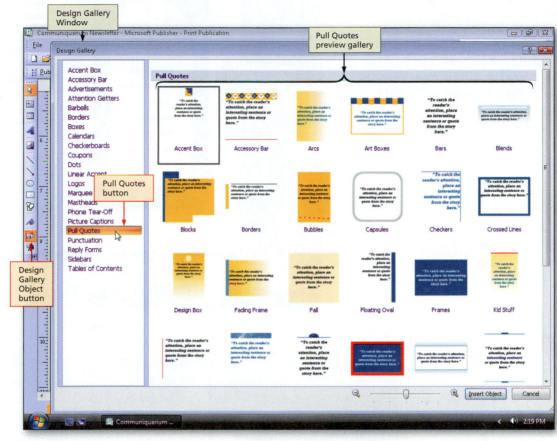

Figure 2–58

2

- Scroll to and then click the Voyage preview shown in Figure 2–59.

Q&A

How do I know which one to choose?

The previews display in alphabetical order in the Pull Quotes pane. Some of them match a specific design set, while others are merely decorative. You should choose one that complements your publication and makes the quote stand out.

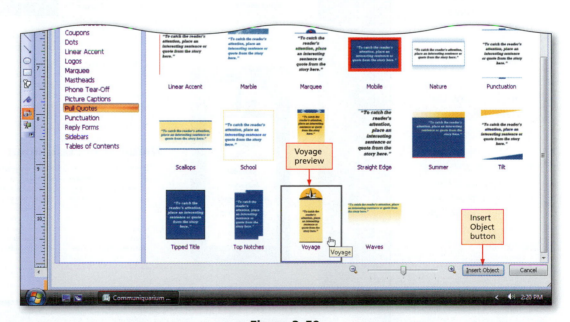

Figure 2–59

3

- Click the Insert Object button to insert the pull quote and close the Design Gallery window.

- Drag the pull quote in front of the blue rounded rectangle (Figure 2–60).

When I drag, text moves instead of the pull quote. What did I do wrong?

When you want to move an object, you must drag it by its border — the gray dotted line surrounding the object. If your text moved, you dragged the text rather than the entire object.

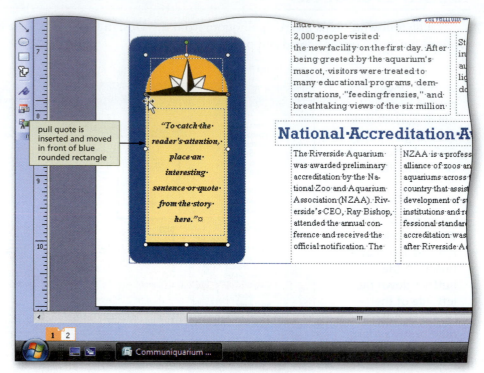

pull quote is inserted and moved in front of blue rounded rectangle

Figure 2–60

4

- Select the first sentence in the second paragraph of the National Accreditation Award story by dragging. Do not include the quotation mark at the beginning of the sentence (Figure 2–61).

Other than dragging, how can I select the sentence?

You can click at the beginning of the sentence — in this case, after the quotation mark — and then SHIFT+click at the end of the sentence.

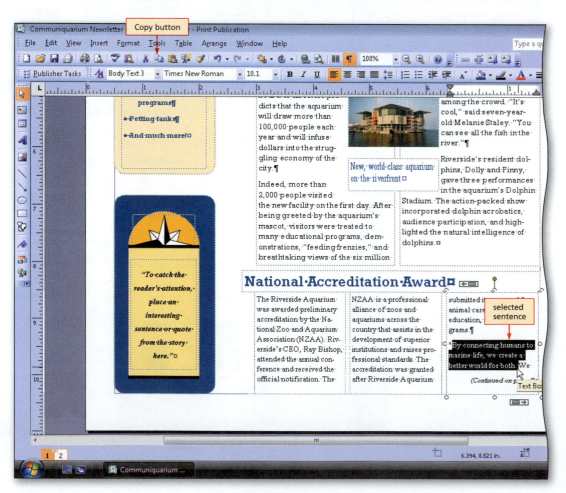

Copy button

selected sentence

Figure 2–61

5

- Click the Copy button on the Standard toolbar to copy the selected text.

- Click the placeholder text in the pull quote to select it (Figure 2–62).

Q&A

Can I use shortcut keys to copy and paste?

Yes, you can use CTRL+C to copy and then CTRL+V to paste. See the Quick Reference at the end of the book for more ways to do these tasks.

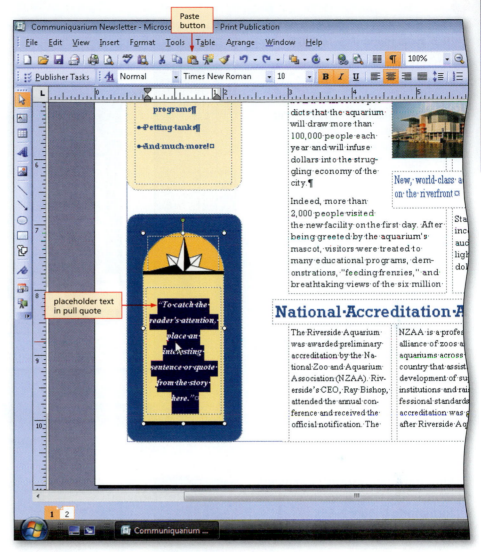

Figure 2–62

6

- Click the Paste button on the Standard toolbar to paste the text from the clipboard (Figure 2–63).

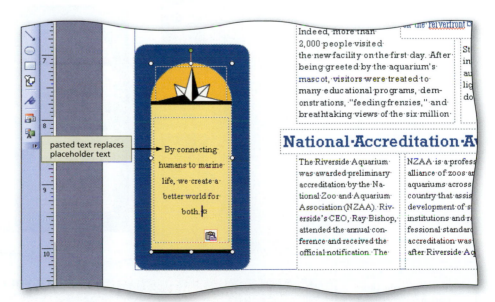

Figure 2–63

7

• Click the Paste Options button to display its menu (Figure 2–64).

Q&A

What if I do not want to display the Paste Options button?

You can choose not to display the Paste Options button by clicking Tools on the menu bar, clicking Options, and then clicking the Edit tab. Finally, clear the Show Paste Options button check box.

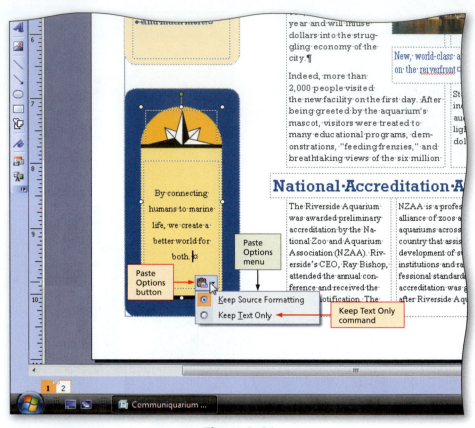

Figure 2–64

8

• Click the Keep Text Only command to maintain the pull quote's formatting (Figure 2–65).

Other Ways

1. On Insert menu, click Design Gallery Object

Figure 2–65

To Finish Formatting the Pull Quote

1 Click at the beginning of the quotation and then type a quotation mark to begin the quote.

2 Click at the end of the quotation. Press the backspace key to remove the space after the period, if necessary. Type a quotation mark to end the quotation.

3 Press the ENTER key to move to the next line.

4 Type `-- Ray Bishop` to finish the pull quote (Figure 2–66).

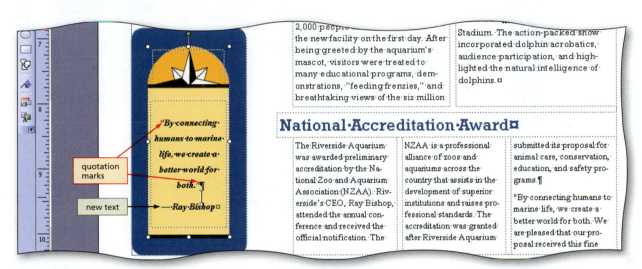

Figure 2–66

Moving Text

To move text, such as words, characters, sentences, or paragraphs, you first select the text to be moved and then use drag-and-drop editing or the cut-and-paste technique to move the selected text. With **drag-and-drop editing**, you drag the selected item to the new location and then insert, or *drop*, it there. Moving text in this manner does not transfer data to either clipboard; neither does it cause Publisher to display the Paste Options button. Any format changes to the text must be made manually.

When moving text between pages, use the cut-and-paste method. When moving text a long distance or between application programs, use the Office Clipboard task pane to cut and paste. When moving text a short distance, the drag-and-drop technique is more efficient. Thus, the steps on the following pages demonstrate drag-and-drop editing.

To Move Text

The editor of the newsletter has decided that two paragraphs should be inverted so the story will read better. The following steps select and move a paragraph on page 2 in the Award story. You will triple-click to select the paragraph and then drag-and-drop it to its new location. You should be sure that drag-and-drop editing is enabled by clicking Options on the Tools menu. On the Edit Tab, make sure the Drag-and-drop text editing check box displays a check mark.

- Go to page 2 of the newsletter.

- If necessary, scroll to display the story in the lower portion of the page (Figure 2–67).

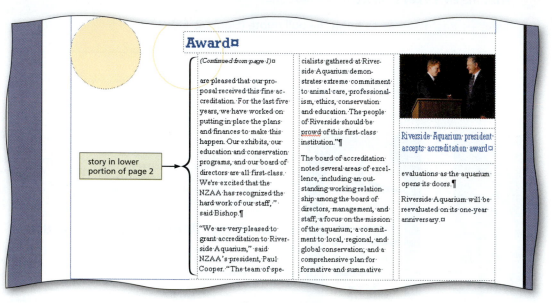

Figure 2–67

- Triple-click the paragraph that begins with the words, The board of accreditation noted, to select the paragraph (Figure 2–68).

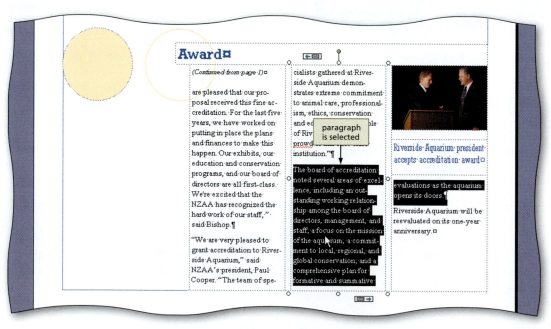

Figure 2–68

3

• Drag the selection to the destination location — before the previous paragraph — as shown in Figure 2–69. Do not release the mouse button.

Q&A What if I accidentally drag text to the wrong location?

Click the Undo button on the Standard Toolbar and try again.

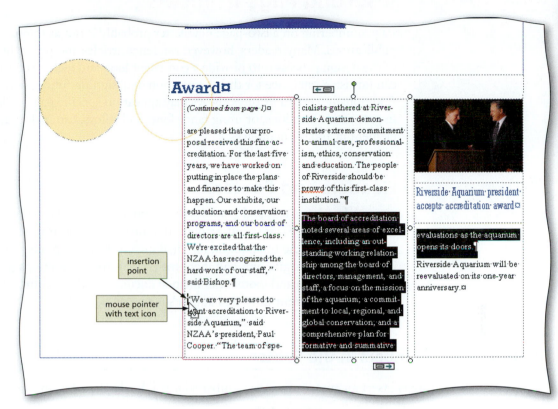

Figure 2–69

4

• Release the mouse button to move the selected text to the location of the mouse pointer.

• To deselect the text, click the workspace (Figure 2–70).

Q&A Can I use drag-and-drop editing to move any selected item?

Yes, you can select words, sentences, phrases, and graphics and then use drag-and-drop editing to move them.

Figure 2–70

Other Ways		
1. Select item, click Cut button on Standard toolbar, click where text is to be pasted, click Paste button on Standard toolbar	2. Right-click selected item, click Cut on shortcut menu, right-click where text is to be pasted, click Paste on shortcut menu	3. Select item, press CTRL+X, position insertion point where text is to be pasted, press CTRL+V

Inserting Page Numbers

Page numbering on a two-page newsletter probably is not as important as it is for longer publications. Many readers, however, reference articles and points by page numbers. Part of the design process is to provide a consistent look and feel to the layout, so page numbers can furnish a reference for the organization in designing future, perhaps longer, newsletters. Additionally, certain features always may appear on specific pages. Placing page numbers in prominent locations, or using fancy fonts and colors, can make page numbers a design element in and of themselves.

Headers and Footers

A **header** is text and graphics that print at the top of each page in a document. Similarly, a **footer** is text and graphics that print at the bottom of every page. In Publisher, headers print in the top margin, one-half inch from the top of every page, and footers print in the bottom margin, one-half inch from the bottom of every page. In addition to text and graphics, headers and footers can include document information, such as the page number, current date, current time, and author's name.

To Insert Page Numbers in the Footer

The following steps insert an automatic page number so it will be displayed in the footer on all pages.

1

- Click Insert on the menu bar and then click Page Numbers to access the Page Numbers dialog box (Figure 2–71).

Q&A

I do not see a Page Numbers dialog box. What did I do wrong?

It is possible that your cursor was positioned inside another text box on the page, so Publisher may have inserted the page number at that point. Click the Undo button on the Standard toolbar, click the workspace so that no text box is selected, and then try again.

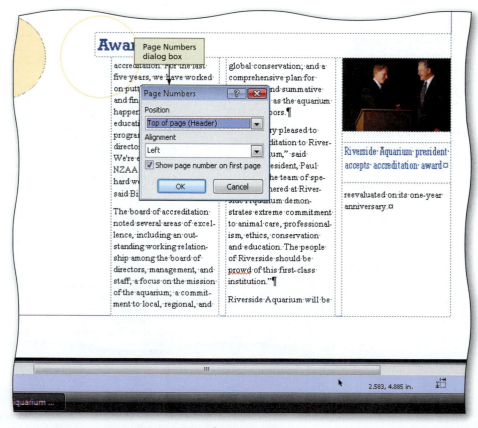

Figure 2–71

2

- Click the Position box arrow and then click Bottom of page (Footer) to position the page number in the footer.

- Click the Alignment box arrow and then click Center to select the alignment within the footer (Figure 2–72).

Q&A Are the headers and footers similar to the ones in Microsoft Word?

They are similar, but not exactly the same. In Word 2007, the headers and footers are chosen from a gallery and then edited. In Publisher 2007, you can access the headers and footers by inserting a page number, or from the View menu.

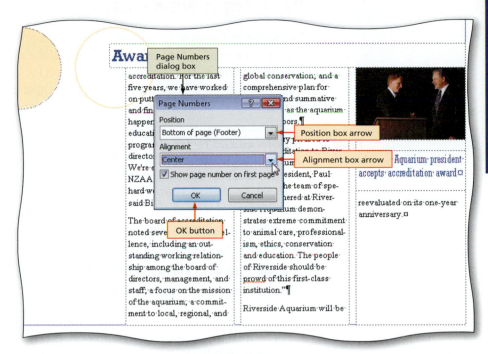

Figure 2–72

3

- Click the OK button to close the Page Numbers dialog box.

 Experiment

- Use the page sorter to move between page 1 and 2 and look at the change in page number.

- Go to page 1 of the newsletter (Figure 2–73).

Q&A How do I place other text or graphics in a header or footer?

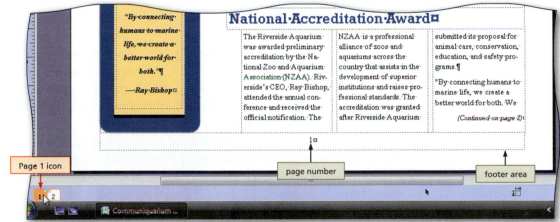

Figure 2–73

You can double-click the header or footer to place the cursor in the header or footer text box. You then can type as you would in any text box, or enter specific pieces of text, such as business information, dates, or times. Options on the Insert menu allow you to insert graphics, as well as dates and times derived from the operating system that update automatically when the publication is edited or printed.

Other Ways

1. Click Insert Page Number button on Header and Footer toolbar

---

BTW

Accessing Headers and Footers

You can access the header and footer areas by clicking Header and Footer on the View menu. Publisher opens a special layout with a text box at the top and bottom that you can use to add additional information. A Header and Footer toolbar helps you insert the page number, date, and time, and it helps you move between the header and footer boxes as well.

Checking a Newsletter for Errors

As discussed in Chapter 1, once you complete a publication, you might find it necessary to make changes to it. Before submitting a newsletter to a customer or printing service, you should proofread it. While **proofreading**, you look for grammatical errors and spelling errors. You want to be sure the layout, graphics, and stories make sense. If you find errors, you must correct, make changes, or edit the newsletter.

<table>
<tr>
<td>

Plan Ahead

</td>
<td>

Proofread and revise the newsletter.

As you proofread the newsletter, look for ways to improve it. Check all grammar, spelling, and punctuation. Be sure the text is logical and transitions are smooth. Where necessary, add text, delete text, reword text, and move text to different locations. Ask yourself these questions:

- Does the title suggest the topic?
- Is the first line of the story enticing the reader to continue?
- Is the purpose of the newsletter clear?
- Are all sources acknowledged?

</td>
</tr>
</table>

The final phase of the design process, therefore, is a synthesis involving proofreading, editing, and publishing. Publisher offers several methods to check for errors in your newsletter. None of these methods is a replacement for careful reading and proofreading.

Spelling Errors

Similar to the spell checking programs in word processing applications, Publisher looks for misspelled words in text boxes. As you type text in a text box, Publisher checks your typing for possible spelling errors. Recall that if a typed word is not in the dictionary, a red wavy underline is displayed below it. You can check the entire newsletter for spelling errors at once or as you are typing.

When a word is flagged with a red wavy underline, it is not in Publisher's dictionary. A flagged word is not necessarily misspelled, as many names, abbreviations, and specialized terms are not in Publisher's main dictionary. In these cases, instruct Publisher to ignore the flagged word. To display a list of suggested corrections for a flagged word, right-click it, and then click a replacement word on the shortcut menu.

When using imported text, as in the newsletter, it may be easier to check all the spelling at once. Publisher's check spelling feature looks through the selected text box for errors. Once errors are found, Publisher offers suggestions and provides the choice of correcting or ignoring the flagged word. If you are creating this project on a personal computer, your text boxes may contain different misspelled words, depending on the accuracy of your typing.

To Check the Newsletter for Spelling Errors

The Spelling command is accessed through the Tools menu. The following steps illustrate how to check your newsletter for spelling errors. You may encounter spelling mistakes you have made while typing. Choose to correct those errors as necessary. The following steps check the newsletter for spelling errors.

1

- With page 1 of the Communiquarium Newsletter still displayed, scroll up, and then click the masthead text box.

- Click the Spelling button on the Standard toolbar to start the spell checking process (Figure 2–74).

Q&A

What if my newsletter did not find the same word as the figure?

If Publisher is flagging a different word, it may be that you already removed the flag on the word Communiquarium by right-clicking the red wavy flag earlier. Or you may not have started in the masthead text box.

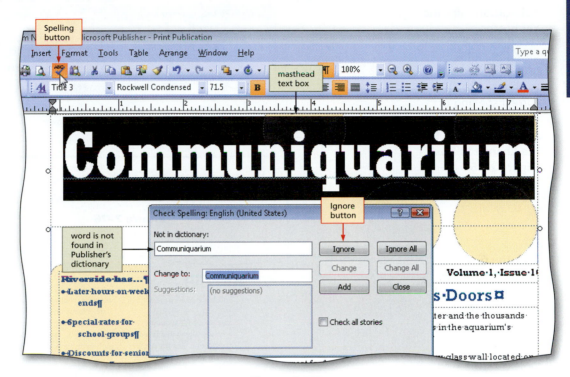

Figure 2–74

2

- Click the Ignore button to ignore the name of the newsletter that is not in Publisher's dictionary (Figure 2–75).

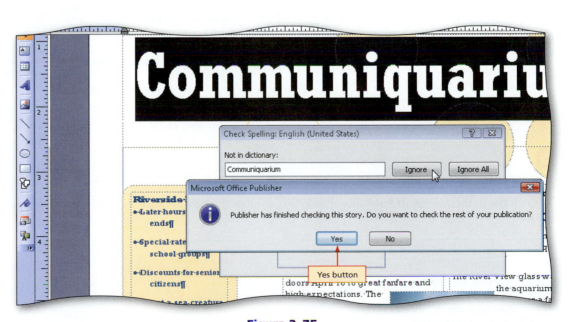

Figure 2–75

3

- If Publisher displays a dialog box asking if you want to check the rest of the publication, click the Yes button.

- Click the word, proud, in the list to choose the correct spelling of the flagged word and to transfer it to the Change to box (Figure 2–76).

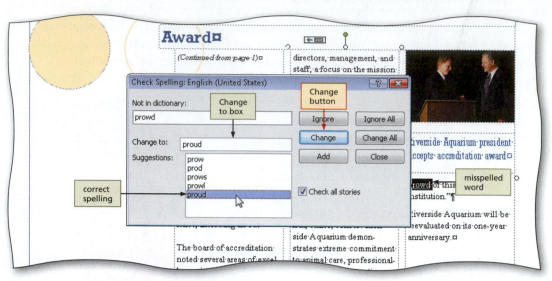

Figure 2–76

4

- Click the Change button to change the word, prowd, to proud (Figure 2–77).

Q&A When should I click the Add button?

Only click the Add button when you are absolutely sure that you want to add the flagged word to Publisher's dictionary, and only on your own computer system. Acceptable additions might be your name, the name of a company you deal with, or foreign words, if you are completely sure of the spelling. Do not click the Add button in a lab setting or on someone else's computer.

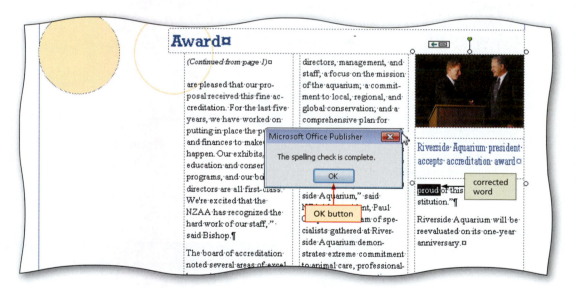

Figure 2–77

5

- If you have other errors, choose the appropriate measure to fix or ignore them.

- Click OK in the Microsoft Publisher dialog box to close the box because the spelling check is complete.

Other Ways

1. On Tools menu, point to Spelling, click Spelling on Spelling submenu

2. Press F7

BTW

Even if text is checked for spelling before it is imported, Publisher flags words, phrases, and punctuation not found in its dictionary. The process is worth the time it takes, but again, there is no substitute for proofreading the text yourself.

Checking the Newsletter for Design Errors

You now are ready to check the newsletter for design errors as you did in Chapter 1. The Design Checker can check single pages or entire publications for a specific type of error or all types of errors. The Design Checker looks for errors related to design issues and object interaction, providing comments and correction choices. Design errors are the most common type of problem when submitting a publication to a professional printer. In a later project, you will learn that, in addition to the interactive Design Checker, Publisher's Pack and Go Wizard checks for errors related to embedded fonts and graphics. Some of the errors flagged by the Design Checker include:

- Empty frames
- Covered objects
- Text in overflow area
- Objects in nonprinting region
- Disproportional pictures
- Spacing between sentences
- Low resolution graphics

To Check the Newsletter for Design Errors

In the following steps, Publisher checks for all kinds of design errors throughout the newsletter.

1 Click Tools on the menu bar and then click Design Checker to start the process.

2 If the Design Checker finds errors, choose to fix or ignore them as necessary. When the Design Checker terminates, close the Design Checker task pane.

To Save an Existing Publication with the Same File Name

The publication now is complete. You should save the newsletter again. The following step saves the publication again.

1 Click the Save button on the Standard toolbar to overwrite the previous Communiquarium Newsletter file on the USB flash drive.

Creating a Template

Newsletters typically retain their masthead, color scheme, font scheme, and other graphics from issue to issue. In a first issue, you must make design choices and implement them to make the newsletter display correctly, which takes time and review. You do not have to do all of that for subsequent issues. Once the decisions have been made, and the publication distributed, you can reuse the same publication as a template. Additionally, Publisher can add it to the templates on your system.

The **Publisher Tasks task pane** offers shortcuts and links to access some of the more powerful Publisher features and information as you design and distribute publications, including the ability to create a template from a newsletter.

To Access the Publisher Tasks Task Pane

The following step accesses the Publisher Tasks task pane.

1

● Click the Publisher Tasks button on the toolbar to open the Publisher Tasks task pane (Figure 2–78).

Q&A

How does the Publisher Tasks task pane assist me?

The task pane offers links and information about creating and distributing publications and tracking a publication's effectiveness in the market. Some of the links open dialog boxes. Others present a list of options or open a Help window. Still, others open a browser and transfer you to a Web page with information.

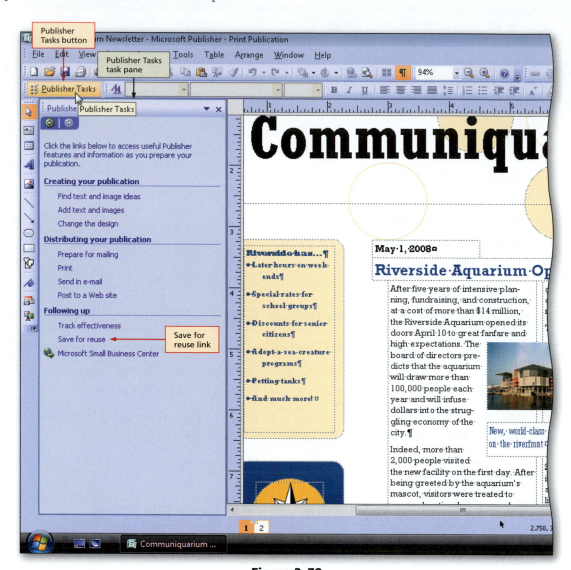

Figure 2–78

Other Ways

1. With any task pane visible, click Other Task Panes button, click Publisher Tasks

2. Press CTRL+F1, click Other Task Panes button, click Publisher Tasks

Setting File Properties at the Time of Creation

Recall that in Chapter 1, you set file properties using the Properties command from the File menu. Two specific properties can be set at the time you create a publication or template. The author and tag properties can be entered into any of the Save As dialog boxes, which can save you several steps. A tag is a custom file property used to help find and organize files. Although there are many properties associated with files, tags are often the most useful because you can add tags to your files that contain words or phrases that make the files easier to find. Adding or changing properties to a file when you create and save it eliminates the need to find the file and apply properties afterwards. Later, to find a file containing a tag, you can type tag words into the Search box of any Windows Vista folder.

To Create a Template with Property Changes

With the Publisher Tasks task pane still open, the following steps create a template. The template will be stored on a USB flash drive. It is not recommended to save templates on lab computers or computers belonging to other people.

1

- With a USB flash drive connected to one of the computer's USB ports, click the link, Save for reuse, to view the Save for reuse tasks (Figure 2–79).

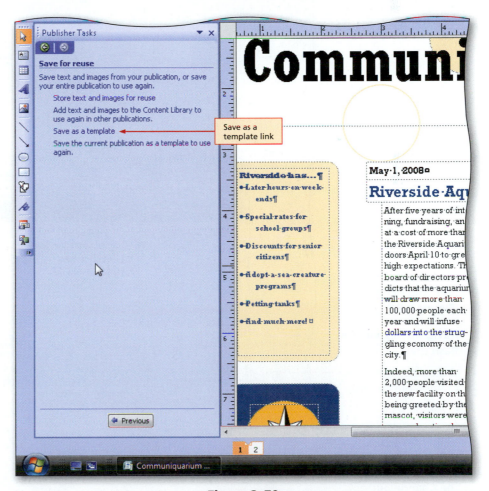

Figure 2–79

2

- Click the link, Save as a template, to open the Save As Template dialog box (Figure 2–80).

🔍 Experiment

- Click the Save as type box arrow to view the many types of file formats available for publications.

- If necessary, click the Save as type box arrow, and then click Publisher Template to select the file format.

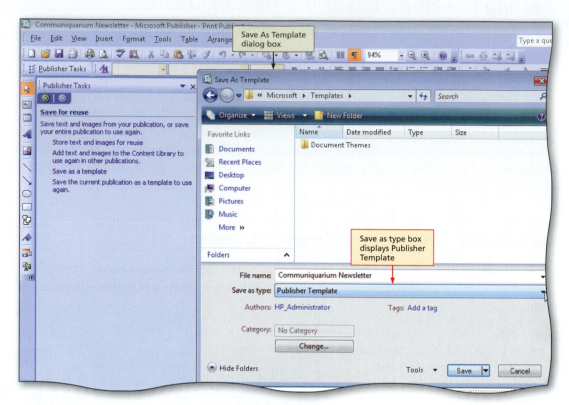

Figure 2–80

3

- If necessary, click the text in the File name text box to select it.

- Type `Communiquarium Newsletter Template` to name the template. Do not press the ENTER key (Figure 2–81).

- Navigate to your USB flash drive.

Q&A

What does the Change button do?

If you plan on creating many templates, you can organize them into categories. Clicking the Change button opens a dialog box that allows you to create or navigate to categories of templates.

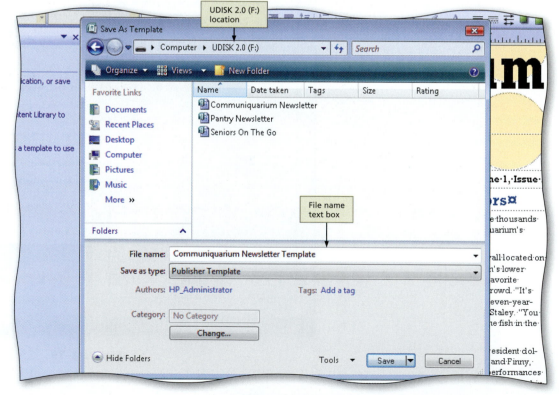

Figure 2–81

4

- If your name does not display next to the word, Authors, in the lower portion of the dialog box, double-click the text and then type your name to replace the text.

- Click the Tags text box and then type `monthly newsletter volume 1` to add the tag words (Figure 2–82). The current text in the Tags text box will disappear as you start to type.

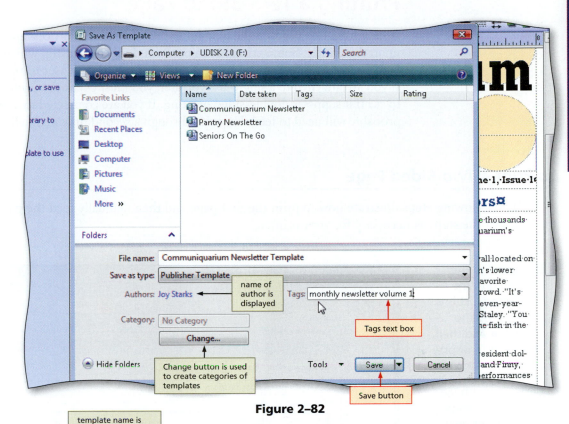

Figure 2–82

5

- Click the Save button to save the template.

- Close the task pane (Figure 2–83).

Where should a company store its templates?

On a business computer, for an organization that routinely uses templates, you should save templates in the default location. Publisher stores templates within the application data in a folder named, Templates. Templates stored in the default location display in the catalog when you click the My Templates button. However, templates can be stored anywhere, on a personal system, on a Web server, or on a common drive for use among employees or students.

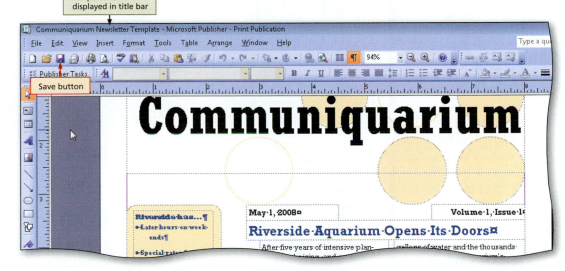

Figure 2–83

Tags are one of many properties available to attach to files to help you find and organize the files. In addition to tags, other properties include the Date Modified, Author, and Subject. Tags are not a part of the actual contents of a file. They become the keywords in the Properties dialog box. Unlike some properties, which are predefined, tags can be anything you choose, such as "Brochures," "Vacation," or "My Stuff."

Printing a Two-Sided Page

Printing the two pages of the newsletter back to back is a process that is highly dependent upon the printer. Some printers can perform **duplex printing**, which prints both sides before ejecting the paper, while other printers require the user to reload the paper manually. If you are attached to a single-user printer, you must check the printer's documentation to see if it supports double-sided printing. If you are connected to a network printer, you probably will need to feed the paper through a second time manually.

To Print a Two-Sided Page

The following steps illustrate how to print the first page and then manually feed the page through a second time. Adjust the steps as necessary for your printer.

- Ready the printer according to the printer instructions. Click File on the menu bar and then click Print to display the Print dialog box.

- Click Current page in the Print range area to print only the current page (Figure 2–84).

Q&A

What if my dialog box is different?

Look for a check box that says current page. If you do not have one, look for a box that allows you to specify a certain page and enter the number 1.

- Click the Print button to begin the printing process.

- When printing is complete, retrieve the printout.

Q&A

Why is it taking so long to print?

Publications with lots of text and graphics take longer to print. As long as progress is being made, your print process is fine. If after several minutes it has not even started to print, consult your instructor or lab technician.

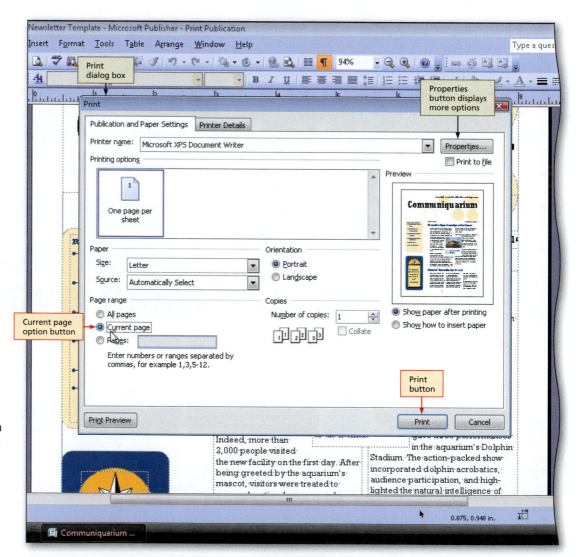

Figure 2–84

3

- After retrieving the printout, wait a few seconds for it to dry. Reinsert the printout in the manual tray of the printer, usually blank side down, top first.

- Navigate to page 2.

- To print the current page, click Print on the File menu, and then choose to print the current page.

Other Ways

1. Press CTRL+P

BTW

If you have an Options button, a Properties button, or an Advanced Print Settings button in your Print dialog box (Figure 2–84), you may be able to duplex print. Check your printer documentation, or click the button for more information. If you are unsure how to load the paper, you can run a test page through the printer. Mark an X in the upper-right corner of a blank sheet and then insert the sheet into the printer, noting where the X is. If your printer has a Manual Feed button or Paper Source list, be sure to click Manual. Print the first page. Note where the X is in relation to the printed page and turn the paper over to print the other side accordingly. In a later project, you will learn more about types of paper best suited for printing on both sides, as well as how to prepare a publication for a printing service.

To Quit Publisher

This project is complete. The following steps quit Publisher.

1 To quit Publisher, click the Close button on the right side of the title bar.

2 If a Microsoft Office Publisher dialog box is displayed, click the No button so that any changes you have made are not saved.

Chapter Summary

In this chapter you have learned how to select template options for a newsletter, edit the masthead and sidebar, import stories and graphics, create original stories using the Edit in Microsoft Word command, insert a pull quote from the Design Gallery, insert a page number in a footer, cut and paste, drag and drop, check the spelling, and use the design checker. The items listed below include all the new Publisher skills you have learned in this chapter.

1. Choose a Newsletter Template and Change Options (PUB 78)
2. Display Formatting Marks (PUB 81)
3. Change and Delete Pages in a Newsletter (PUB 83)
4. Edit the Masthead (PUB 85)
5. Edit a Headline and Import a Text File (PUB 89)
6. Import Text for the Secondary Story and Continue It on Page 2 (PUB 92)
7. Format with Continued Notices (PUB 95)
8. Replace the Back Page Story Headline (PUB 97)
9. Edit a Story Using Word (PUB 98)
10. Change the Font Size (PUB 101)
11. Use the Color Scheme Colors (PUB 102)
12. Delete the Logo and Edit Other Text Boxes on Page 2 (PUB 103)
13. Replace a Graphic and Edit the Caption (PUB 106)
14. Replace a Graphic on Page 2 and Edit the Caption (PUB 109)
15. Insert a New Picture from Clip art (PUB 110)
16. Move and Resize a Graphic (PUB 112)
17. Edit a Sidebar (PUB 113)
18. Delete the Sidebar (PUB 115)
19. Insert a Pull Quote (PUB 117)
20. Finish Formatting the Pull Quote (PUB 121)
21. Move Text (PUB 122)
22. Insert Page Numbers in the Footer (PUB 124)
23. Check the Newsletter for Spelling Errors (PUB 127)
24. Access the Publisher Tasks Task Pane (PUB 130)
25. Create a Template with Property Changes (PUB 131)
26. Print a Two-Sided Page (PUB 134)

Learn It Online

Test your knowledge of chapter content and key terms.

Instructions: To complete the Learn It Online exercises, start your browser, click the Address bar, and then enter the Web address `scsite.com/pub2007/learn`. When the Office 2007 Learn It Online page is displayed, click the link for the exercise you want to complete and then read the instructions.

Chapter Reinforcement TF, MC, and SA

A series of true/false, multiple choice, and short answer questions that test your knowledge of the chapter content.

Flash Cards

An interactive learning environment where you identify chapter key terms associated with displayed definitions.

Practice Test

A series of multiple choice questions that test your knowledge of chapter content and key terms.

Who Wants To Be a Computer Genius?

An interactive game that challenges your knowledge of chapter content in the style of a television quiz show.

Wheel of Terms

An interactive game that challenges your knowledge of chapter key terms in the style of the television show *Wheel of Fortune*.

Crossword Puzzle Challenge

A crossword puzzle that challenges your knowledge of key terms presented in the chapter.

Apply Your Knowledge

Reinforce the skills and apply the concepts you learned in this chapter.

Revising Text and Paragraphs in a Publication

Instructions: Start Publisher. Open the publication, Apply 2-1 Pantry Shelf Newsletter Draft, from the Data Files for Students. See the inside back cover of this book for instructions on downloading the Data Files for Students, or contact your instructor for more information about accessing the required files.

The publication you open is a four-page newsletter. You are to revise the publication as follows: enter the date in the masthead, move a paragraph, delete pages, enter a caption, insert a pull quote with text, insert page numbers, resize a graphic, and check the publication for errors. The revised publication is shown in Figure 2–85.

Perform the following tasks:
1. Enter the current date in the empty text box below the volume in the masthead.
2. Select the second paragraph in the lead story. Use drag-and-drop editing to move this paragraph so that it is the next to the last paragraph in the publication.
3. Below the graphic in the lead story, enter the following caption in the text box: `Guardian Angel Award`. Center the caption text.
4. Use the Design gallery to select the Tilt pull quote. Move the pull quote to a position above the Dates to Remember sidebar.
5. From the first paragraph in the lead story, select the words on the plaque, beginning with the text, 2008 Guardian Award. Copy the selection. Paste the selection, replacing the text in the pull quote.
6. Select the graphic of the line on the right side of page 1. Use the Line Color box arrow on the Formatting toolbar to change the color to the Accent 3 (Blue) color of the Wildflower color scheme.

(a)

(b)

Figure 2–85

7. Delete pages 2 and 3 of the publication.

8. Insert page numbers in the lower-right corner of the footer on both of the remaining pages.

9. Repeat Step 6 for the graphic of the line on the left side of page 2.

10. On page 2, resize the cornucopia graphic to fill the space below the last line of the article.

11. Use Publisher's thesaurus to change the Publisher, incorporated, to the Publisher, integrated, in the first sentence of the second paragraph.

12. Run the publication through the Design Checker and check the spelling. Fix any errors you find. Choose to ignore names of people and businesses.

13. Change the publication properties, as specified by your instructor.

14. Save the publication using the file name, Apply 2-1 Pantry Shelf Newsletter Modified.

15. Print the publication using duplex printing.

Extend Your Knowledge

Extend the skills you learned in this chapter and experiment with new skills. You may need to use Help to complete the assignment.

Working with Text in Overflow and the Design Gallery

Instructions: Start Publisher. Open the publication, Extend 2-1 Evergreen Newsletter Draft, from the Data Files for Students. See the inside back cover of this book for instructions on downloading the Data Files for Students, or contact your instructor for more information about accessing the required files.

You will link a text box from page 1 that has text in overflow with an empty box on page 2, format both with continued notices, insert a headline and picture with a caption for the new text box, insert and format page numbers in the header, and fix any spelling and design errors.

Perform the following tasks:

1. In the second story on page 1, click the third text box. Notice that the Text in Overflow symbol is displayed.

2. Edit the story in Microsoft Word. Insert a blank line before the last paragraph, which begins a second internship listing in the story.

3. Return to Publisher. Select the third text box in the secondary story.

4. Use the Create Text Box Link button in the Connect Text Boxes toolbar to begin the process of making the story flow to page 2. Notice the mouse pointer change after clicking the button.

5. Move to page 2 of the publication and click the large, empty text box to indicate the location to which the story should flow.

6. Add continued notices on page 1 and page 2.

7. Create an appropriate headline for the second part of the story on page 2.

8. Insert a page number only on page 2, in the header, centered.

9. Make other appropriate changes to the publication, such as inserting a graphic with a caption from the design gallery and then searching for an appropriate clip art using the task pane.

10. Use the spelling and design checking features of Publisher.

11. Save the newsletter with a new name and print the newsletter using duplex printing (Figure 2–86).

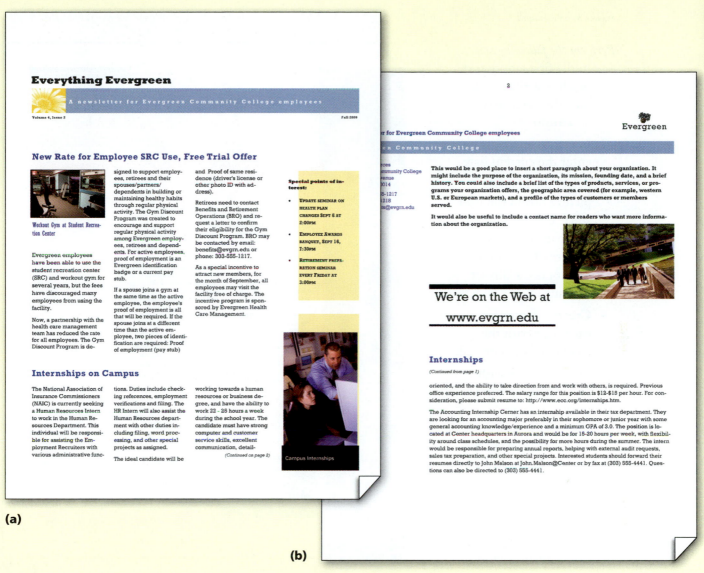

Figure 2–86

Make It Right

Analyze a publication and correct all errors and/or improve the design.

Inserting Missing Continued Notices and Masthead Elements

Instructions: Start Publisher. Open the publication, Make It Right 2-1 History Newsletter Draft, from the Data Files for Students. See the inside back cover of this book for instructions on downloading the Data Files for Students, or contact your instructor for more information about accessing the required files.

The publication is a newsletter that is missing several elements, as shown in Figure 2–87 on the next page. You are to insert these missing elements: masthead volume number, issue number and date, a graphic for the lead story, a footer with a page number, and continued notices.

Continued >

Make It Right *continued*

Perform the following steps:

1. In the first empty text box below the newsletter title, enter `Volume 7 Issue 4`.
2. In the second text box, enter the current date.
3. Select the empty picture box in the lead story. Use the clip art task pane to find a picture of a building. Do not use a clip art drawing.
4. Create a footer for each page with the page number centered.
5. Find the story with text that flows from page 1 to page 2. Format the appropriate boxes with continued notices. Insert an appropriate title on page 2.
6. Change the publication properties, as specified by your instructor.
7. Run the publication through the Design Checker and check the spelling. Fix any errors you find. Choose to ignore names of people and businesses.
8. Save the revised publication and then submit it in the format specified by your instructor.

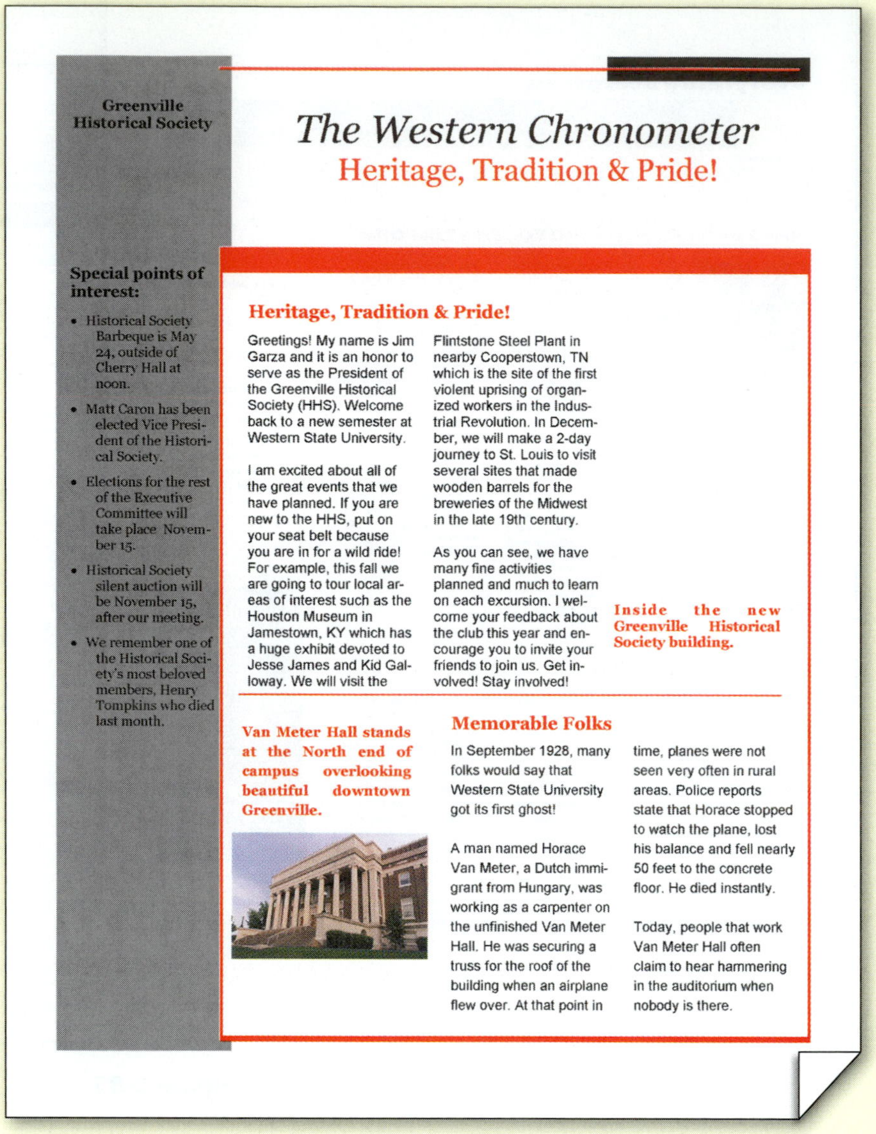

Greenville Historical Society

The Western Chronometer

Heritage, Tradition & Pride!

Special points of interest:

- Historical Society Barbeque is May 24, outside of Cherry Hall at noon.
- Matt Caron has been elected Vice President of the Historical Society.
- Elections for the rest of the Executive Committee will take place November 15.
- Historical Society silent auction will be November 15, after our meeting.
- We remember one of the Historical Society's most beloved members, Henry Tompkins who died last month.

Heritage, Tradition & Pride!

Greetings! My name is Jim Garza and it is an honor to serve as the President of the Greenville Historical Society (HHS). Welcome back to a new semester at Western State University.

I am excited about all of the great events that we have planned. If you are new to the HHS, put on your seat belt because you are in for a wild ride! For example, this fall we are going to tour local areas of interest such as the Houston Museum in Jamestown, KY which has a huge exhibit devoted to Jesse James and Kid Galloway. We will visit the Flintstone Steel Plant in nearby Cooperstown, TN which is the site of the first violent uprising of organized workers in the Industrial Revolution. In December, we will make a 2-day journey to St. Louis to visit several sites that made wooden barrels for the breweries of the Midwest in the late 19th century.

As you can see, we have many fine activities planned and much to learn on each excursion. I welcome your feedback about the club this year and encourage you to invite your friends to join us. Get involved! Stay involved!

Inside the new Greenville Historical Society building.

Van Meter Hall stands at the North end of campus overlooking beautiful downtown Greenville.

Memorable Folks

In September 1928, many folks would say that Western State University got its first ghost!

A man named Horace Van Meter, a Dutch immigrant from Hungary, was working as a carpenter on the unfinished Van Meter Hall. He was securing a truss for the roof of the building when an airplane flew over. At that point in time, planes were not seen very often in rural areas. Police reports state that Horace stopped to watch the plane, lost his balance and fell nearly 50 feet to the concrete floor. He died instantly.

Today, people that work Van Meter Hall often claim to hear hammering in the auditorium when nobody is there.

Figure 2–87

In the Lab

Design and/or create a publication using the guidelines, concepts, and skills presented in this chapter. Labs are listed in order of increasing difficulty.

Lab 1: Creating a Blank Newsletter Template with a Masthead

Problem: As a student working in the English department, you have been asked to create a template for the College of Liberal Arts monthly alumni newsletter. The College wants a four-page newsletter in black and white, with space for many articles (including one where they highlight a member of the COLA alumni), a masthead, pictures with captions, and an attention getter. Each month a faculty member from the English department will work with the template, replacing default text. You prepare a newsletter template similar to the one whose first page is shown below (Figure 2–88).

Perform the following tasks:

1. Start Publisher. Select the Refined newsletter template with a two-column format. Choose the Black and White color scheme and the Literary font scheme.
2. The title of the newsletter is `The COLA Alumnus`. The Business Name text will be `A Newsletter from the College of Liberal Arts`. Use Volume X and Issue X as the text in the template boxes, which will be replaced each month. Use the Insert menu's Date and Time command to enter a template date. (*Hint*: Click the Update Automatically check box.)
3. On pages 2 and 3, replace the quotation text boxes with the Marquee pull quote from the Design Gallery.
4. On page 2, delete the graphic and insert an attention getter from the Design Gallery. Replace the default text of the attention getter with the words, `Attention Getter`, so template users will understand the purpose.
5. On page 3, change one of the headlines to `Alumni of the Month`.
6. Insert page numbers at the bottom of pages 1 and 4, centered.
7. Save the publication on a USB flash drive, using Lab 2-1 COLA Newsletter Template as the file name. E-mail the newsletter as an attachment to your instructor.

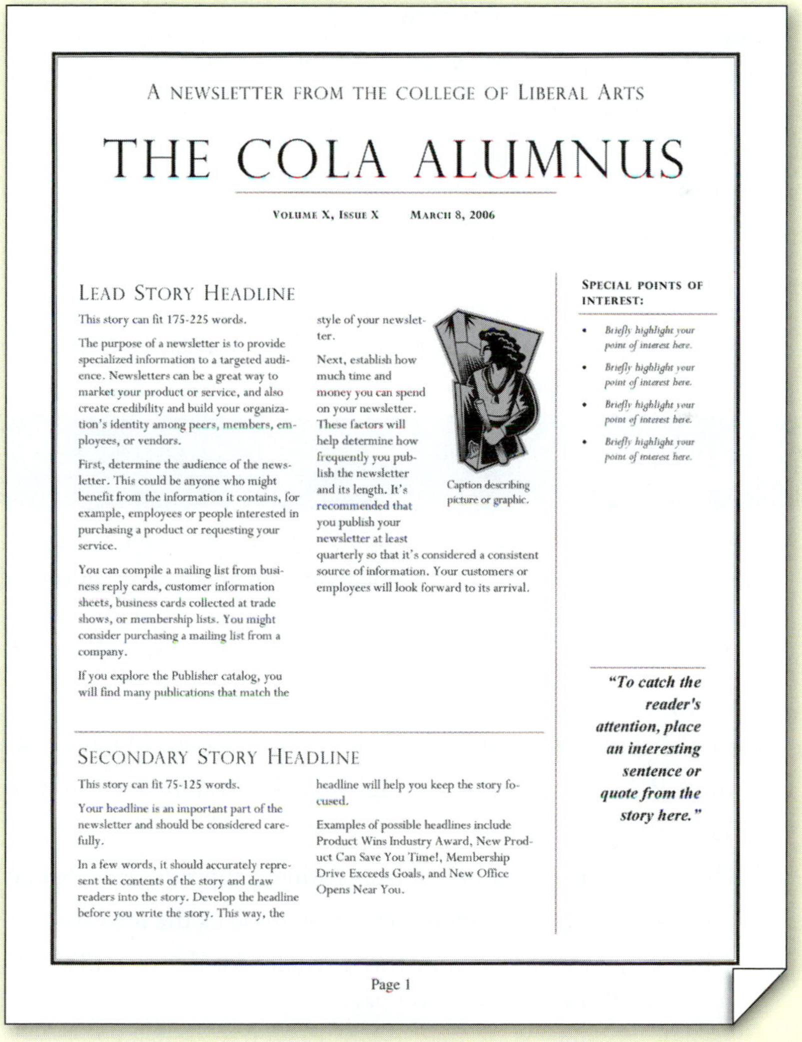

A NEWSLETTER FROM THE COLLEGE OF LIBERAL ARTS

THE COLA ALUMNUS

VOLUME X, ISSUE X   MARCH 8, 2006

LEAD STORY HEADLINE

This story can fit 175-225 words.

The purpose of a newsletter is to provide specialized information to a targeted audience. Newsletters can be a great way to market your product or service, and also create credibility and build your organization's identity among peers, members, employees, or vendors.

First, determine the audience of the newsletter. This could be anyone who might benefit from the information it contains, for example, employees or people interested in purchasing a product or requesting your service.

You can compile a mailing list from business reply cards, customer information sheets, business cards collected at trade shows, or membership lists. You might consider purchasing a mailing list from a company.

If you explore the Publisher catalog, you will find many publications that match the style of your newsletter.

Next, establish how much time and money you can spend on your newsletter. These factors will help determine how frequently you publish the newsletter and its length. It's recommended that you publish your newsletter at least quarterly so that it's considered a consistent source of information. Your customers or employees will look forward to its arrival.

Caption describing picture or graphic.

SPECIAL POINTS OF INTEREST:

- *Briefly highlight your point of interest here.*
- *Briefly highlight your point of interest here.*
- *Briefly highlight your point of interest here.*
- *Briefly highlight your point of interest here.*

"To catch the reader's attention, place an interesting sentence or quote from the story here."

SECONDARY STORY HEADLINE

This story can fit 75-125 words.

Your headline is an important part of the newsletter and should be considered carefully.

In a few words, it should accurately represent the contents of the story and draw readers into the story. Develop the headline before you write the story. This way, the headline will help you keep the story focused.

Examples of possible headlines include Product Wins Industry Award, New Product Can Save You Time!, Membership Drive Exceeds Goals, and New Office Opens Near You.

Page 1

Figure 2–88

In the Lab

Lab 2: Newsletter Analysis

Problem: Obtain a copy of a newsletter that you regularly receive or one from a friend, company, or school. Using the principles in this chapter, analyze the newsletter.

Instructions: Start Publisher. Open the publication, In the Lab 2-2 Newsletter Analysis Table, from the Data Files for Students. See the inside back cover of this book for instructions on downloading the Data Files for Students, or contact your instructor for more information about accessing the required files. Use a word processing program to fill in each empty cell in the table as it applies to your selected newsletter. The table is displayed below:

Newsletter Name:	Your Name:
Purpose:	
Audience:	
Paper:	
Distribution:	
Font & Color Scheme:	
Consistency:	
Alignment:	
Repeated Elements:	
Jump Lines, Sidebars, Pull Quotes, etc.:	

Print the table and attach a copy of the newsletter. Turn in both to your instructor.

In the Lab

Lab 3: Researching Computer-Related Jobs

Problem: You are a college student currently enrolled in an introductory business class. Your assignment is to prepare a short newsletter about computer-related jobs. Research three computer-related jobs, using journals, interviews, or the Web, and prepare a two-page newsletter.

Instructions: Perform the following tasks:
1. Gather your data and prepare electronic versions of your research.
2. Start Publisher. Choose a template, column style, font style, and color style.
3. Delete pages 2 and 3.
4. Replace the masthead text boxes with appropriate data. Name your newsletter.
5. Choose your favorite computer-related job as the lead story.
6. Choose the longest of your three articles for the secondary story and have Publisher flow the text into one of the text boxes on page 2.
7. Import the third story into a vacant text box on page 2.
8. Delete any text boxes that have to do with a company name, address, or phone. Delete a logo if it is displayed.
9. Use the design gallery to insert an attention getter. Replace the attention getter text with your name.
10. Check the spelling and design of the newsletter.
11. Save the publication on a USB flash drive, using Lab 2-3 Computer Jobs Newsletter as the file name.
12. Print the newsletter using duplex printing and turn it in to your instructor.

Cases and Places

Apply your creative thinking and problem-solving skills to design and implement a solution.

• Easier   •• More Difficult

• 1: Create a Vacation Club Newsletter

Use the Voyage Newsletter template to create a two-page newsletter for the Seniors Abroad Club. This local club of senior citizens gets together to take group trips. For the newsletter title, use Seniors On The Go, and place today's date in the masthead. Include an article heading for the lead story, which concerns the club's most recent trip to London (you may use the default text in the story itself), and a secondary article heading that tells how to pack lightly for trips overseas. Add a list of dates for the upcoming trips to Paris, the Caribbean, and Tokyo in the Special points of interest sidebar. Replace the graphics with suitable pictures using the Clip Art task pane.

• 2: Create a Band Booster Quarterly Newsletter

The two-page newsletter will be sent to band students, parents, and other interested parties. Use the Rhythm template, the Concourse color scheme, and the Literary font scheme. The name of the newsletter is High Notes. Use the name of your school as the business name. The newsletter should feature the most recent performance as the lead story. You may write a story about a recent musical performance at your school. The secondary story should be about a "Band Member of the Month." You may use yourself as the band member or a friend who plays an instrument. If either story flows onto the back page, create jump lines. If necessary, create a story related to an individual band in the school system to include on the back page. Include a sidebar with upcoming competitions and events. Use another sidebar for a future trip payment schedule. Incorporate clip art or photographs. Make sure that any graphics downloaded from the Web have no copyright restrictions. Save the newsletter as a template for the band boosters to use next quarter. For extra credit on this assignment, create a list of instructions for template users.

•• 3: Create a Restaurant Review Newsletter

You are a member of a restaurant and food review club. Because you have a background in desktop publishing, you prepare the monthly two-page newsletter for club members. Your assignment is to design the newsletter and develop the next issue. The newsletter should have a feature article and some announcements for club members. Your feature article could discuss/review a restaurant, a deli, an online or in town grocery store, a recipe, or any other aspect of food or food service. Use the Internet, visit a restaurant, interview restaurant or grocery store patrons, prepare a dish using a new recipe, and so on, to obtain information for the articles. The feature article should be continued on page 2. Enhance the newsletter with color and font schemes, graphics, sidebars, and pull quotes.

•• 4: Create a Newsletter about the Month You Were Born

Make It Personal

Did you ever wonder what world events took place during the month you were born (besides your birth)? For example, what happened with respect to politics, world affairs, and the economy? What made headline news? Were there any scientific breakthroughs? What was on television and at the box office? Were any famous people born? Did anyone famous die? What songs topped the charts? What was happening in the world of sports? Research the newsworthy events that took place during the month and year you were born (i.e., July 1985) by looking through newspapers, magazines, searching the Web, and/or interviewing family and friends. Create a two-page newsletter with articles about that month. Include the date in the masthead. Use appropriate graphics, a sidebar, a pull quote, WordArt, and other newsletter objects.

Continued >

Cases and Places *continued*

•• 5: Create a Newsletter about Spring Break Vacation Destinations

Working Together

Your school newspaper is planning a four-page insert to review spring break destinations. Your team is to design and write that insert, using a Publisher newsletter template. The newsletter should have a lead story that reviews the most popular destination. Other articles could review locations, transportation, group rates, new passport or travel regulations, security at the airport, etc. As a group, decide on the name of the newsletter and design the masthead. Each team member independently is to write at least three paragraphs for a story. Then, the team should meet as a group to combine all of the documents so you can place them into the newsletter on appropriate pages. If articles are too long to fit in a template box, decide where to continue the stories. Use jump lines. On the first page, include a sidebar, listing the top five destinations. Use appropriate graphics, sidebars, and pull quotes. Make sure that any graphics downloaded from the Web have no copyright restrictions. Run the publication through the Design Checker and check the spelling. Fix any errors you find. Choose to ignore names of people and businesses.

3 | Publishing a Tri-Fold Brochure

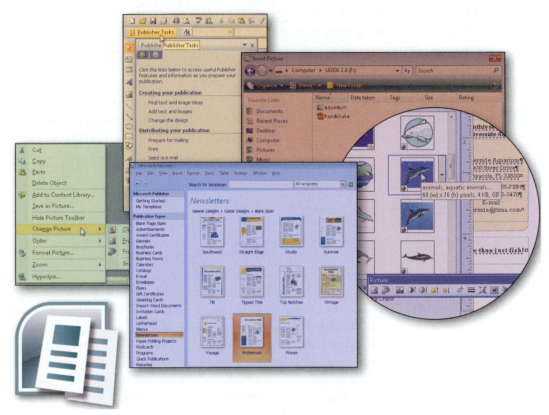

Objectives

You will have mastered the material in this project when you can:

- Discuss advantages of the brochure medium
- Choose brochure options
- Create a custom color scheme
- Edit brochure template text boxes
- Use AutoCorrect options and the Format Painter
- Create a font style and format paragraphs
- Edit a Sign-up form
- Describe the use of graphic formats
- Wrap text around a graphic
- Create a logo from scratch using AutoShapes

- Format AutoShapes in the scratch area
- Duplicate, resize, and reposition objects
- Create a composite object in the scratch area
- Create a WordArt object
- Create a watermark on the Master Page
- Choose appropriate printing services, paper, and color libraries
- Prepare a publication for outside printing
- Use the Pack and Go Wizard

3 | Publishing a Tri-Fold Brochure

Introduction

Whether you want to advertise a service, event, or product, or merely want to inform the public about a current topic of interest, brochures are a popular type of promotional publication. A **brochure**, or pamphlet, usually is a high-quality document with lots of color and graphics, created for advertising purposes. Businesses that may not be able to reach potential clientele effectively through traditional advertising, such as newspapers and radio, can create a long-lasting advertisement with a well-designed brochure.

Brochures come in all shapes and sizes. Colleges and universities produce brochures about their programs. The travel industry uses brochures to entice tourists. In addition, service industries and manufacturers display their products using this visual, hands-on medium.

Project — Brochure

The project in this chapter shows you how to build the two-page, tri-fold brochure shown in Figure 3–1. The brochure informs secondary school teachers about a Tech Camp summer program, held at the local college. Each side of the brochure has three panels. Page 1 (Figure 3–1a) contains the front and back panels, as well as the inside fold. Page 2 (Figure 3–1b) contains a three-panel display that, when opened completely, provides the reader with more details about the event and a sign-up form.

On page 1, the front panel contains shapes, text boxes, and a graphic designed to draw the reader's attention and inform the reader of the intent of the brochure. The back panel, which displays in the middle of page 1, contains the name of the school, the address, telephone numbers, and the organization logo. The inside fold, on the left, contains an article about the details of the program.

The three inside panels on page 2 contain more information about the camp, a list of topics or tracks, and a form the reader may use to register.

Overview

As you read through this chapter, you will learn how to create the newsletter shown in Figure 3–1 by performing these general tasks:

- Select a brochure template and specify the layout options.
- Create a new color scheme and style for the brochure.
- Copy formatting, using styles and the Format Painter button.
- Create a logo from an AutoShape and format it.
- Use WordArt to create a watermark on page 2 of the brochure.
- Proof the brochure with spell checking and the design checker.
- Prepare the brochure for commercial printing.

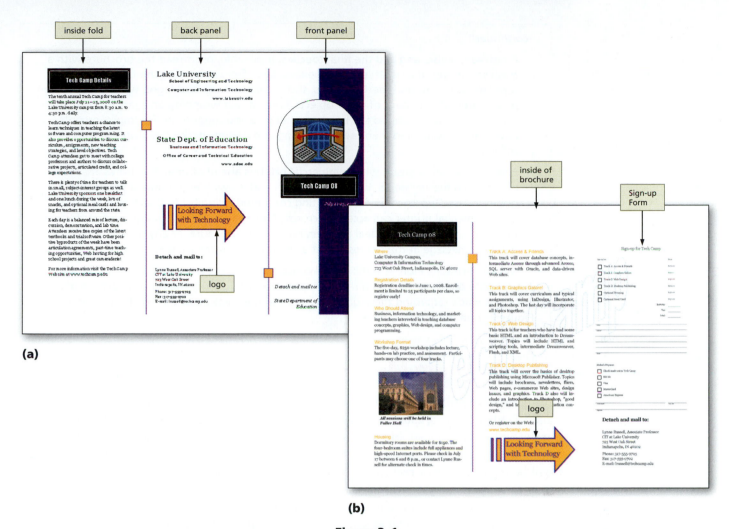

Figure 3–1

General Project Guidelines

Plan Ahead

When creating a Publisher brochure, the actions you perform and decisions you make will affect the appearance and characteristics of the finished publication. As you create a brochure, such as the project shown in Figure 3–1, you should follow these general guidelines:

1. **Decide on the purpose, shelf life, and layout.** Spend time brainstorming ideas for the brochure. Think about why you want to create one. Decide on the purpose of the brochure. Is it to inform, sell, attract, or advertise an event? Adjust your template, fonts, colors, and graphics to match that purpose. Brochures commonly have a wider audience than newsletters and flyers. They need to last longer. Carefully consider whether to add dated material or prices. Create a timeline of effectiveness and plan to have the brochure ready far in advance. Decide how many panels your brochure should be, and how often you are going to produce it. If you are working for someone, draw a storyboard and get it approved before you begin. Think about alignment of objects, proximity of similar data, contrast, and repetition.

2. **Create the brochure.** Gather all the information, such as stories, graphics, logos, colors, shapes, style information, and watermarks. Use a template until you are very experienced in designing brochures. Save copies or versions along the way. If you have to create objects from scratch, have someone else evaluate your work and give you constructive feedback. If you are using forms in your brochure, verify the manner in which the viewer will return the form. Check and double-check all prices, addresses, and phone numbers.

(continued)

(continued)

3. **Proofread, revise, and add the final touches.** If possible, proofread the brochure with a fresh set of eyes, that is, at least one to two days after completing the first draft. Insert repeated elements and special objects, such as watermarks and logos, which need to be placed around or in back of other objects. Look at text wrapping on every graphic. Ask someone else to proofread the brochure and give you suggestions for improvements. Revise as necessary and then use the spelling and design checking features of the software.

4. **Plan for printing.** Consult with commercial printers ahead of time. Brochures are more effective on heavier paper, with strong colors and glossy feels. Choose a paper that is going to last. Discuss commercial printing color modes and fonts. Check to make sure the commercial printer can accept Microsoft Publisher 2007 files. Designing an effective brochure involves a great deal of planning. A good brochure, or any publication, must deliver a message in the clearest, most attractive, and effective way possible.

When necessary, more specific details concerning the above guidelines are presented at appropriate points in the chapter. The chapter also will identify the actions performed and decisions made regarding these guidelines during the creation of the brochure shown in Figure 3–1 on the previous page.

The Brochure Medium

Brochures are professionally printed on special paper to provide long-lasting documents and to enhance the graphics. The brochure medium intentionally is tactile. Brochures are meant to be touched, carried home, passed along, and looked at, again and again. Newspapers and fliers usually are produced for short-term readership on paper that soon will be thrown away or recycled. Brochures frequently use a heavier stock of paper so that they can stand better in a display rack.

The content of a brochure needs to last longer, too. On occasion, the intent of a brochure is to educate, such as a brochure on health issues in a doctor's office. More commonly, though, the intent is to market a product or sell a service. Prices and dated materials that are subject to frequent change affect the usable life of a brochure.

Typically, brochures use a great deal of color, and they include actual photographs instead of drawings or graphic images. Photographs give a sense of realism to a publication and should be used to show people, places, or objects that are real, whereas images or drawings more appropriately are used to convey concepts or ideas.

Many brochures incorporate newspaper features, such as columns and a masthead, and the added eye appeal of logos, sidebars, shapes, and graphics. Small brochures are separated into panels and folded. Larger brochures resemble small magazines, with multiple pages and a stapled binding.

Brochures, designed to be in circulation for longer periods as a type of advertising, ordinarily are published in greater quantities and on more expensive paper than newsletters and are, therefore, more costly. The cost, however, is less prohibitive when produced **in-house** using desktop publishing rather than hiring an outside service. The cost per copy sometimes is less than a newsletter because brochures are produced in mass quantities.

Table 3–1 lists some benefits and advantages of using the brochure medium.

Table 3–1 Benefits and Advantages of Using the Brochure Medium

Aspect	Benefits and Advantages
Exposure	An attention getter in displays A take-along document encouraging second looks A long-lasting publication due to paper and content An easily distributed publication — mass mailings, advertising sites
Information	An in-depth look at a product or service An opportunity to inform in a nonrestrictive environment An opportunity for focused feedback using tear-offs and forms
Audience	Interested clientele and retailers
Communication	An effective medium to highlight products and services A source of free information to build credibility An easier method to disseminate information than a magazine

Besides the intent and content of the brochure, you must consider the shape and size of the page when designing this type of publication. Publisher can incorporate a variety of paper sizes, from the standard 8½ × 11-inch to the 8½ × 24-inch. You also can design smaller brochures, such as those used as liner notes for CD jewel cases or inserts for videotapes. In addition, you need to think about how the brochure or pamphlet will be folded. Publisher's brochure templates can create three or four panels. Using the page setup options, you can even create special folds, such as book or card folds.

Decide on the purpose, shelf life, and layout.
The first impression of a company sometimes is through its brochure. Thus, it is important that your brochure appropriately reflects the essence of the business, item, or event. Determine the shelf life of your brochure and its purpose.

Choose your template, font, colors, panels, and forms. Choose a template that matches the feeling of your topics. Use colors and fonts already in use in graphics from the company, school, or event organizers.

Plan Ahead

After starting Publisher, the following pages choose a template and select font and color schemes.

To Start Publisher

If you are using a computer to step through the project in this chapter, and you want your screens to match the figures in this book, you should change your computer's resolution to 1024 × 768. For information about how to change a computer's resolution, read Appendix D.

The following steps, which assume Windows is running, start Publisher based on a typical installation. You may need to ask your instructor how to start Publisher for your computer.

Note: If you are using Windows XP, please see Appendix F for alternate steps.

1 Click the Start button on the Windows Vista taskbar to display the Start menu, and then click All Programs at the bottom of the left pane on the Start menu to display the All Programs list.

2 Click Microsoft Office in the All Programs list to display the Microsoft Office list, and then click Microsoft Office Publisher 2007 to start Publisher and display the Getting Started with Microsoft Office Publisher 2007 catalog.

3 If the Publisher window is not maximized, click the Maximize button next to the Close button on its title bar to maximize the window.

Plan
Ahead

> **Create the brochure.**
> Gather all the information and objects. Once you make a few changes, save a copy as the rough draft version. As you add new objects, verify the accuracy of all your information. Get a second opinion on anything created from scratch.

Creating a Tri-Fold Brochure

Publisher-supplied templates use proven design strategies and combinations of objects, which are placed to attract attention and disseminate information effectively. The options for brochures differ from other publications in that they allow you to choose from page sizes, special kinds of forms, and panel/page layout options.

Making Choices about Brochure Options

For the Tech Camp brochure, you will use an informational brochure template, named Spotlight, making changes to its page size, customer address, sign-up form, color scheme, and font scheme. **Page size** refers to the number of panels in the brochure. The **Customer address** selection offers choices about whether to include the customer's address in the brochure. **Form options**, which display on page 2 of the brochure, include None, Order form, Response form, and Sign-up form. The **Order form** displays fields for the description of items ordered as well as types of payment information, including blank fields for entering items, quantities, and prices. The **Response form** displays check box choices and fields for comments, and blanks for up to four multiple-choice questions and a comment section. The **Sign-up form** displays check box choices, fields for time and price, as well as payment information.

All three forms are meant to be detached and mailed in as turnaround documents. Each form contains blanks for the name and address of prospective customers or clients. The company not only verifies the marketing power of its brochure but also is able to create a customer database with the information.

To Choose Brochure Options

The following steps choose a brochure template and make design choices. In the Customize area, the Spotlight template and the Impact font scheme are used to highlight the topic of the brochure. The color scheme will be created later in the project. In the Options area, a 3-panel format is used, and a sign-up form is inserted.

BTW

How Brochures Differ
Each brochure template produces two pages of graphics, business information text boxes, and story boxes. The difference is in the look and feel of the front panel, the location and style of the shapes and graphics, the design of any panel dividers, and the specific kind of decorations unique to each publication set.

- Click Brochures in the list of publication types to display the catalog of brochure templates.

- At the top of the catalog, click Classic Designs. Scroll to display the informational brochure previews. Click the Spotlight preview to select it (Figure 3–2).

Figure 3–2

- In the Customize area, click the Font scheme box arrow to display the list of font schemes.

 **Experiment**

- Scroll in the list of font schemes and click various schemes to see the previews change.

- Click Impact in the list to change the font scheme for the publication (Figure 3–3).

Q&A

Why does my customize area look different?

The customize area displays the most recently used color and font schemes.

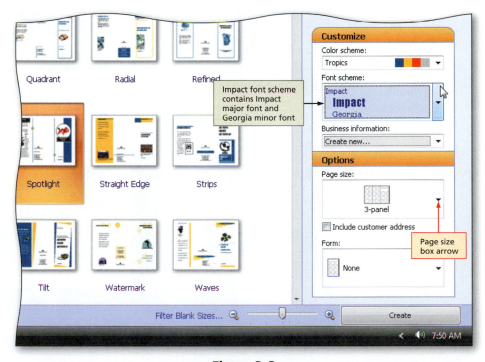

Figure 3–3

3

- In the Options area, if necessary, click the Page size box arrow and then click 3-panel in the list to choose a tri-fold brochure.

- Click the Form box arrow (Figure 3–4).

Do I need to change the color scheme?

Publisher by default chooses the color scheme from the previous editing session on your system. Because you will create a custom color scheme later in the project, it does not make any difference which color scheme displays at this point.

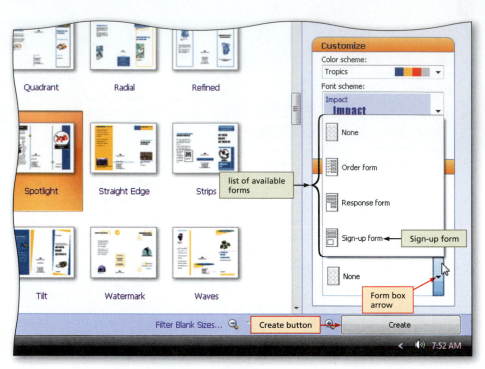

Figure 3–4

4

- Click Sign-up form in the list to choose the Sign-up form option.

- Click the Create button in the lower-right corner of the window to create the publication based on the template settings (Figure 3–5).

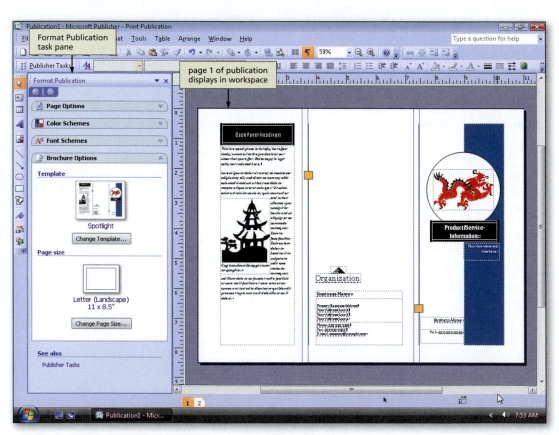

Figure 3–5

Custom Color Schemes

Recall that a color scheme is a predefined set of harmonized colors that you can apply to text and objects. Text and objects with an applied color scheme will change automatically when you switch to a new color scheme or modify the current color scheme. Publisher provides an option for users to create their own color schemes rather than using one of the predefined sets. Creating a **custom color scheme** means choosing your own colors to use in a publication. You may choose one main color, five accent colors, a hyperlink color, and a followed hyperlink color. The **main color** commonly is used for text in major eye-catching areas of the publication. The first accent color is used for graphical lines, boxes, and separators. The second accent color typically is used as fill color in prominent publication shapes. Subsequent accent colors may be used in several ways, including shading, text effects, and alternate font color. The hyperlink color is used as the font color for hyperlink text. After a hyperlink is clicked, the color changes to show users which path, or trail, they have clicked previously.

Custom color schemes can be given a name that will appear in the Apply a color scheme list. The chosen colors also appear on the Fill Color, Line Color, and Font Color button menus.

The Tech Camp brochure will use accent colors of blue and gold, which are the school colors, other accent colors of light blue and tan, as well as a basic black main color for text. Publisher displays an option to create a custom color scheme on the task pane. Publisher then allows users to choose the various colors and name the scheme.

To Open the Create New Color Dialog Box

The following steps create a custom color scheme.

1

- If the Special Characters button on the Standard toolbar is not selected already, click it to display formatting marks on the screen.

- With the Format Publication task pane still displayed, click Color Schemes to access the color scheme options (Figure 3–6).

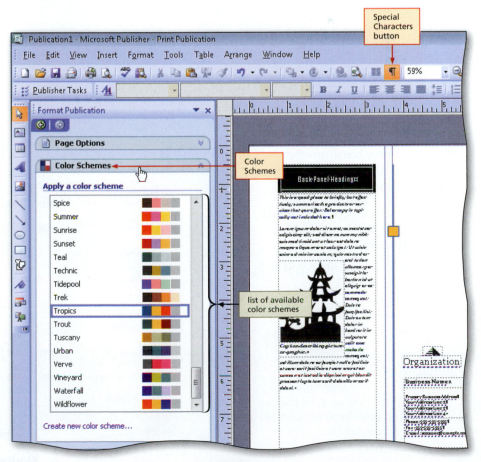

Figure 3–6

- Click the Create new color scheme link to open the Create New Color Scheme dialog box (Figure 3–7).

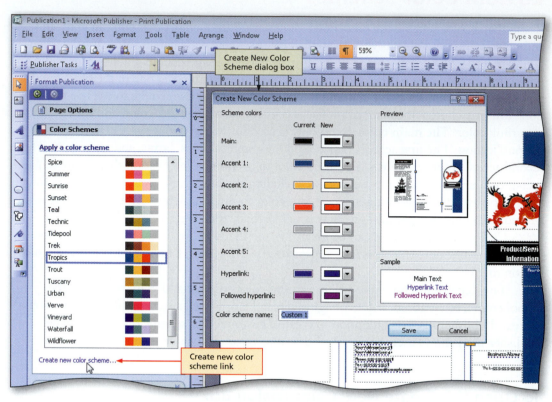

Figure 3–7

To Change an Accent Color

The following steps select an accent color for the custom color scheme.

- In the Scheme colors area, click the second New box arrow that corresponds to the Accent 1 color to display a palette of color choices.

- When the color palette is displayed, point to Dark Blue to display the screentip (Figure 3–8).

Q&A

What colors display when you click the New box arrow?

Publisher presents 40 of the common printing colors for desktop printers in a small palette. You can click the More Colors button to display the Colors dialog box, where you can choose other colors, create your own colors by entering color numbers, or choose a publishing color system, such as **Pantone**, a popular color system for professional printing.

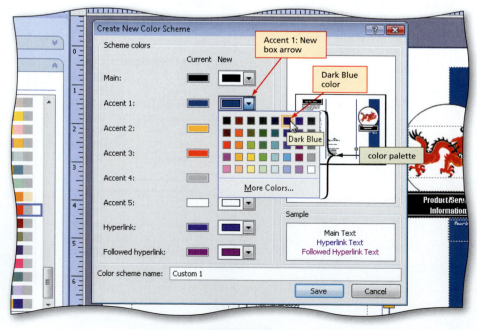

Figure 3–8

2

- Click Dark Blue to select the Accent 1 color (Figure 3–9).

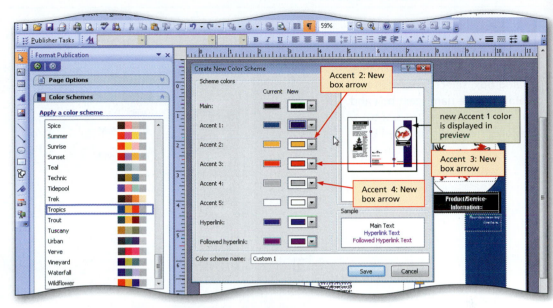

Figure 3–9

To Select More Accent Colors

The following steps select more accent colors.

1 Click the Accent 2, New box arrow. Click Gold.

2 Click the Accent 3, New box arrow. Click Pale Blue.

3 Click the Accent 4, New box arrow. Click Tan (Figure 3–10).

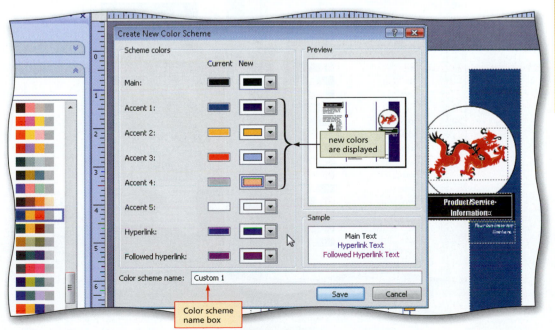

Figure 3–10

To Save a New Color Scheme

The following steps save the new color scheme for the Tech Camp brochure.

- In the Create New Color Scheme dialog box, select the text in the Color scheme name text box and then type School Colors to replace the text (Figure 3–11).

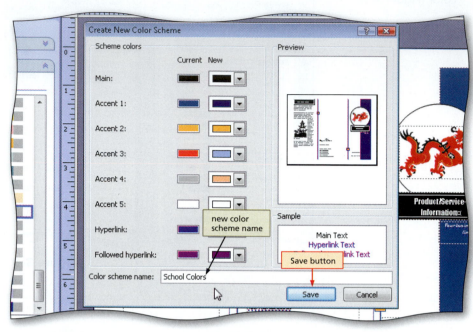

Figure 3–11

- Click the Save button to save the color scheme (Figure 3–12).

- Close the Format Publication task pane by clicking the Close button.

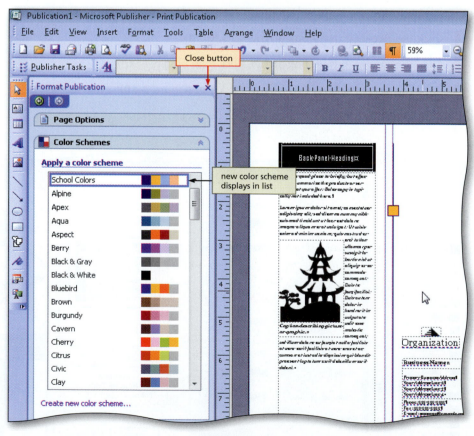

Figure 3–12

To Save the Publication

Now that several important options have been chosen, it is a good practice to save the publication. The following steps save the publication with the file name, Tech Camp Brochure. For a detailed example of the procedure summarized below, refer to pages PUB 31 through PUB 33 in Chapter 1.

1 With a USB flash drive connected to one of the computer's USB ports, click the Save button on the Standard toolbar.

2 Type `Tech Camp Brochure` in the File name text box to change the file name. Do not press the ENTER key.

3 Navigate to your USB flash drive.

4 Click the Save button in the Save As dialog box to save the publication on the USB flash drive with the file name, Tech Camp Brochure.

BTW

Automatic Saving
Publisher can save your publication at regular intervals for you. On the Tools menu, click Options, and then click the Save tab. Select the Save AutoRecover info every check box. In the minutes box, specify how often you want Publisher to save files. Do not use AutoRecover as a substitute for regularly saving your work.

Deleting Objects on Page 1

In the Tech Camp brochure, you will not use a graphic in the left panel on page 1, so it can be deleted. You also will create a new logo for the brochure, so the logo in the middle panel of page 1 can be deleted.

To Delete Objects

The following steps delete objects on page 1.

1 In the left panel of page 1, right-click the grouped picture and caption. On the shortcut menu, click Delete Object.

2 In the middle panel, right-click the organization logo. On the shortcut menu, click Delete Object.

Replacing Text

Recall that editing text in the brochure involves selecting the current text and replacing it with new, appropriate text in one of two ways: editing text directly in Publisher or using Word to facilitate editing. If you need to edit only a few words, it is faster to use a Publisher text box with the accompanying Publisher tools. If you need to edit a long story, however, perhaps one that appears on different pages in a publication, it might be easier to edit the story in Word.

Publisher inserts placeholder text on page 1 of its supplied templates. This placeholder text may be selected by a single click. Alternately, personal information components, designed to be changed or personalized for a company, are best selected by dragging through the text. When you change a personal information component, all matching components in the publication change due to the synchronization that is built into those special text boxes.

Table 3–2 displays the text that needs to be replaced on page 1 of the brochure.

Table 3–2 Page 1 Text

Location	Publisher-Supplied Text and Text Boxes	New Text
Right Panel	Public/Service Information	Tech Camp 08
	Your business tag line here.	July 21–25, 2008
	Business Name	Co-sponsored by: Lake University
	Tel: 555 555 5555	State Department of Education
Middle Panel	Business Name	For more information contact:
	Address	Lynne Russell, Associate Professor CIT at Lake University 723 West Oak Street Indianapolis, IN 46202
	Phone/Fax/E-mail	Phone: 317-555-9705 Fax: 317-555-9702 E-mail: lrussell@techcamp.edu
Left Panel	Back Panel Heading	Tech Camp Details
	Back Panel Story	The tenth annual Tech Camp for teachers will take place July 21 – 25, 2008, on the Lake University campus from 8:30 a.m. to 4:30 p.m. daily. Tech Camp offers teachers a chance to learn techniques in teaching the latest software and computer programming. It also provides opportunities to discuss curriculum, assignments, new teaching strategies, and level objectives. Tech Camp attendees get to meet with college professors and authors to discuss collaborative projects, articulated credit, and college expectations. There is plenty of time for teachers to talk in small, subject-interest groups as well. Lake University sponsors one breakfast and one lunch during the week, lots of snacks, and optional housing and meal cards for teachers from around the state. Each day is a balanced mix of lecture, discussion, demonstration, and lab time. Attendees receive free copies of the latest textbooks and trial software. Other positive byproducts of the week have been articulation agreements, part-time teaching opportunities, Web hosting for high school projects, and great camaraderie! For more information, visit the Tech Camp Web site at www.techcamp.edu

To Edit Text in the Brochure

The following steps edit both placeholder and personal information text on page 1 of the brochure.

 1

- Click the Product/Service Information text box in the right panel on page 1. Press the F9 key to zoom the placeholder text box (Figure 3–13).

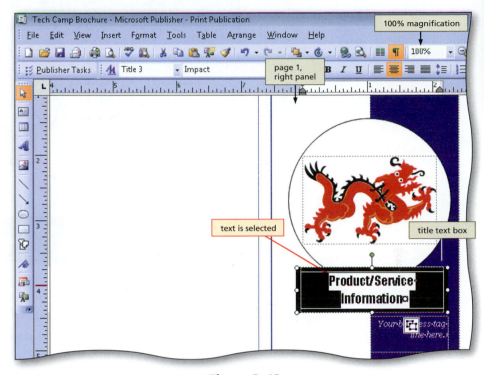

Figure 3–13

2

- Type Tech Camp 08 to replace the title text.

- Drag through the text in the tag line text box to select it (Figure 3–14).

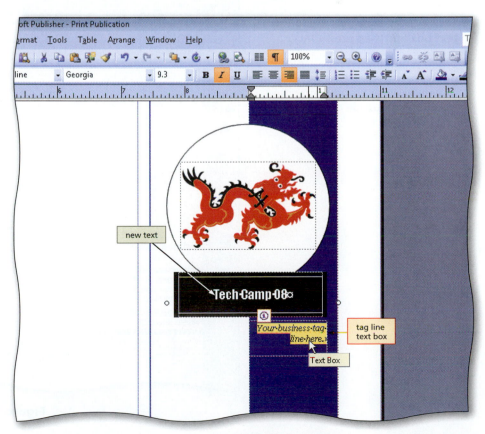

Figure 3–14

3

- Type `July 21-25, 2008` to replace the text (Figure 3–15).

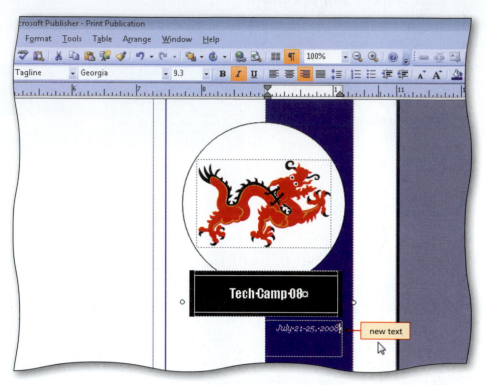

Figure 3–15

4

- Scroll down in the right panel to display the business name text box.

- To select the text, click inside the text box and then press CTRL+A.

- Type `Co-sponsored by: Lake University` to replace the text.

- Do not click outside of the text box (Figure 3–16).

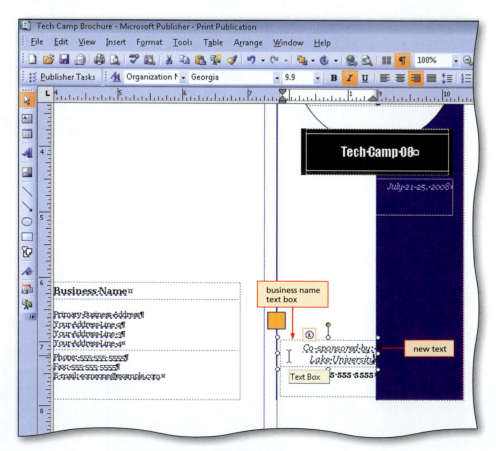

Figure 3–16

To Undo Synchronization

Recall that the business name text box is a synchronized object, which means that all business name text boxes change when you edit any one of them. Other synchronized objects include the personal information boxes, such as the address and telephone text boxes, as well as tear-offs, which you synchronized in Chapter 1. Because you want to edit each business name text box individually, the following steps use the Undo button on the Standard toolbar to undo synchronization.

1 Click outside of the business name text box.

2 Click the Undo Update Fields button on the Standard toolbar.

3 Zoom to Whole Page (Figure 3–17).

BTW

The Undo Button
The Undo button takes on a new name depending upon the previous task. If you have just changed the font scheme, the screentip will say Undo Font Schemes. In Figure 3–17, the synchronization was an example of updating a field, so the button is called the Undo Field Update button. The same is true for the Redo button.

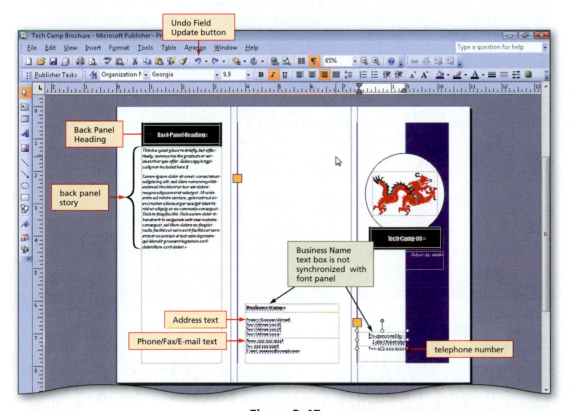

Figure 3–17

To Replace the Other Text Boxes on Page 1

The following step replaces the rest of the placeholder text on page 1. Alternately, you can import the text for the back panel story from the Data Disk associated with this book. The name of the file is Tech Camp Details. For a detailed example of the import procedure, refer to pages PUB 89 through PUB 91 in Chapter 2.

1 Zoom, scroll, and select as necessary to replace the other text boxes on page 1 with the new text from Table 3–2 on page PUB 158. After you edit the business name text box in the middle panel, do not forget to click the Undo button to cancel the synchronization. You may keep the synchronization of the address and telephone text boxes.

Font Styles

Each of the font schemes contains numerous styles. In Publisher, a **style** is a combination of formatting characteristics, such as font size, colors, effects, and formatting, which are named and stored for each font scheme. When you select a font scheme, Publisher creates styles for titles, headings, accent text, body text, list bullets, normal text, and personal information components, using the fonts from the font scheme. For example, in the Impact font scheme, Heading 2 uses the Georgia font, black and bolded, with a font size of 16 and a line spacing of 1.14 spaces.

Applying a Style

When you apply a style, all of the formatting instructions in that style are applied at one time. To apply a style to new text, select the style from the Style list on the Formatting toolbar and then type the text. Alternately, you can select the text first and then select the style. In a later chapter, you will learn that Publisher also has a Styles task pane to help you edit and import styles.

To Insert a Text Box and Apply a Font Scheme Style

The following steps create a new text box for the middle panel of page 1, apply styles, and then insert text. In the Impact font scheme, the Heading 2 style is used for the first line of text, which is bold with a font size of 16. The other lines use Heading 4, which is bold, aligned right, with a font size of 8.3.

- With page 1 of the brochure still displayed, scroll to the upper portion of the middle panel. If necessary, type 100% in the Zoom box to increase the magnification.

- Click the Text Box button on the Objects toolbar and then drag a text box approximately 3 inches × 1.5 inches, as shown in Figure 3–18.

Q&A

How do I know how big the text box is?

As you drag to create the text box, you can watch the Object Size area of the status bar. Your text box measurements do not have to be exact.

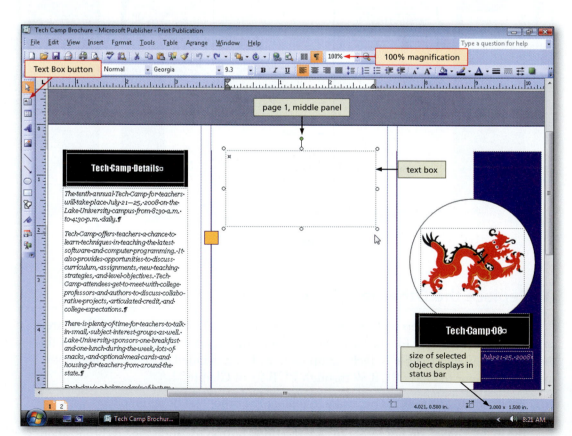

Figure 3–18

Later, you will learn to use the Measurements toolbar, or the Format Text Box dialog box to set exact measurements.

2

- Click the Style box arrow on the Formatting toolbar to display the styles.

 Experiment

- Scroll in the list of styles to view the various font sizes, alignments, and formatting.

- Scroll, if necessary, and then point to Heading 2 in the list (Figure 3–19).

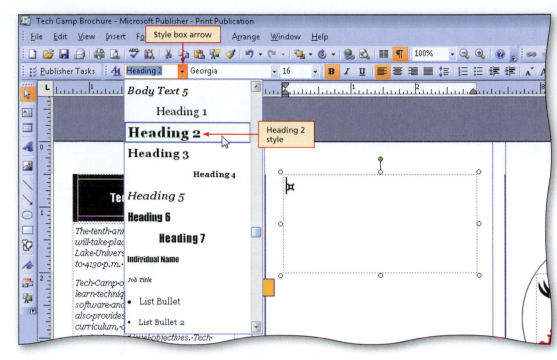

Figure 3–19

3

- Click Heading 2 to select the style.

- Type Lake University and then press the ENTER key (Figure 3–20).

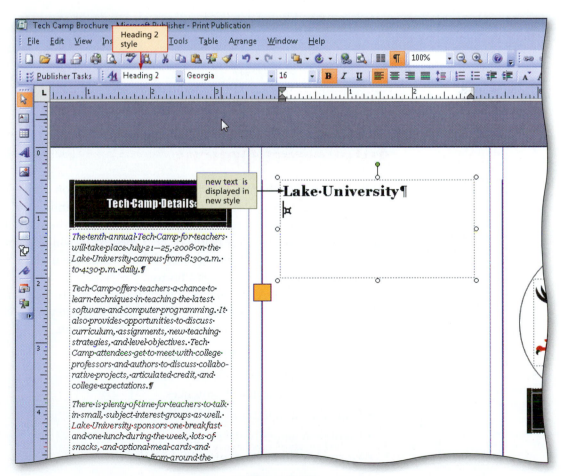

Figure 3–20

4
- Click the Style box arrow on the Formatting toolbar to display the styles.

- Scroll and then click Heading 4 to select the style.

- Type School of Engineering and Technology and then press the ENTER key.

- Type Computer and Information Technology and then press the ENTER key.

- Type www. lakeuniv.edu to complete the text (Figure 3–21).

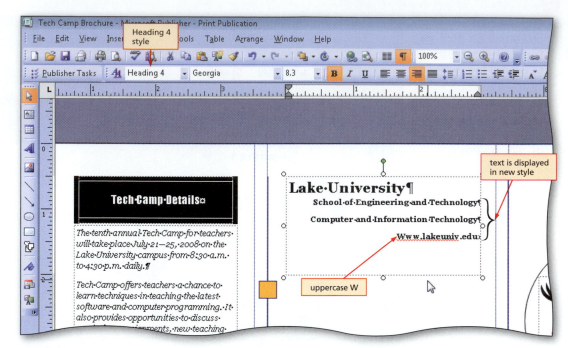

Figure 3–21

Q&A

Why did the first letter of the Web page address capitalize itself?

Publisher tries to help you by capitalizing the beginning of sentences and paragraphs for you. As you will learn in the next series of steps, this autocorrect feature can be reversed for individual occurrences or turned off for all occurrences.

Autoformatting
In addition to the AutoCorrect options, Publisher autoformats some text as you type. Publisher replaces two hyphens with a dash and straight quotes with smart quotes when you type the closing quotation marks. Publisher also continues bullets and numbered list formatting. These options and the AutoCorrect options can be changed by clicking AutoCorrect Options on the tools menu.

AutoCorrect Options

Publisher assists you by correcting certain kinds of common errors. While these **AutoCorrect options** can be turned on or off from the Tools menu, individual occurrences can be edited with the **AutoCorrect Options button**, one of the smart tags in Publisher. Recall that a smart tag displays just below or near the text to which it applies. The AutoCorrect Options smart tag first displays as a small blue rectangle under the correction. When you point to the smart tag, it displays a button.

The following AutoCorrect options typically are turned on in an initial installation of Publisher. You can create specific exceptions or define your own automatic replacement text by clicking AutoCorrect Options on the Tools menu.

- Show AutoCorrect Options button
- Correct TWo INtial CApitals
- Capitalize first letter of sentences
- Capitalize first letter of table cells
- Capitalize names of days
- Correct accidental use of cAPS LOCK key
- Replace text as you type
- Automatically use suggestions from the spelling checker

To Use the AutoCorrect Options Button

The next steps turn off autocorrection for capitalization of the first letter in the URL. **URL** is an acronym for Uniform Resource Locator that refers to a Web address. Web addresses typically begin with the letters www.

1

- Move the mouse pointer near the capital W in the URL to display the smart tag (Figure 3–22).

Q&A

My Web page address does not have a capital W. What should I do?

If your Web page address does not have a capital W, it is possible that someone already has turned that feature off on your system. You can skip to the next section or turn the feature back on by clicking AutoCorrect Options on the Tools menu. Make sure the Capitalize first letter of sentences check box displays a check mark.

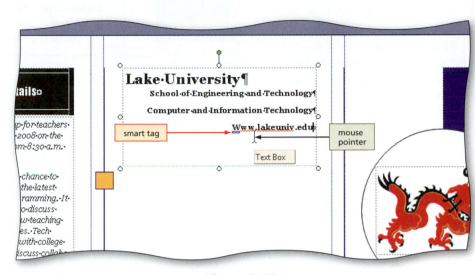

Figure 3–22

2

- Point to the smart tag to display the AutoCorrect Options button (Figure 3–23).

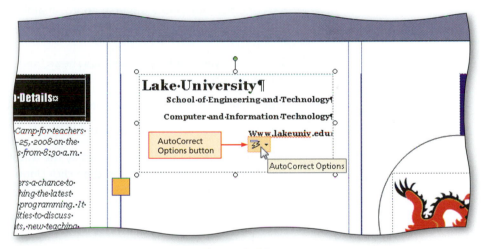

Figure 3–23

3

- Click the AutoCorrect Options button to display its menu (Figure 3–24).

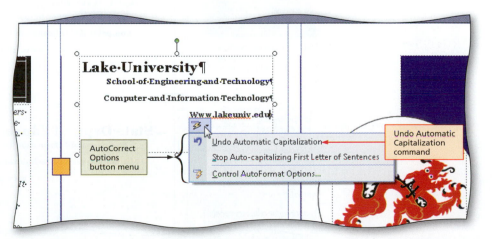

Figure 3–24

4

- Click Undo Automatic Capitalization to cancel the capital first letter (Figure 3–25).

Q&A

Why did the red wavy line disappear?

By default, Publisher does not flag text that begins with the lowercase letters, www, because it is normally a URL. When it was uppercase, Publisher warned you that it might be the beginning of a sentence with a misspelled word.

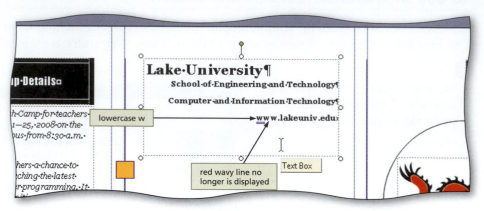

Figure 3–25

To Create Another Text Box

A second text box with styles is created in the following steps.

1 To create another text box, click the Text Box button on the Objects toolbar and then drag a second text box below the first, approximately the same size.

2 Select the style, Heading 2. Type `State Dept. of Education` and then press the ENTER key.

3 Select the style, Heading 4. Type `Business and Information Technology` and press the ENTER key.

4 Type `Office of Career and Technical Education` and then press the ENTER key.

5 Type `www.sdoe.edu` to complete the text.

6 Point to the smart tag button to display the AutoCorrect Options button. Click the AutoCorrect Options button and then click Undo Automatic Capitalization to cancel the capital first letter (Figure 3–26).

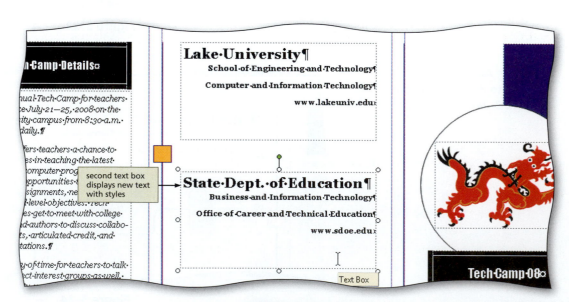

Figure 3–26

To Apply a Style to Existing Text

In the previous steps, you chose a style and then typed the text. Now you will apply a style to existing text. You first select the text, and then select the style.

1 Select the text in the left panel story.

2 Zoom to Whole Page using the F9 key.

3 Select the Body Text 3 style (Figure 3–27).

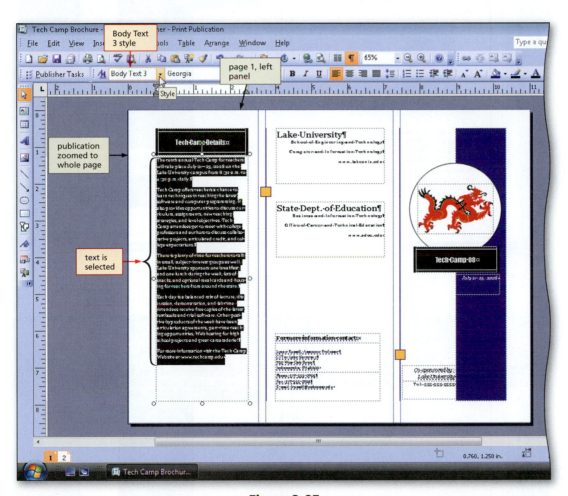

Figure 3–27

The Format Painter

Another way to apply specific formatting other than using a style is to copy the formatting from existing text or objects with the Format Painter button on the Standard toolbar. When using the Format Painter with text, click the Format Painter button, click anywhere in the source text, click the Format Painter button, and then click the destination text. The Format Painter changes all of the text in the destination paragraph. To format smaller or larger portions of text, drag the destination text. To apply formatting to multiple locations, double-click the Format Painter button so that it stays on. In those cases, when you finish, click the Format Painter to turn it off.

To Use the Format Painter

The following steps copy the formatting from one text box to another, in the lower part of the right panel on page 1.

- With page 1 of the brochure still displayed, scroll to the lower portion of the right panel and zoom to 100%.

- Click the text in the co-sponsored by text box (Figure 3–28).

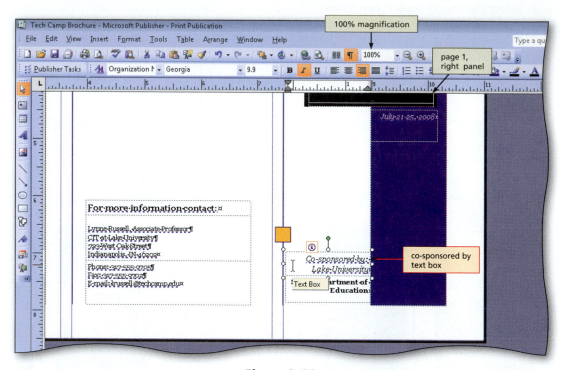

Figure 3–28

2

- Click the Format Painter button on the standard toolbar to copy the formatting.

- Position the mouse pointer inside the state department text box (Figure 3–29).

Q&A

Why does the mouse pointer display a paintbrush?

The mouse pointer changes when a format has been copied. Once you apply the format by clicking somewhere else, the paintbrush will disappear.

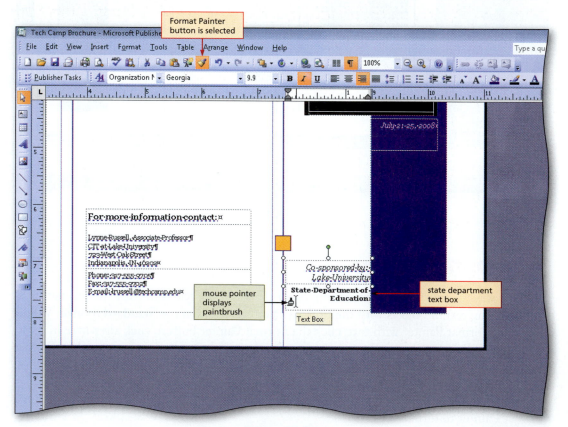

Figure 3–29

3

- Click the text in the state department text box to copy the formatting.

- If necessary, click the Align Text Right button on the Standard toolbar to align the text on the right side (Figure 3–30).

Q&A

Can I use the format painter on objects other than text?

Yes. You can copy applied formatting of a graphic, WordArt, shapes, fills, or any object from the Design Gallery. If you can change the style or set formatting options, you can copy them from one object to another.

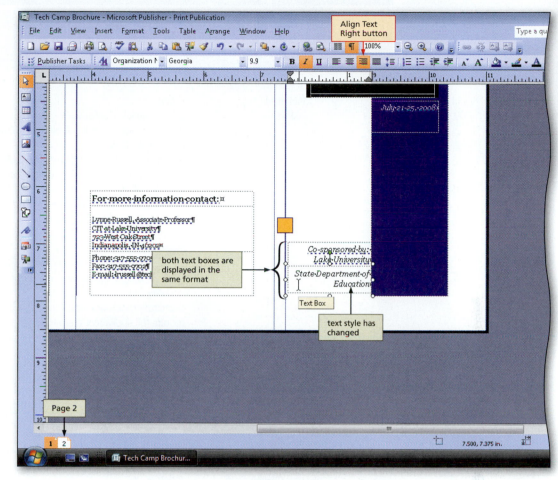

Figure 3–30

To Switch to Page 2

1 Click Page 2 on the page sorter.

2 Zoom to Whole Page.

Creating a New Style

Publisher allows you to create a new style from scratch or based on a current style or text selection. Creating a new style is a good idea when you have multiple text passages that have to be formatted identically, and the desired attributes are not saved as a current style.

In the Tech Camp brochure, first you will enter the text shown in Table 3–3 on the next page. Then, you will create a style for the inside, secondary headings. The text in italics will be formatted as headings later in this project.

BTW

Font Scheme Options
The Font scheme options link in the lower portion of the Font Schemes task pane includes options to update custom text styles in order to match one of the fonts used in the current font scheme. It also allows you to override applied text formatting, which changes only the font; it does not affect any other text formatting. A third option allows users to adjust font sizes to maintain the same area covered by the original block of text. This option may cause the font size to increase or decrease from the size set in the style, but it will prevent the text from reflowing.

Table 3–3 Text for Page 2, Left and Middle Panels

Location	Publisher-Supplied Text and Text Boxes	New Text
Left Panel	Main Inside Heading	Tech Camp 08
	Main Inside Story	*Where* Lake University Campus, 723 West Oak St., Indianapolis, IN 46202 *Registration Details* Registration deadline is June 1, 2008. Enrollment is limited to 25 participants per class, so register early! *Who Should Attend* Business, information technology, and marketing teachers interested in teaching database concepts, graphics, Web design, and computer programming. *Workshop Format* The five-day, $250 workshop includes lecture, hands-on lab practice, and assessment. Participants may choose one of four tracks. *Housing* Dormitory rooms are available for $150. The four-bedroom suites include full appliances and high-speed Internet ports. Please check in July 17 between 6 and 8 p.m., or contact Lynne Russell for alternate check in times.
	Caption	All sessions will be held in Fuller Hall.
Middle Panel	Secondary Story	*Track A: Access & Friends* This track will cover database concepts, intermediate Access through advanced Access, SQL server with Oracle, and data-driven Web sites. *Track B: Graphics Galore!* This track will cover curriculum and typical assignments, using InDesign, Illustrator, and Photoshop. The last day will incorporate all topics together. *Track C: Web Design* This track is for teachers who have had some basic HTML and an introduction to Dreamweaver. Topics will include HTML and scripting tools, intermediate Dreamweaver, Flash, and XML. *Track D: Desktop Publishing* This track will cover the basics of desktop publishing, using Microsoft Publisher. Topics will include brochures, newsletters, fliers, Web pages, e-commerce Web sites, design issues, and graphics. Track D also will include an introduction to Photoshop, "good design," and technical communication concepts. Complete and mail the attached form, or register on the Web at www.techcamp.edu.

To Enter Text on Page 2

The following steps enter text with styles for page 2 of the brochure. The new text displays in Table 3–3. Do not try to create the italics in your publication. You will format the headings later in the chapter. Zoom and select text as necessary.

1 In the left pane, click the Main Inside Heading text and then type `Tech Camp 08` to replace the text.

2 Select the story below the heading.

3 To select a style, click the Style box arrow, and then if necessary, click Body Text 3.

④ Replace the text by typing the main inside story text from Table 3–3.

⑤ Select the text in the caption below the picture in the left panel. Type the new caption text from Table 3–3 to replace the text.

⑥ Select all of the text in the middle panel text box using CTRL+A.

⑦ To select a style, click the Style box arrow and then click Accent Text 6.

⑧ Replace the text by typing the main inside story text from Table 3–3. Use the AutoCorrect Options button as necessary.

⑨ Zoom to Whole Page (Figure 3–31).

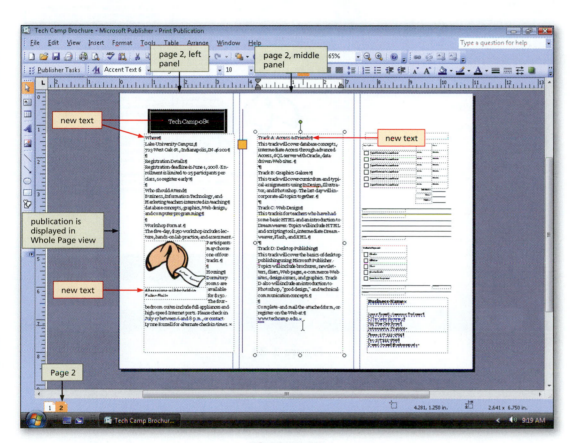

Figure 3–31

To Open the Styles Task Pane

Now that text has been entered, the step on the next page opens the Styles task pane, in preparation for formatting the headings with a new style.

1

- Click the Styles button on the Formatting toolbar to display the Styles task pane (Figure 3–32).

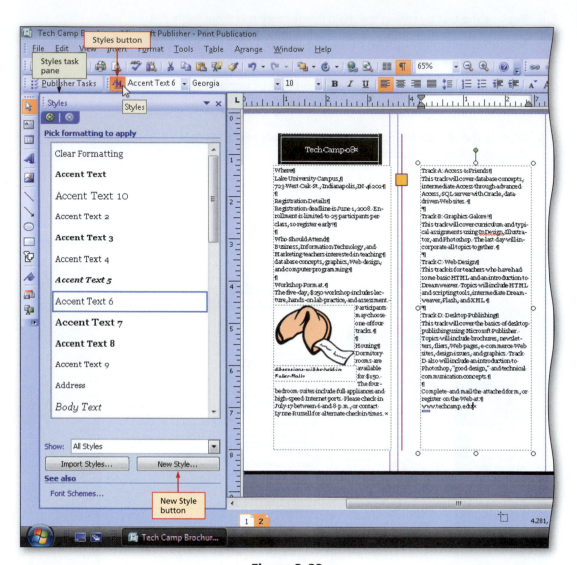

Figure 3–32

To Create a New Style

The following steps create a new Style named Tech Camp, setting the font to Arial Rounded MT Bold, the font style to Regular, the font size to 10, and the font color to Light Orange.

1

- In the Styles task pane, click the New Style button to display the New Style dialog box.

- In the Enter new style name box, type Tech Camp to name the style (Figure 3–33).

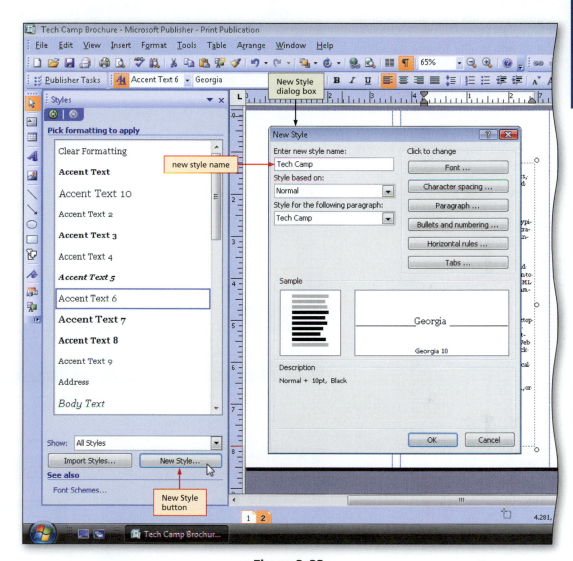

Figure 3–33

- Click the Font button to display the Font Dialog box.

- When the Font dialog box is displayed, click the Font box arrow and then click Arial Rounded MT Bold or a similar font in the list.

- If necessary, click the Font style box arrow and then click Regular in the list to specify the font style.

- If necessary, click the Size box arrow and then click 10 in the list to set the size.

- Click the Color box arrow and then click Accent 2 (Gold) in the list to set the color for the new style (Figure 3–34).

Q&A What if I do not have that particular font?

You can use any font that is bold and contrasts the text in the stories.

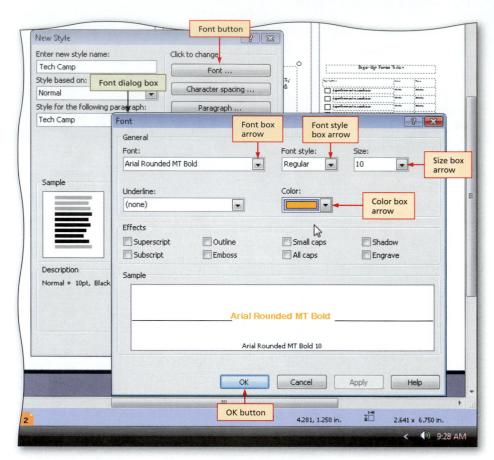

Figure 3–34

- Click the OK button to close the Font dialog box.

- Click the OK button to close the New Style dialog box.

- Scroll in the Styles task pane to display the Tech Camp style (Figure 3–35).

Q&A Will the new style appear in the drop-down list in the Formatting toolbar?

Yes, Publisher will add the new style and display its name in the Styles list, both in the Styles task pane and when clicking the Style box arrow.

4

- Close the Styles task pane.

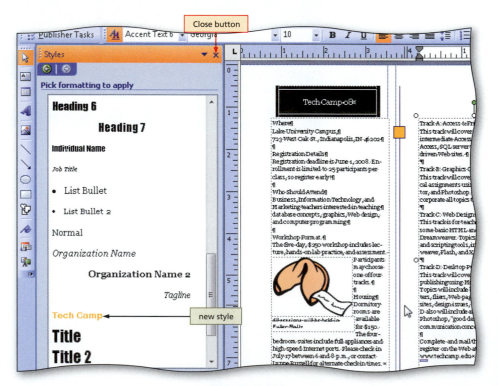

Figure 3–35

To Apply the New Style

- Select the first heading text in the main inside story. Headings are identified by italics in Table 3–3 on page PUB 170.

- Zoom to 100%.

- Click the Style box arrow. Scroll as necessary and click Tech Camp in the list to apply the new style.

- Click outside the selection to view the new formatting (Figure 3–36).

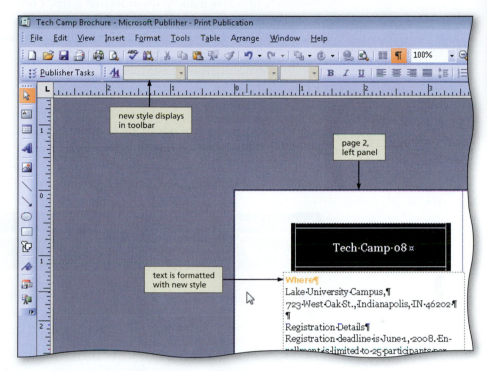

Figure 3–36

- Repeat step 1 for each of the headings italicized in Table 3–3 (Figure 3–37).

Q&A

Could I use the Format Painter to copy the formatting attributes to all of the other headings?

Yes, you can edit the formatting either way, or you could use the Styles task pane.

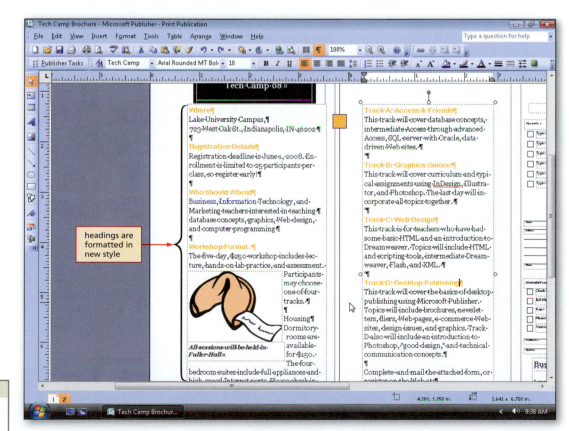

Figure 3–37

Other Ways

1. Select text, in Styles task pane, click desired style.
2. Click desired format, click Format Painter button, click new text.

Formatting Fonts

Publisher provides many ways to format fonts. Font schemes assist with major and minor fonts. Styles further specify sizes and formatting. Publisher also provides several font effects and line spacing options using menu options and toolbar buttons.

Font Effects

You have learned about font schemes, fonts, font sizes, formatting, and styles. Another way to format fonts is to use an effect. An **effect** is a special font option to add distinction to your text, including such ornamentation as outlining, embossing, and shadows.

Table 3–4 lists the font effects available in Publisher. The specific appearances of the font effects are printer- and screen-dependent.

Table 3–4 Font Effects	
Font Effect	**Description**
All caps	Formats lowercase letters as capitals. All caps formatting does not affect numbers, punctuation, nonalphabetic characters, or uppercase letters.
Emboss	The selected text appears to be raised off the page in relief.
Engrave	The selected text appears to be imprinted or pressed into the page.
Outline	Displays the inner and outer borders of each character.
Shadow	Adds a shadow beneath and to the right of the selected text.
Small caps	Formats selected lowercase text as capital letters and reduces their size. Small caps formatting does not affect numbers, punctuation, nonalphabetic characters, or uppercase letters.
Subscript	Lowers the selected text below the baseline.
Superscript	Raises the selected text above the baseline.

BTW

Superscripts and Subscripts
Two special font effects are superscript and subscript. A superscript is a character that appears slightly higher than other text on a line, such as that used in footnotes (reference[1]). A subscript describes text that is slightly lower than other text on a line, such as that used in scientific formulas (H_2O).

Using a Font Effect

The following steps apply an Outline font effect as new text is entered for the Sign-Up Form Title in the right panel of page 2.

To Apply a Font Effect

- In the right panel on page 2, right-click the text, Sign-Up Form Title, to display the shortcut menu.

- Point to Change Text to display the submenu (Figure 3–38).

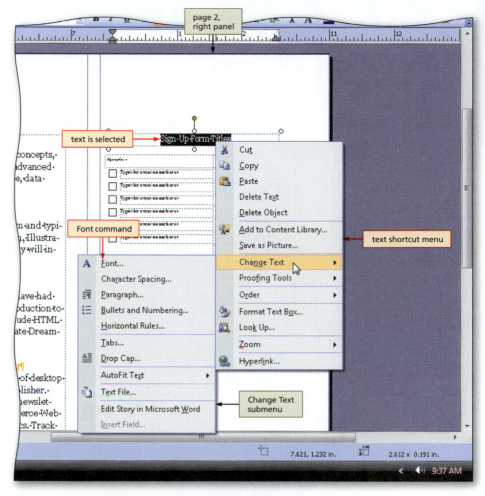

Figure 3–38

- Click Font on the Change Text submenu to display the Font dialog box.

- Click Outline in the Effects area (Figure 3–39).

Figure 3–39

3

- Click the OK button.

- Type `Sign-up for Tech Camp` to replace the text.

- Zoom to 200% (Figure 3–40).

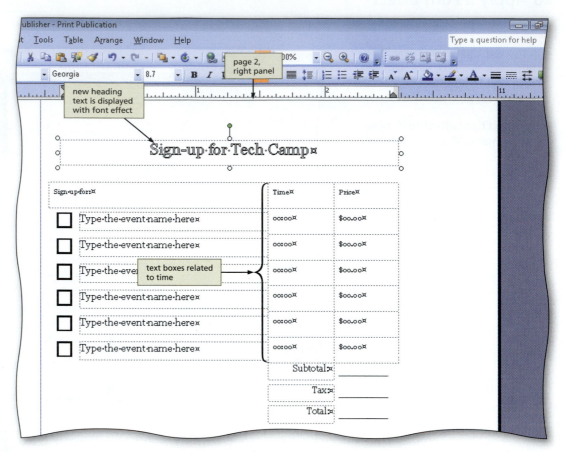

Figure 3–40

Editing the Sign-Up Form

To complete the text editing on page 2, the following steps describe how to edit the Sign-up form. Table 3–5 displays the text for event titles and prices. In the form, you will delete the text in the boxes related to time.

Table 3–5 Text for Sign-up Form	
Item Description	**Price**
Track A: Access & Friends	$250.00
Track B: Graphics Galore	$250.00
Track C: Web Design	$250.00
Track D: Desktop Publishing	$250.00
Optional Housing	$150.00
Optional Meal Card	$150.00

To Edit the Sign-Up Form

- One at a time, select the text in each of the center text boxes related to time. Press the DELETE key to delete the text.

- One at a time, click each event and price text box and then enter the new text from Table 3–5 (Figure 3–41).

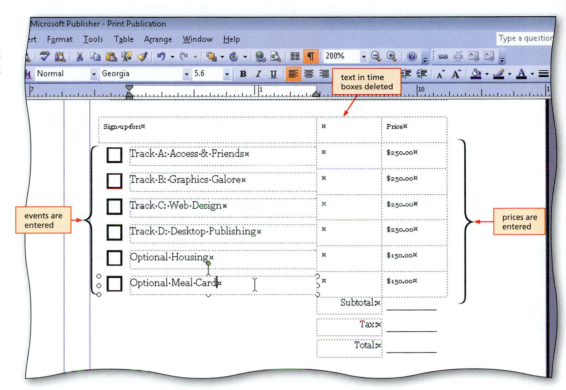

Figure 3–41

- Scroll down and select the text, Check, in the Method of Payment area.

- Type `Check made out to Tech Camp` to replace the text (Figure 3–42).

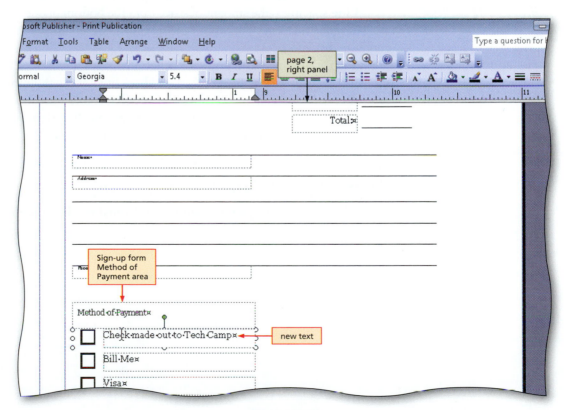

Figure 3–42

To Finish Text Replacement on Page 2

1 On page 2, in the right panel, select the text in the business name text box.

2 Type `Detach and mail to:` to replace the text.

Formatting Paragraphs

A **paragraph** in Publisher, as well as in most word processing programs, consists of the text you type until you press the ENTER key. Pressing the ENTER key creates a **hard return**, or paragraph, in a text box. Recall that certain kinds of formatting are paragraph-dependent, such as bullets and numbering.

Publisher allows users to change the indentation, alignment, line spacing, baseline guides, and paragraph spacing of paragraphs. **Indentation** determines the distance of the paragraph from either the left or right margins. Within margins, you can increase or decrease the indentation of a paragraph or group of paragraphs. You also can create a negative indent (also known as an exdent), which pulls the paragraph out toward the left margin. You also can create a hanging indent, in which the first line of the paragraph is not indented, but subsequent lines are.

Alignment refers to horizontal appearance and orientation of the edges of the paragraph: left-aligned, right-aligned, centered, or justified. For example, in a left-aligned paragraph (the most common alignment), the left edge of the paragraph is flush with the left margin. **Justified alignment** adjusts the horizontal spacing of text within text boxes, so that all lines, except the last line of the paragraph, align evenly along both the left and right margins. Justifying text creates a smooth edge on both sides. Publisher also allows users to create a rarely used **Distribute** alignment, which justifies even the last line of the paragraph.

Line spacing is the amount of space from the bottom of one line of text to the bottom of the next line. Publisher adjusts the line spacing to accommodate the largest font or the tallest graphic in that line.

You can use **baseline guides** to align text lines precisely across multiple columns. Publisher also allows you to set when and how lines and paragraphs break across text boxes. For example, you may want to specify that if one line of a paragraph moves to a new column, text box, or page, the entire paragraph should move.

Paragraph spacing determines the amount of space above or below a paragraph.

Changing the Paragraph Spacing

The following steps illustrate how to adjust the line spacing of the paragraphs to 1.5 inches.

BTW

Line Spacing
If you need to adjust the line spacing of a text box in order to make it fit or display better, you can change the line spacing. In the Paragraph dialog box, the Line spacing area contains three options. You may change the spacing before paragraphs, after paragraphs, or between lines. Pressing CTRL+1 or CTRL+2 changes the line spacing to single or double, respectively. You also can add a Line Spacing button to the Formatting toolbar.

To Change the Paragraph Spacing

1
- Zoom and scroll as necessary to select all of the text in the middle panel text box.

- Right-click the selection and then point to Change Text (Figure 3–43).

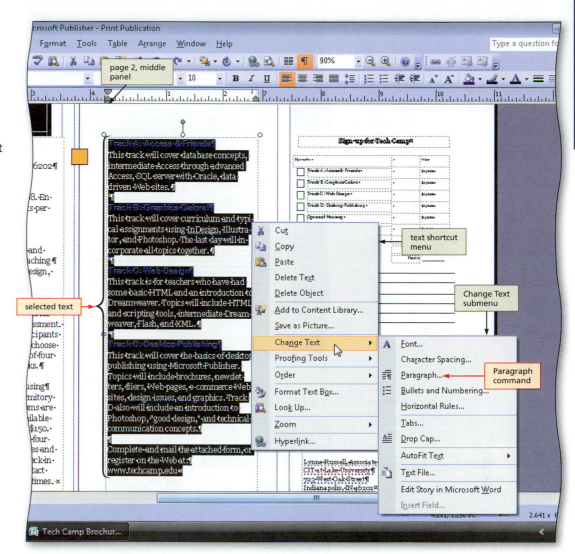

Figure 3–43

2

- On the Change Text submenu, click Paragraph to display the Paragraph dialog box.

- In the Line spacing area, select the text in the After paragraphs box, if any, and then type 1.5 to enter the new value (Figure 3–44).

Q&A

Why does the Between lines box say 1.14sp?

The template text was set to 1.14 spaces between lines for easier reading. When you typed in the new text, you did not change the line spacing.

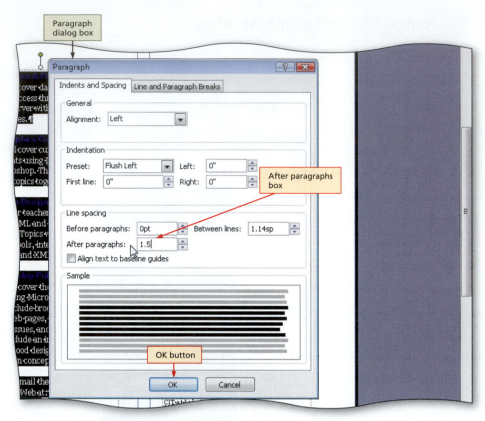

Figure 3–44

3

- Click the OK button to close the dialog box.

- Click outside the text box to remove the highlighting (Figure 3–45).

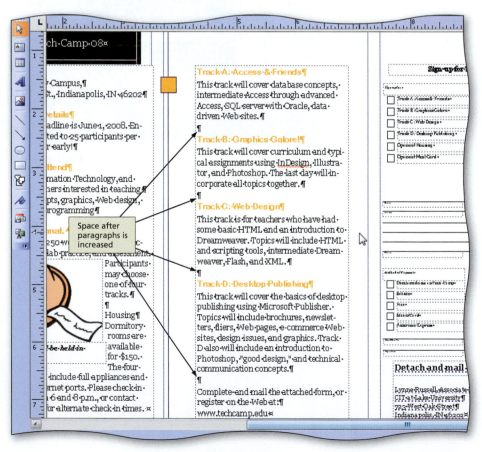

Other Ways

1. On Format menu, click Paragraph

Figure 3–45

Using Photographs in a Brochure

The advent of inexpensive photo CDs, along with Web access, has increased exponentially the possibilities for photographic reproduction in publications. Regular cameras using popular types of film now can take pictures that are ultimately digitized, a process that previously required digital cameras. **Digitizing** means converting colors and lines into digital impulses capable of being read by a computer. Digitized photos and downloaded graphics from the Web, combined with high-resolution production from scanners, create endless possibilities. Small businesses now can afford to include photographs in their brochures and other types of publications.

Publisher can accept photographs and images from a variety of input sources. Each graphic you import has a file name, followed by a dot or period, followed by a three-letter extension. Publisher uses **extensions** to recognize individual file formats.

You can choose from a number of common graphics file formats, including the **bitmap** format (which creates a picture made from a series of small dots), scanned pictures, and photographs. Publisher supports all the major file formats. However, each year, new graphic formats are introduced, and older graphic formats are retired. Depending on your installation of Publisher, you may need to install a filter for some formats. A **filter** is a set of instructions that the operating system and Publisher use to import and display graphics. Not all filters are installed in order to save disk space. Table 3–6 displays a list of supported file formats.

Table 3–6 Supported Graphic Formats	
Graphic Formats	**Filter May Be Needed**
Compressed Macintosh PICT (.pcz)	X
Computer Graphics Metafile (.cgm)	X
CorelDraw (.cdr)	X
Encapsulated PostScript (.eps)	X
Graphics Interchange Format, CompuServe format (.gif or .gfa)	
JPEG File Interchange Format (.jpeg, .jpg, .jfif, or .jpe)	
Macintosh PICT (.pct or .pict)	X
Microsoft Windows Bitmap (.bmp)	
Portable Network Graphics (.png)	
TIFF, Tagged Image File Format (.tif or .tiff)	
Windows Enhanced Metafile (.emf)	
Windows Metafile (.wmf)	
WordPerfect Graphics (.wpg)	X

BTW

Widows and Orphans
The Paragraph dialog box contains a Line and Paragraph Breaks tab where you can set widow and orphan control. A **widow** is the last line of a paragraph printed by itself at the top of a connected text box. An **orphan** is the first line of a paragraph printed by itself at the bottom of a connected text box. Choices include keeping the lines together and starting the paragraph in a new text box.

BTW

More Graphics
Microsoft supplies many free graphics and add-ins for your Microsoft Office products, which you may download from the Microsoft Web site. To do this, click Help on the menu bar and then click Microsoft Office Online. When your browser displays the Web page, follow the links to Products and then click Check for free updates.

Inserting a Photograph from a File

Publisher can insert a photograph into a publication by accessing the Clip Art task pane, by externally importing from a file, by directly importing an image from a scanner or camera, or by creating a new drawing.

Recall that when a Publisher template has grouped a picture with its caption, clicking either will select both. To further select only the picture or only the caption text box, a second click is required.

To Insert a Photograph

BTW

Illustration Software
Another common method of creating new image files, other than scanning, is to use **illustration software**. Designed for artists, illustration software packages, such as Photoshop and Adobe Illustrator, create graphics to import into desktop publishing software.

1. Click the picture/caption grouped object in the left panel of page 2.
2. Double-click the picture to display the Clip Art task pane.
3. Type `university` in the Search for box. If necessary, click the Search in box arrow and then click Everywhere in the list. To search for only pictures, click the Results should be box arrow and then make sure Photographs is the only box with a check mark.
4. Click the Go button to search for clip art related to the term, university.
5. When the clips are displayed, scroll to find a picture of a building similar to the one shown in Figure 3–46. To insert the picture into the brochure, click the picture.
6. Close the Clip Art task pane.

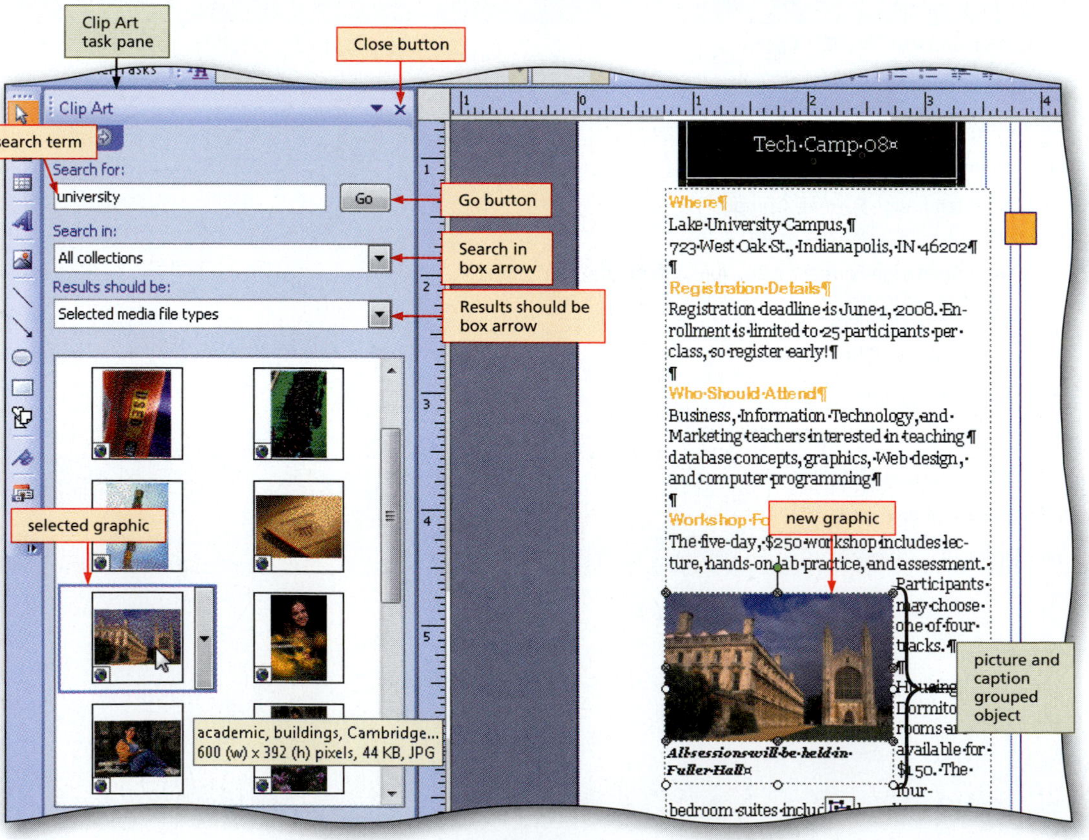

Figure 3–46

Wrapping Text around Pictures

The way that text wraps, or adjusts itself around objects, is called **text wrapping**. Text wrapping applies to text boxes, graphics, and all other kinds of shapes that are close to, or overlapping, other Publisher objects. You can choose how you want the text to wrap around an object using one of the following **wrapping styles**. **Square** wraps text around all sides of the selected object. **Tight** wraps text as closely as possible to the object. **Through** wraps text around the perimeter and inside any open portions of the object. **Top and bottom** wraps text above and below the object, but not on either side. The **None** option removes all text wrapping formatting so that text does not wrap around the object. If the object is transparent, the text behind it will show through. Otherwise, the text will be hidden behind the object.

BTW

Text Wrapping
Publisher text boxes automatically wrap around other objects on the page. The Format dialog box associated with most objects also contains text wrapping options on the Layout sheet. If text wrapping appears to be unavailable, one of the objects may be transparent. In that case, press CTRL+T.

To Text Wrap

- If necessary, select the object you wish to text wrap, in this case the picture and caption grouped object.

- Click the Text Wrapping button on the Picture toolbar to display its options (Figure 3–47).

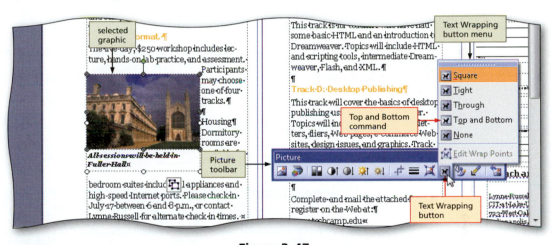

Figure 3–47

- Click Top and Bottom to select the text wrapping style.

- Drag to reposition the picture and caption to a location between paragraphs, as shown in Figure 3–48.

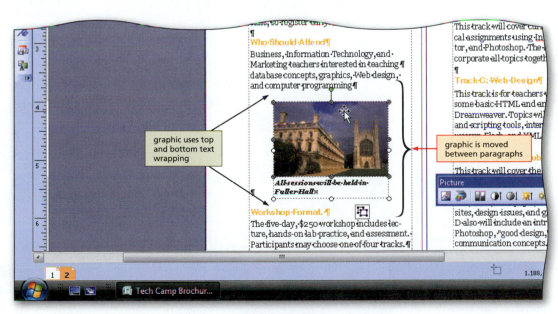

Figure 3–48

Replacing Graphics on Page 1

The following steps describe how to use the Clip Art task pane to replace the graphics on page 1.

To Replace the Graphics in the Left Panel of Page 1

1 Click Page 1 on the page sorter.

2 Zoom and scroll as necessary to display the right panel.

3 Click the grouped graphic in the right panel, and then double-click the picture to display the Clip Art task pane.

4 Type technology in the Search for box.

5 If necessary, click the Search in box arrow and then click Everywhere in the list.

6 Click the Results should be box arrow and click All media types.

7 Click the Go button to search for clip art related to the term, technology.

8 When the clips are displayed, scroll to find a graphic similar to the one shown in Figure 3–49.

9 To insert the picture into the brochure, click the picture (Figure 3–49).

10 Close the Clip Art task pane.

Clip Art Sources
In addition to the clip art images included in the previews, other sources for clip art include retailers specializing in computer software, the Internet, bulletin board systems, and online information systems. A **bulletin board system** is a computer system that allows users to communicate with each other and share files. Microsoft has created a special page on its Web site where you can add new clips to the Clip Organizer.

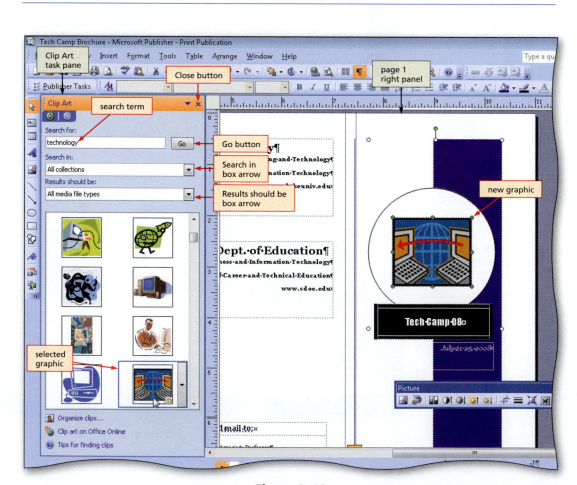

Figure 3–49

Creating a Logo from Scratch

Many types of publications use logos to identify and distinguish the page. A **logo** is a recognizable symbol that identifies a person, business, or organization. A logo may be composed of a name, a picture, or a combination of symbols and graphics. In a later project, you will learn how to add a permanent logo to an information set for a company.

Creating a Shape for the Logo

The logo in the Tech Camp brochure is a shape with colors and text. Created individually in the workspace, the logo easily is positioned and sized to the proper places in the brochure. The logo appears both on the back of the brochure (middle panel of page 1) and on the inside of the brochure (middle panel of page 2).

The background of the logo is from the AutoShapes menu. Accessed through the Objects toolbar, the AutoShapes menu displays seven categories of shapes you may use as graphics in a publication. These shapes include lines, connectors, basic shapes, block arrows, stars, and banners, among others. **AutoShapes** differ from WordArt in that they do not contain text; rather, they are graphic designs with a variety of formatting options, such as color, border, size, and shadow.

The workspace, also called the **scratch area**, can serve as a kind of drawing board to create new objects. Without disturbing any object already on the publications page, you can manipulate and edit objects in the workspace and then move them to the desired location. The rulers and status bar display the exact size of the new object. Moving objects off the page and into the workspace sometimes is advantageous as well. Small objects that are difficult to revise on the publication can be moved into the workspace, magnified and edited, and then moved back. As you place new objects in the workspace, more workspace room is allocated.

The steps on the next page illustrate creating the logo in Publisher's workspace to the right of the brochure.

BTW

Logos
A logo is a recognizable symbol that identifies you or your business. If you do not want to create one from scratch, the Design Gallery contains many logo styles from which you may choose. Although Publisher's logo styles are generic, commercial logos typically are copyrighted. Consult with a legal representative before you commercially use materials bearing clip art, logos, designs, words, or other symbols that could violate third-party rights, including trademarks.

BTW

Formatting Options
You can set the fill color, line weight, and line color for new AutoShapes or drawing objects, such as curves, lines, and WordArt, in the current publication, using the Format dialog box. Right-click an AutoShape or drawing object that has the attributes, such as line fill or text color, that you want to use as the default. Then, on the shortcut menu, click the Format option. In the dialog box, click the Colors and Lines tab. Finally, select the Apply settings to new AutoShapes check box.

To Create a Shape for the Logo

- On page 1, zoom to Whole Page.

- Drag the horizontal scroll box to the right, to view more of the workspace (Figure 3–50).

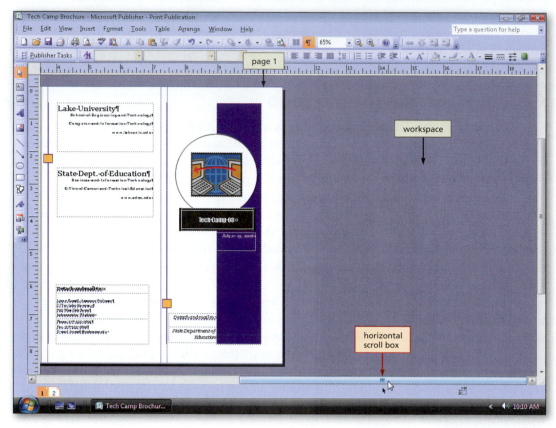

Figure 3–50

2

- Click the AutoShapes button on the Objects toolbar to display the available groups of shapes.

- Point to Block Arrows on the AutoShapes menu to display the submenu.

- Point to the Striped Right Arrow shape (Figure 3–51).

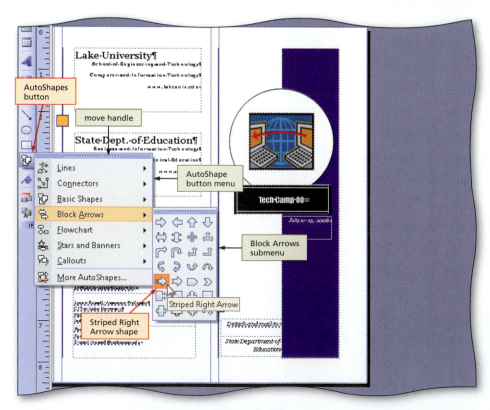

Figure 3–51

3

- Click the Striped Right Arrow shape and then move the mouse pointer to the workspace to the right of the brochure.

- Drag down and to the right until the shape is approximately 2.5 × 1.5 inches. Release the mouse button.

- To quickly zoom to 100%, press the F9 key (Figure 3–52).

BTW

Floating Toolbars
The AutoShape menu can be changed to a floating toolbar by dragging the move handle at the top of the menu (shown in Figure 3–51).

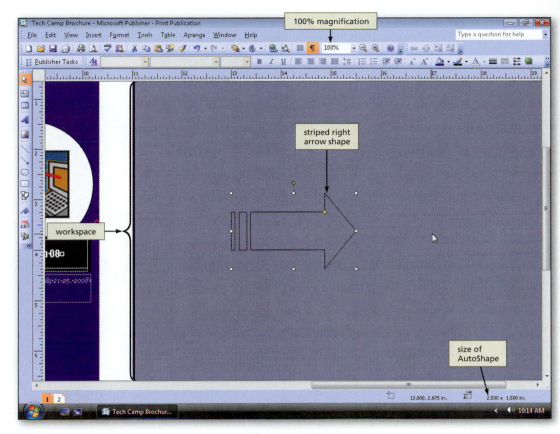

Figure 3–52

To Fill a Shape with Color

The following steps fill the AutoShape with the gold color from the color scheme.

1

- With the AutoShape still selected, click the Fill Color button arrow on the Formatting toolbar to display the scheme colors (Figure 3–53).

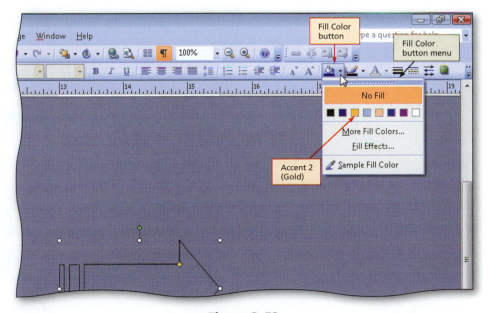

Figure 3–53

- Click Accent 2 (Gold) in the list to change the fill color (Figure 3–54).

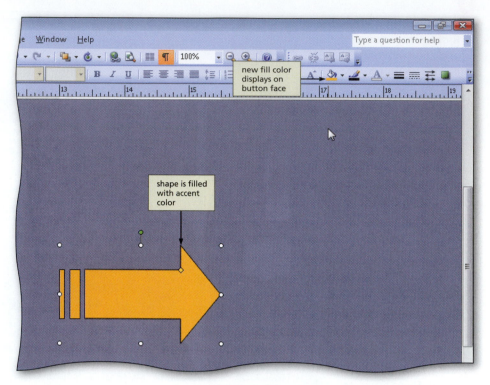

Figure 3–54

To Edit AutoShape Lines

The following steps edit both the color and style of the lines around the AutoShape.

- With the AutoShape still selected, click the Line Color button arrow on the Formatting toolbar to display the colors in the color scheme (Figure 3–55).

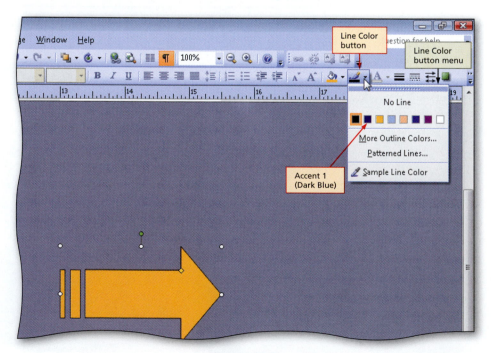

Figure 3–55

2
• Click Accent 1 (Dark Blue) in the list to change the line color (Figure 3–56).

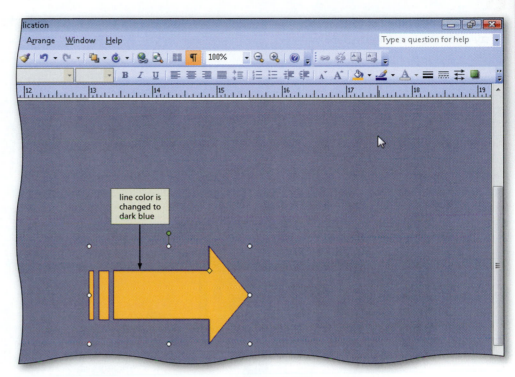

Figure 3–56

3
• With the AutoShape still selected, click the Line/Border Style button on the Formatting toolbar to display the list (Figure 3–57).

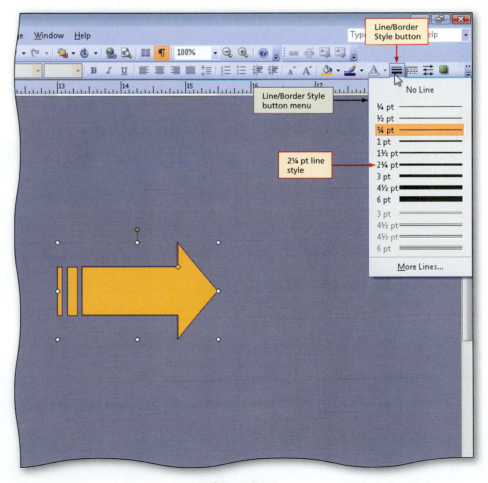

Figure 3–57

- Click 2 ¼ pt in the list to choose a style for the line (Figure 3–58).

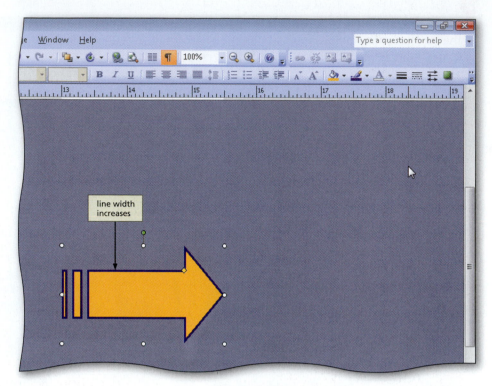

Figure 3–58

To Add Text to an AutoShape

The following steps add text to the AutoShape using the Accent 1 (Dark Blue) color.

- Right-click the AutoShape to display its shortcut menu (Figure 3–59).

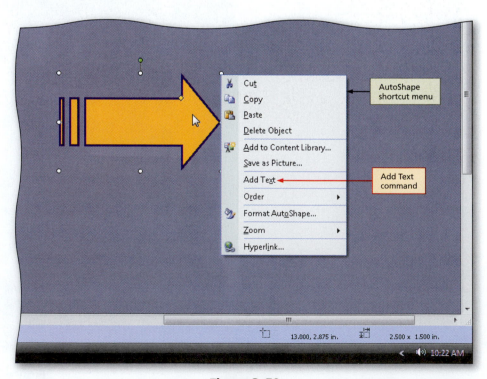

Figure 3–59

2

- Click Add Text to position the cursor inside the AutoShape.

- Click the Font color button arrow and then click Accent 1 (Dark Blue) in the list to select the font color.

- Type `Looking Forward with Technology` to enter the text (Figure 3–60).

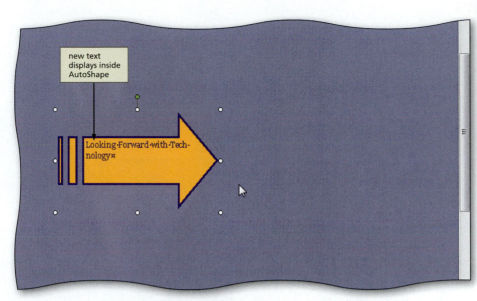

Figure 3–60

To Fit Text

Publisher has three **AutoFit Text** options to adjust the size of text in text boxes or shapes. The default value is **Do Not AutoFit**, where text is displayed in the exact font size selected in the Formatting toolbar. A second way is to use the **Best Fit** option in which Publisher adjusts the size of the text to as big a size as possible to fit the box or shape. The third way, **Shrink Text On Overflow**, allows Publisher to adjust the size of your text only when it is necessary to keep text from overflowing.

1

- Right-click the AutoShape to display its shortcut menu.

- Point to Change Text to display the Change Text submenu.

- Point to AutoFit Text to display the AutoFit Text submenu (Figure 3–61).

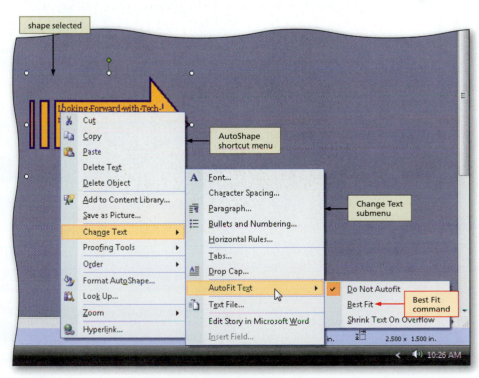

Figure 3–61

2

- Click Best Fit to adjust the size of the text (Figure 3–62).

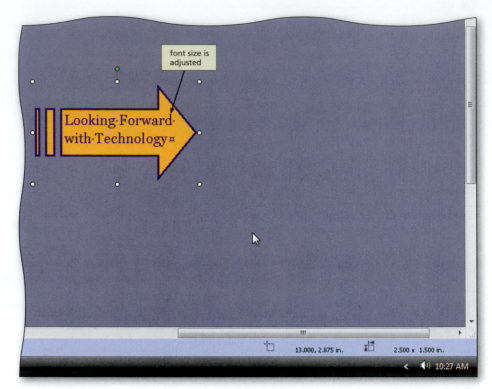

Figure 3–62

AutoFit Text
Some Publisher template text boxes, such as titles, mastheads, and tag lines, are preset to Shrink Text On Overflow. Objects created from the Objects toolbar and most story text boxes are preset to Do Not AutoFit.

To Copy the Logo

The next step makes a copy of the logo by pressing the CTRL key while dragging.

1

- Point to the logo. When the mouse pointer changes to a double two-headed arrow, CTRL+DRAG to an empty location in the workspace (Figure 3–63).

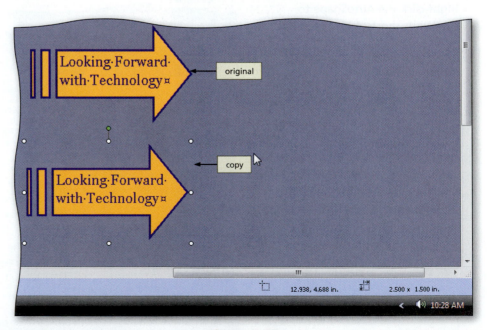

Figure 3–63

To Reposition and Resize the Logos

1

- Click the Zoom Out button on the Standard toolbar several times until the entire page layout and workspace area are visible.

- Point to one of the logos. When the mouse pointer changes to a double two-headed arrow, drag the logo to a position above the contact information in the middle panel of page 1.

- If necessary, to resize the logo and make it fit in the empty space, SHIFT+DRAG a corner. Drag to reposition, if necessary, and position the logo as shown in Figure 3–64.

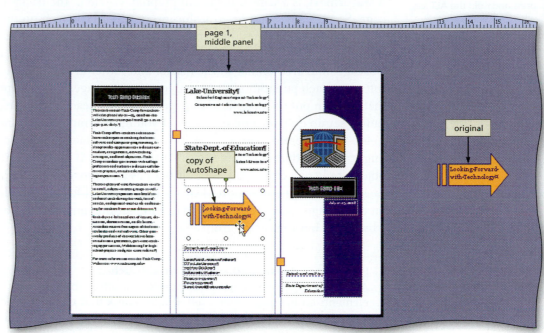

Figure 3–64

2

- Click Page 2 on the page sorter.

- Point to the logo in the workspace. When the mouse pointer changes to a double two-headed arrow, drag the logo to a position below the URL in the middle panel of page 2.

- To resize the logo and make it fit in the empty space, SHIFT+DRAG a corner. Drag to reposition, if necessary, and position the logo as shown in Figure 3–65.

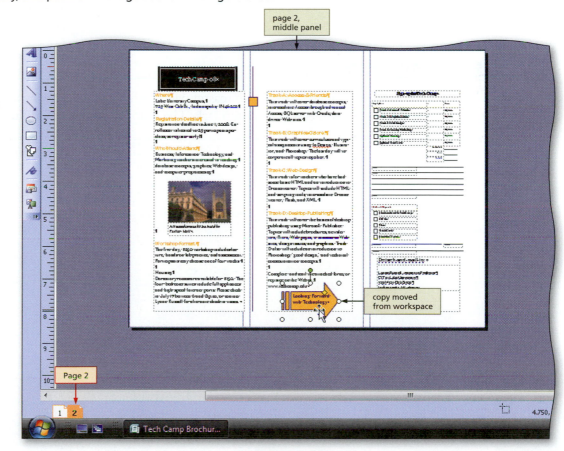

Figure 3–65

Nudging
You can drag objects to new positions, or you can press and hold the ALT key while pressing the arrow keys to **nudge** objects to new positions. If you increase the magnification of the screen, you can resize and reposition objects precisely. For instance, at 400% magnification, you can move an object .003 inch by pressing and holding the ALT key and then pressing an arrow key. The Arrange menu also contains options for nudging and aligning. The Measurements toolbar allows you to enter exact horizontal and vertical positions, as well.

Plan Ahead

Creating a Watermark with WordArt

A **watermark** is a semi-transparent graphic, visible in the background on the printed page. Some watermarks are translucent; others can be seen on the paper when held up to the light. Other times the paper itself has a watermark when it is manufactured. In Publisher, watermarks are created by placing text or graphics on a **master page**, which is a background area similar to the header and footer area in traditional word processing software. Each publication starts with one master page. A master page can contain anything that you can put on a publication page, as well as headers, footers, and layout guides that can be set up only on a master page. If you have a multipage document, you can choose to use two different master pages for cases such as facing pages in a book, in which you might want different graphics in the backgrounds. If you want to display master page objects only on certain pages, Publisher has an **Ignore Master Page command** that causes the master page not to display. This is useful for cases such as background images on every page except the title page in a longer document, or a watermark on the inside of a brochure but not on the front.

Proofread, revise, and add the final touches.
Add logos, watermarks, headers, footers, and other objects on the master page or repeated elements on the publication itself. Double-check that each repeated element is exactly alike.

Proofread the brochure several times before using the Pack and Go Wizard to take your publication to the printer. Proofreading involves reading the brochure with the intent of identifying errors and looking for ways to improve it. Ask someone else to proofread the paper and give you suggestions for improvements. Revise as necessary and then use the spelling and design checking features of the software.

To Access the Master Page

In the Tech Camp brochure, you will create two master pages. The master page for page 1 will contain no objects. The master page for page 2 will contain a watermark. The following steps access the master page.

1

- Click Page 1 on the page sorter.

- Click View on the menu bar to display the View menu (Figure 3–66).

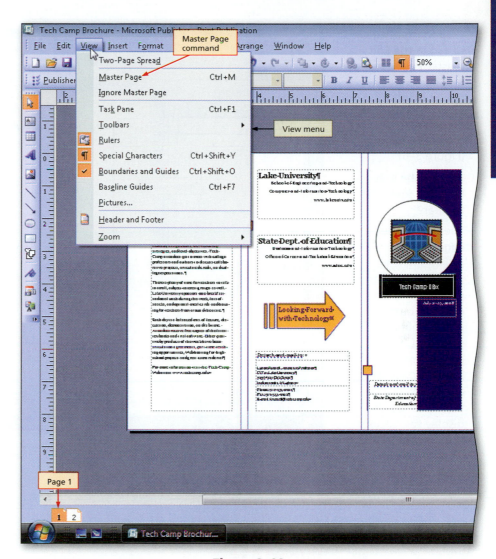

Figure 3–66

2

- Click Master Page to access the Edit Master Pages task pane.

- Zoom and scroll as necessary to display the entire page (Figure 3–67).

Q&A

What is the Edit Master Pages toolbar?

The Edit Master Pages toolbar displays when viewing a master page. The toolbar contains buttons to insert, delete, duplicate, and change master pages, as well as options to display the layout guides, display two facing master pages, and close the master page view entirely.

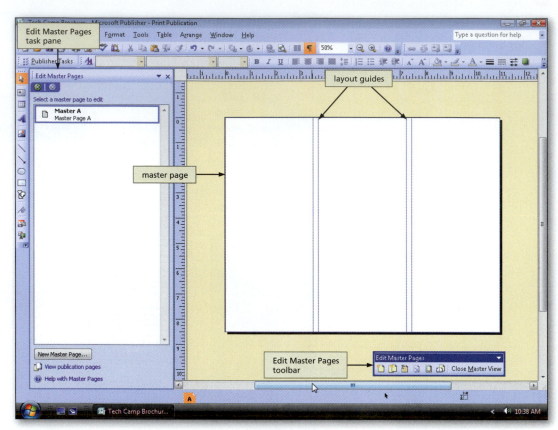

Figure 3–67

BTW

Multiple Master Pages
You can create multiple master pages if you want a variety of layouts in a publication that has more than one page. The Apply Master Page task pane will allow you to apply the new master page to any or all of the publication pages. By default, master pages are named with letters of the alphabet, such as Master Page A, Master Page B, and so on; however, you can rename any master page by using the Rename Master Page button on the Edit Master Pages toolbar.

WordArt

WordArt is a gallery of text styles that works with Publisher to create fancy text effects. A WordArt object actually is a graphic and not text. Publication designers typically use WordArt to create eye-catching headlines and banners or watermark images. WordArt uses its own toolbar to add effects to the graphic.

Inserting a WordArt Object

The Tech Camp brochure will use a WordArt object, with the text, Tech Camp, as a watermark on page 2. A text box with font effects could be formatted to create a similar effect, but using WordArt increases the number of special effect possibilities and options.

To Insert a WordArt Object

The following steps explain how to add a WordArt object as the watermark on the master page of the brochure.

 1

- Click the Insert WordArt button on the Objects toolbar.

- When the WordArt Gallery dialog box is displayed, click the first WordArt style in the top row, if necessary (Figure 3–68).

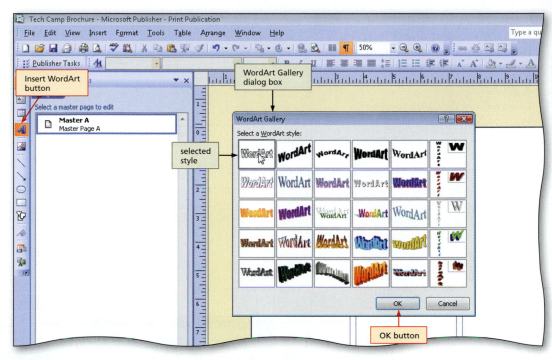

Figure 3–68

2

- Click the OK button.

- When Publisher displays the Edit WordArt Text dialog box, type `Tech Camp` as the new text (Figure 3–69).

- Click the OK button.

BTW

WordArt Spelling
Keep in mind that WordArt objects are drawing objects; they are not treated as Publisher text. Thus, if you mis-spell the contents of a WordArt object and then check the publication, Publisher will not flag the misspelled word(s) in the WordArt text.

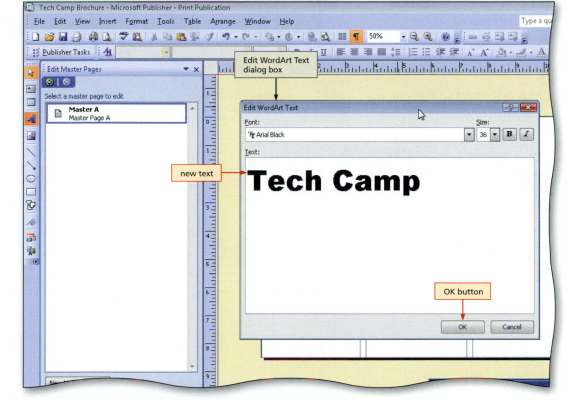

Figure 3–69

To Format WordArt

The WordArt toolbar contains several buttons to help you format WordArt objects. The following steps use the WordArt Shape button to change the general shape of the WordArt object.

- With the WordArt object selected, click the WordArt Shape button on the WordArt toolbar (Figure 3–70).

Q&A

Where is my WordArt toolbar?

The WordArt toolbar usually displays when a WordArt object is selected. If your toolbar does not display, you may have closed it by accident. To redisplay the WordArt toolbar, point to Toolbars on the View menu, and then click WordArt on the Toolbars submenu.

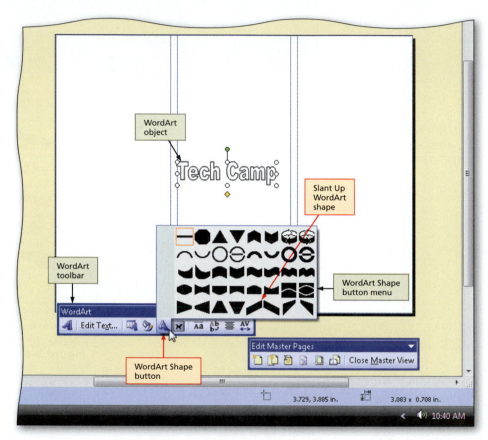

Figure 3–70

2

- Click the Slant Up shape on the bottom row of the displayed shapes.

- Drag a corner handle to resize the object to approximately 6 inches wide and 6 inches tall, as noted on the status bar.

- Drag the WordArt object to the upper-center part of the page (Figure 3–71).

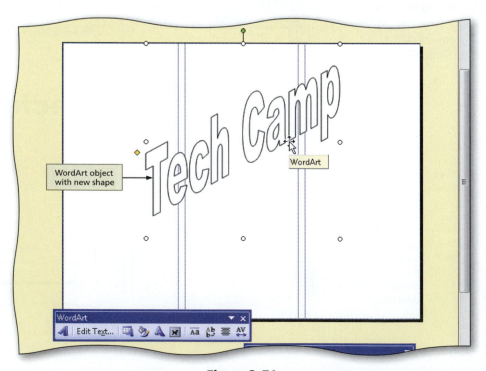

Figure 3–71

3
- Click the Format WordArt button on the WordArt toolbar to display the Format WordArt dialog box.

- In the Line area, click the Color box arrow and then click Accent 3 (Pale Blue) in the list.

- Click the Dashed box arrow (Figure 3–72).

Q&A

What do the other buttons on the WordArt toolbar do?

Each button displays its name in a screen tip when you point to it. The buttons toward the left create a new WordArt object and change the basic text, style, format, and shape. The buttons toward the right change how the text and characters are displayed, with features such as text wrapping, letter heights, vertical text, alignment, and character spacing.

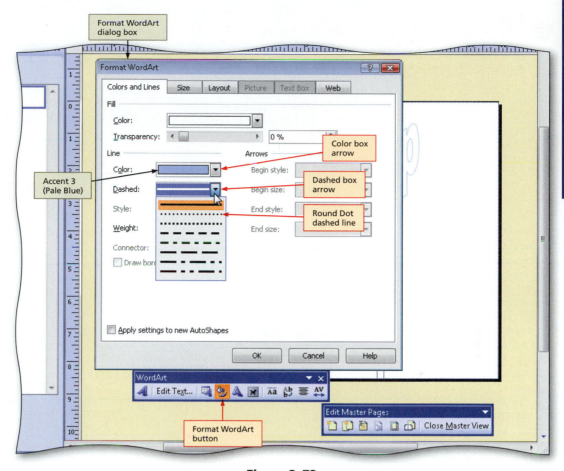

Figure 3–72

4
- Click the Round Dot dashed line (Figure 3–73).

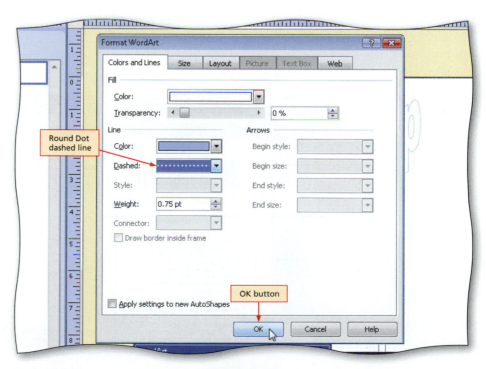

Figure 3–73

5
- Click the OK button to close the Format WordArt dialog box (Figure 3–74).

Formatting WordArt
When you click the Format WordArt button on the WordArt toolbar, Publisher displays options for fill color, lines, size, spacing, rotating, shadows, and borders, as well as many of the same features Publisher provides on its Formatting toolbar, such as text wrapping, alignment, bold, italics, underline, and fonts.

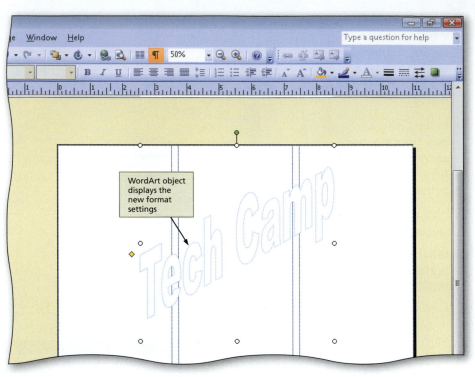

Figure 3–74

Other Ways

1. Click Insert WordArt button on the WordArt toolbar

To Close the Master Page

1 On the Edit Master Pages toolbar, click the Close Master View button to return to the document.

2 Close the task pane, if necessary, and then zoom to Whole Page (Figure 3–75).

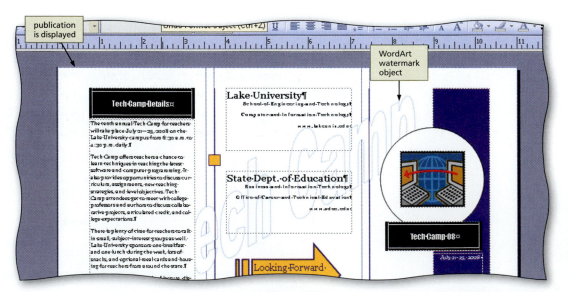

Figure 3–75

Completing the Watermark

The final step in creating the watermark is to change the transparency of the text boxes on page 2 and then choose to ignore the master page so that it does not display on page 1. Text box transparency refers to whether the area around the text is a solid color, such as white, or clear. To make a text box transparent, you can press CTRL+T. Pressing CTRL+T a second time toggles back to a solid background.

To Remove the Watermark from Page 1

The next step removes the watermark from page 1 by choosing to ignore the master page.

1

- With page 1 displayed, click View on the menu bar and then click the Ignore Master Page command (Figure 3–76).

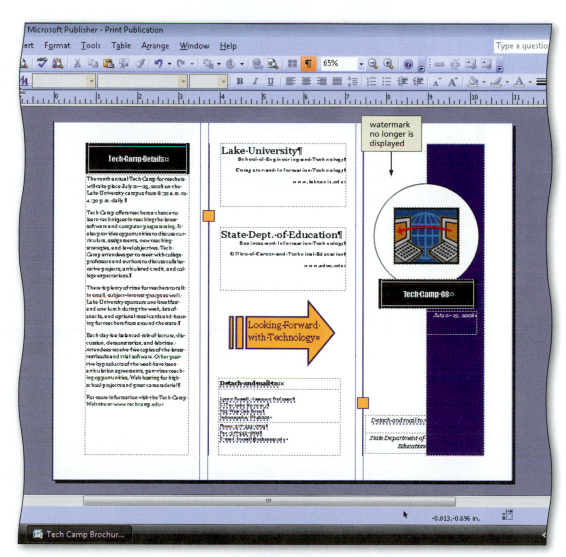

Figure 3–76

To Make Text Boxes Transparent

The next steps change the transparency of the two text boxes in the left and middle panel of page 2.

1

- Click Page 2 on the page sorter and then zoom to Whole Page.

- Select the text box in the left panel and then press CTRL+T to make it transparent.

- Select the text box in the middle panel and then press CTRL+T to make it transparent (Figure 3–77).

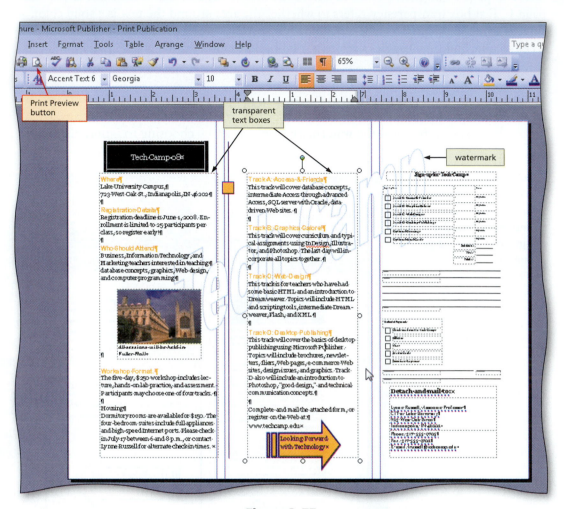

Figure 3–77

Checking and Saving the Publication

The publication now is complete. You should check for spelling errors in the publication, run the Design Checker, and then save the publication again.

To Check the Publication and Save Again

1 Click the Spelling button on the Standard toolbar. If Publisher flags any words, fix or ignore them as appropriate.

2 When Publisher asks to check the entire document, click the Yes button.

3 Click Tools on the menu bar and then click Design Checker. Ignore any messages about extra space, empty text boxes, or picture resolution.

4 If the Design Checker identifies any other errors, fix them as necessary.

5 Close the Design Checker task pane.

6 Click the Save button on the Standard toolbar.

Outside Printing

When they need mass quantities of publications, businesses generally **outsource**, or submit their publications to an outside printer, for duplicating. You must make special considerations when preparing a document for outside printing.

Previewing the Brochure before Printing

The first step in getting the publication ready for outside printing is to examine what the printed copy will look like from your desktop. The following steps preview the brochure before printing.

To Preview the Brochure before Printing

1 Click the Print Preview button on the Standard toolbar (Figure 3–78).

2 Click the Page Up button in the toolbar to view page 1.

3 Click the Close button on the Print Preview toolbar.

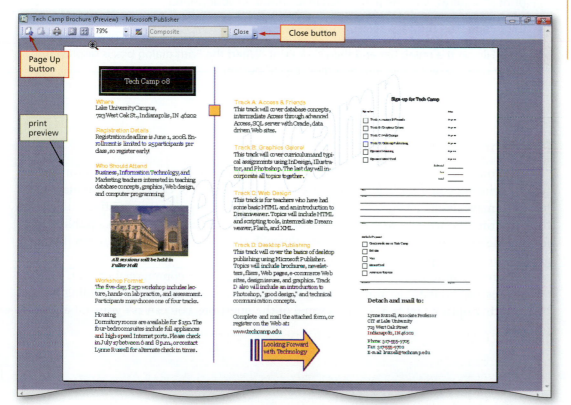

Figure 3–78

Printing the Brochure

The next sequence of steps recommends publishing this brochure on a high grade of paper to obtain a professional look. A heavier stock paper helps the brochure to stand up better in display racks, although any paper will suffice. If you do use a special paper, be sure to click the Properties or Advanced Settings button in the Print dialog box for your printer and then specify the paper you are using. Following your printer's specifications, print one side of the paper, turn it over, and then print the reverse side. The completed brochure prints as shown in Figure 3–1 on page PUB 147. You then can fold the brochure to display the title panel on the front.

Plan Ahead

> **Plan for printing.**
> Make a firm decision that quality matters and consult with several commercial printers ahead of time. Get prices, color modes, copies, paper, and folding options in writing before you finish your brochure. Brochures are more effective on heavier paper, with strong colors and glossy feels. Together with the commercial printer, select a paper that is going to last. Check to make sure the commercial printer can accept Microsoft Publisher 2007 files.

To Print the Brochure

BTW

Printer Memory
Some printers do not have enough memory to print a wide variety of images and color. In these cases, the printer prints up to a certain point on a page and then chokes — resulting in only the top portion of the publication printing. Check with your instructor to see if your printer has enough memory to work with colors.

1 Ready the printer according to the printer instructions, and insert paper.

2 With page 1 displaying in the workspace, click File on the menu bar and then click Print. When the Print dialog box is displayed, click Current page. If necessary, click the Properties button to choose a special paper. Click the OK button.

3 When page 1 finishes printing, turn the page over and reinsert it top first (or as your printer requires) into the paper feed mechanism on your printer.

4 Click Page 2 on the page sorter.

5 Click File on the menu bar and then click Print. When the Print dialog box is displayed, again click Current page and then click the OK button.

Printing Considerations

If you start a publication from scratch, it is best to **set up** the publication for the type of printing you want before you place objects on the page. Otherwise, you may be forced to make design changes at the last minute. You also may set up an existing publication for a printing service. In order to provide you with experience in setting up a publication for outside printing, this project takes you through the preparation steps — even if you are submitting this publication only to your instructor.

Printing options, such as whether to use a copy shop or commercial printer, have advantages and limitations. You may have to make some trade-offs before deciding on the best printing option. Table 3–7 shows some of the questions you can ask yourself about printing.

Table 3–7 Picking a Printing Option

Consideration	Questions to Ask	Desktop Option	Professional Options
Color	Is the quality of photographs and color a high priority?	Low- to medium-quality	High quality
Convenience	Do I want the easy way?	Very convenient and familiar	Time needed to explore different methods, unfamiliarity
Cost	How much do I want to pay?	Printer supplies and personal time	High-resolution color/high quality is expensive; the more you print, the less expensive the per copy price
Quality	How formal is the purpose of my publication?	Local event; narrow, personal audience	Business, marketing, professional services
Quantity	How many copies do I need?	1 to 10 copies	10 to 500 copies: use a copy shop; 500+ copies: use a commercial printer
Turnaround	How soon do I need it?	Immediate	Rush outside printing is probably an extra cost

Paper Considerations

Professional brochures are printed on a high grade of paper to enhance the graphics and provide a longer lasting document. Grades of paper are based on weight. Desktop printers commonly use **20 lb. bond paper**, which means they use a lightweight paper intended for writing and printing. A commercial printer might use 60 lb. glossy or linen paper.

The finishing options and their costs are important considerations that may take additional time to explore. **Glossy paper** is a coated paper, produced using a heat process with clay and titanium. **Linen paper**, with its mild texture or grain, can support high-quality graphics without the shine and slick feel of glossy paper. Users sometimes pick a special stock of paper, such as cover stock, card stock, or text stock. This textbook is printed on 45 lb., blade-coated paper. **Blade-coated paper** is coated and then skimmed and smoothed to create the pages you see here.

These paper and finishing options may sound burdensome, but they are becoming conveniently available to desktop publishers. Local office supply stores have shelf after shelf of special computer paper specifically designed for laser and ink-jet printers. Some of the paper you can purchase has been prescored for special folding.

Color Considerations

When printing colors, desktop printers commonly use a color scheme called **RGB**. RGB stands for the three colors — red, green, and blue — that are used to print the combined colors of your publication. Professional printers, on the other hand, can print your publication using color scheme processes, or **libraries**. These processes include black and white, spot color, and process color.

BTW

Spot Colors

If you choose black plus one spot color in a publication, Publisher converts all colors except for black to tints of the selected spot color. If you choose black plus two spot colors, Publisher changes only exact matches of the second spot color to 100 percent of the second spot color. All other colors in the publication, other than black, are changed to tints of the first spot color. You then can apply tints of the second spot color to objects in the publication manually.

BTW

Offset Printing

Your printing service may use the initials SWOP, which stand for Standard for Web Offset Printing — a widely accepted set of color standards used in Web offset printing. Web offset printing has nothing to do with the World Wide Web. It is merely the name for an offset printing designed to print thousands of pieces in a single run from a giant roll of paper.

BTW

T-Shirts

You can use Publisher to create T-shirt designs with pictures, logos, words, or any of the Publisher objects. You need thermal T-shirt transfer paper that is widely available for most printers. Then create your design in Publisher. On the File menu, click Page Setup. On the Printer & Paper sheet, select Letter. If your design is a picture, clip art, or WordArt, flip it horizontally. If your design includes text, cut it from the text box, and insert it into a WordArt object; then flip it horizontally.

In **black-and-white printing**, the printer uses only one color of ink (usually black, but you can choose a different color if you want). You can add accent colors to your publication by using different shades of gray or by printing on colored paper. Your publication can have the same range of subtleties as a black-and-white photograph.

A **spot color** is used to accent a black-and-white publication. Newspapers, for example, may print their masthead in a bright, eye-catching color on page 1 but print the rest of the publication in black and white. In Publisher, you may apply up to two spot colors with a color matching system called **Pantone**. **Spot-color printing** uses semi-transparent, premixed inks typically chosen from standard color-matching guides, such as Pantone. Choosing colors from a **color-matching library** helps ensure high-quality results, because printing professionals who license the libraries agree to maintain the specifications, control, and quality.

In a spot-color publication, each spot color is **separated** to its own plate and printed on an offset printing press. The use of spot colors has become more creative in the last few years. Printing services use spot colors of metallic or florescent inks, as well as screen tints, to get color variations without increasing the number of color separations and cost. If your publication includes a logo with one or two colors, or if you want to use color to emphasize line art or text, then consider using spot-color printing.

Process-color printing means your publication can include color photographs and any color or combination of colors. One of the process-color libraries, called **CMYK**, or **four-color printing**, is named for the four semi-transparent process inks — cyan, magenta, yellow, and black. CMYK process-color printing can reproduce a full range of colors on a printed page. The CMYK color model defines color as it is absorbed and reflected on a printed page rather than in its liquid state.

Process-color printing is the most expensive proposition; black-and-white printing is the cheapest. Using color increases the cost and time it takes to process the publication. When using either the spot-color or process-color method, the printer first must output the publication to film on an **image setter**, which recreates the publication on film or photographic paper. The film then is used to create color **printing plates**. Each printing plate transfers one of the colors in the publication onto paper in an offset process. Publisher can print a preview of these individual sheets showing how the colors will separate before you take your publication to the printer.

A new printing technology called **digital printing** uses toner instead of ink to reproduce a full range of colors. Digital printing does not require separate printing plates. Although not yet widely available, digital printing promises to become cheaper than offset printing without sacrificing any quality.

Publisher supports all three kinds of printing and provides the tools commercial printing services need to print the publication. You should ask your printing service which color-matching system it uses.

Choosing a Commercial Printing Tool

After making the decisions about printing services, paper, and color, you must prepare the brochure for outside printing. The first task is to assign a color library from the commercial printing tools, as illustrated in the following steps.

To Choose a Commercial Printing Tool

1

- Click Tools on the menu bar.

- Point to Commercial Printing Tools (Figure 3–79).

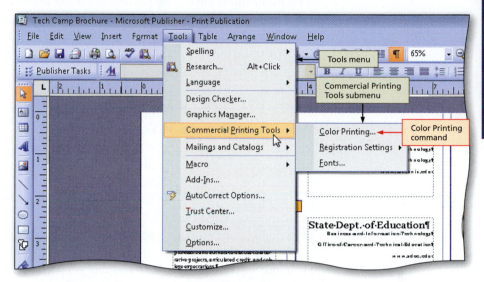

Figure 3–79

2

- Click Color Printing on the Commercial Printing Tools submenu.

- When the Color Printing dialog box is displayed, click Process colors (CMYK) (Figure 3–80).

3

- Click the OK button in the information dialog box.

- Click the OK button in the Color Printing dialog box.

BTW

CMYK Colors
When Process Colors are selected, Publisher converts all colors in text, graphics, and other objects to CMYK values and then creates four plates, regardless of the color scheme originally used to create the publication. Some RGB colors, including some of Publisher's standard colors, cannot be matched exactly to a CMYK color. After setting up for process-color printing, be sure to evaluate the publication for color changes. If a color does not match the color you want, you will have to include the new color library when you pack the publication.

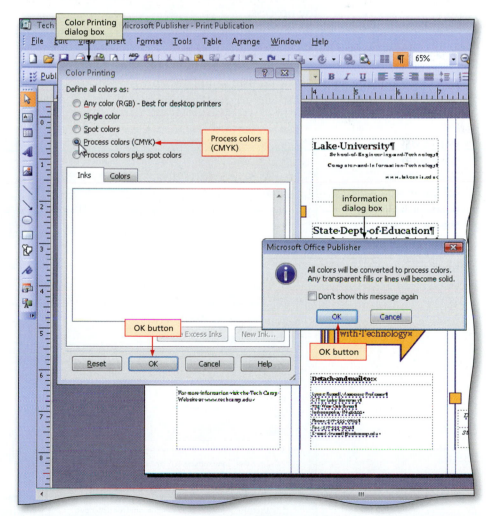

Figure 3–80

Packaging the Publication for the Printing Service

The publication file can be packaged for the printing service in two ways. The first way is to give the printing service the Publisher file in Publisher format using the Pack and Go Wizard. The second way is to save the file in a format called Encapsulated PostScript. Both of these methods are discussed in the following sections.

Using the Pack and Go Wizard

The **Pack and Go Wizard** guides you through the steps to collect and pack all the files the printing service needs and then compress the files to fit on one or more disks. Publisher checks for and embeds the TrueType fonts used in the publication. **Embedding** ensures that the printing service can display and print the publication with the correct fonts. The Pack and Go Wizard compresses all necessary files and fonts to take to the printing service. At the end of Publisher's packing sequence, you are given the option of printing a composite color printout or color separation printout on your desktop printer.

You need either sufficient space on a floppy disk or another formatted disk readily available when using the Pack and Go Wizard. Graphic files and fonts require a great deal of disk space. In the next series of steps, if you use a storage device other than the one on which you previously saved the brochure, save it again on the new disk before beginning the process.

To Use the Pack and Go Wizard

The following steps illustrate using the Pack and Go Wizard to ready the publication for submission to a commercial printing service. As you progress through the wizard, read each screen for more information.

1

- With a USB flash drive connected to one of the computer's USB ports, click File on the menu bar.

- Point to Pack and Go to display its submenu (Figure 3–81).

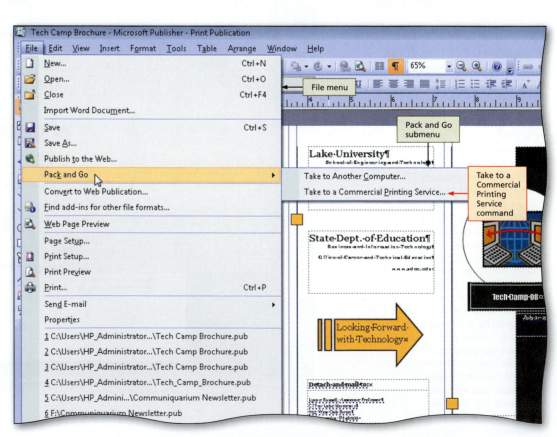

Figure 3–81

2

- Click Take to a Commercial Printing Service on the Pack and Go submenu to begin the process (Figure 3–82).

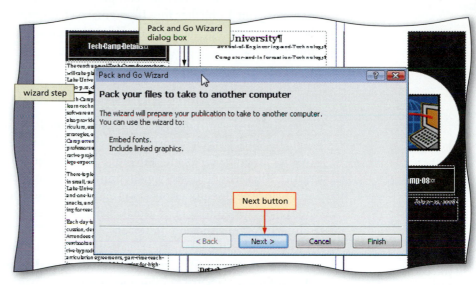

Figure 3–82

3

- Click the Next button to display the second dialog box in the wizard.

- Click the Browse button, navigate to your USB flash drive, and then click the OK button (Figure 3–83).

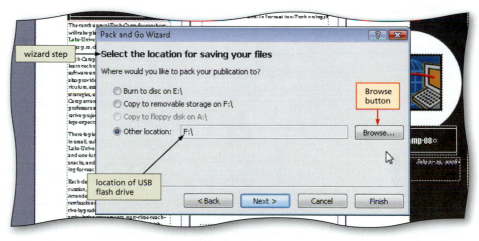

Figure 3–83

4

- Click the Next button to display the Include fonts and graphics dialog box.

- Click the Next button to display the Pack my publication dialog box.

- Click the Finish button.

- When the final dialog box is displayed, remove the check mark in the 'Print a composite proof' box, if necessary (Figure 3–84).

- Click the OK button.

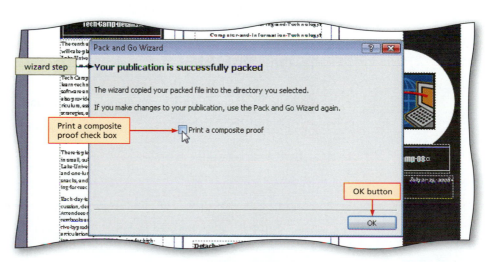

Figure 3–84

The files are saved in a compressed format on the USB flash drive, with the same name as your Publisher file. If you make changes to the publication after packing the files, be sure to run the Pack and Go Wizard again so that the changes are part of the packed publication.

Using PostScript Files

If your printing service does not accept Publisher files, you can hand off, or submit, your files in PostScript format. **PostScript** is a page definition language that describes the document to be printed in language that the printer can understand. The PostScript printer driver includes a page definition language translator to interpret the instructions and print the document on a printer or a PostScript output device, such as an image setter. Because you cannot open or make changes directly to a PostScript file, everything in the publication must be complete before saving it.

Nearly all printing services can work with some type of PostScript file, either regular PostScript files, known as **PostScript dumps**, or **Encapsulated PostScript** (**EPS**) files, which are graphic pictures of each page. If you hand off a PostScript file, you are responsible for updating graphics, including the necessary fonts, and ensuring that you have all the files your printing service needs. Publisher includes several **PostScript printer drivers** (**PPD**) and their description files to facilitate printing at the publisher. You must install a PPD before saving in PostScript form. Because the most common installation of Publisher is for a single user in a desktop environment, this project will not take you through the steps involved to install a PostScript printer driver. That process would necessitate using original operating system disks and a more thorough knowledge of PostScript printers. Ask your printing service representative for the correct printer driver, and see your Windows documentation for installing it. Then use the Save As command on the File menu to save the publication in PostScript format.

Another question to ask your printing service is whether it performs the **prepress tasks** or a **preflight check**. You may be responsible for making color corrections, separations, setting the printing options, and other printing tasks.

BTW

PostScript Files
If you decide to hand off a PostScript dump, or file, to an outside printer or service bureau, include a copy of the original document as well — for backup purposes. Many shops slowly are changing over from Macintosh-based to cross-platform based operations. If something happens, the printer technician can correct the error from the original without another trip by you to the print shop.

Quitting Publisher

The following steps quit Publisher.

To Quit Publisher

1 Click the Close button on the Publisher title bar.

2 If a dialog box displays reminding you to save the document, click the No button.

Chapter Summary

In this chapter you were introduced to the brochure medium. You learned how to create custom color schemes, apply font effects, and change paragraph formatting. You learned about the use of photographs versus images, and how to insert a photograph from a file. After entering new text and deleting unwanted objects, you created a logo using a formatted shape and autofitted text. You used WordArt to create a watermark on the master page. You also learned about design and printing considerations, such as overlapping, separations, color libraries, paper types, and costs. In anticipation of taking the brochure to a professional publisher, you previewed and printed your publication and then used the Pack and Go Wizard to create the necessary files. The items listed below include all the new Publisher skills you have learned in this chapter.

1. Choose Brochure Options (PUB 150)
2. Open the Create New Color Dialog Box (PUB 153)
3. Change an Accent Color (PUB 154)
4. Save a New Color Scheme (PUB 156)
5. Edit Text in the Brochure (PUB 159)
6. Insert a Text Box and Apply a Font Scheme Style (PUB 162)
7. Use the Auto Correct Options Button (PUB 165)
8. Use the Format Painter (PUB 168)
9. Open the Styles Task Pane (PUB 171)
10. Create a New Style (PUB 173)
11. Apply the New Style (PUB 175)
12. Apply a Font Effect (PUB 177)
13. Edit the Sign-Up Form (PUB 179)
14. Change the Paragraph Spacing (PUB 181)
15. Text Wrap (PUB 185)
16. Create a Shape for the Logo (PUB 188)
17. Fill a Shape with Color (PUB 189)
18. Edit AutoShape Lines (PUB 190)
19. Add Text to an AutoShape (PUB 192)
20. Fit Text (PUB 193)
21. Copy the Logo (PUB 194)
22. Reposition and Resize the Logos (PUB 195)
23. Access the Master Page (PUB 196)
24. Insert a WordArt Object (PUB 199)
25. Format WordArt (PUB 200)
26. Remove the Watermark from Page 1 (PUB 203)
27. Make Text Boxes Transparent (PUB 204)
28. Choose a Commercial Printing Tool (PUB 209)
29. Use the Pack and Go Wizard (PUB 210)

Learn It Online

Test your knowledge of chapter content and key terms.

Instructions: To complete the Learn It Online exercises, start your browser, click the Address bar, and then enter the Web address scsite.com/pub2007/learn. When the Office 2007 Learn It Online page is displayed, click the link for the exercise you want to complete and then read the instructions.

Chapter Reinforcement TF, MC, and SA
A series of true/false, multiple choice, and short answer questions that test your knowledge of the chapter content.

Flash Cards
An interactive learning environment where you identify chapter key terms associated with displayed definitions.

Practice Test
A series of multiple choice questions that test your knowledge of chapter content and key terms.

Who Wants To Be a Computer Genius?
An interactive game that challenges your knowledge of chapter content in the style of a television quiz show.

Wheel of Terms
An interactive game that challenges your knowledge of chapter key terms in the style of the television show *Wheel of Fortune.*

Crossword Puzzle Challenge
A crossword puzzle that challenges your knowledge of key terms presented in the chapter.

Apply Your Knowledge

Reinforce the skills and apply the concepts you learned in this chapter.

Revising Text and Paragraphs in a Publication
Instructions: Start Publisher. Open the publication, Apply 3-1 Fall Concert Series Brochure Draft, from the Data Files for Students. See the inside back cover of this book for instructions on downloading the Data Files for Students, or contact your instructor for more information about accessing the required files.

You are to revise the publication as follows: enter new text and text boxes, replace some graphics, create a logo, delete objects, create a fancy heading, and check the publication for errors. Finally, you will pack the publication for a commercial printing service. The revised publication is shown in Figure 3–85.

Perform the following tasks:
1. On page 1, make the following text changes, zooming as necessary:
    a. Click the text, Seminar or Event Title. Type `Music Among the Maples` to replace the text.
    b. Drag through the text, Business Name. Type `The Performing Arts Center` to replace the text.
    c. In the lower portion of the right panel of page 1, insert a text box below Performing Arts Center. Click the Font Color button arrow on the Formatting toolbar and then click white on the color palette. Press CTRL+E to center the text. Press F9 to increase the magnification. Type `In conjunction with the Kansas City Symphonic Orchestra` and then press the enter key. Type `2009 Fall Concert Series` to complete the entry.
    d. Use the Format Painter button to copy the formatting from the Performing Arts Center text box to the new text box.
    e. Delete the organization logo in the middle panel.
2. In the left panel, double-click each of the three graphics, one at a time. Use the keywords, violin, conductor, and entertainment, respectively, to search for pictures similar to Figure 3–85a.

(a)

(b)

Figure 3–85

3. Click Page 2 on the page sorter. Delete the text box in the middle panel by right-clicking the text box and then clicking Delete Object on the shortcut menu. Delete the picture of the graduate and its caption. Drag the instruments picture upward to the center of the panel.

4. Select the entire story in the left panel on page 2. Change the line spacing to 1.5 and the alignment to justified.

5. Create a 5-point Star AutoShape button in the workspace. Use the Accent 1 scheme color to fill the star. Create a centered text box using the Best Fit option and a white font color. Insert the letters KCSO, the abbreviation for the Kansas City Symphonic Orchestra. Autofit the text for best fit. Drag the object to an empty location in the middle panel.

6. In the right panel, select the Sign-up Form Heading. Type the text, `Order Fall Concert Series Tickets`. Apply an emboss font effect.

7. Check spelling and run the Design Checker. Correct errors if necessary.

8. Click File on the menu bar and then click Save As. Use the file name, Apply 3-1 Fall Concert Series Brochure Modified.

9. Click Tools on the menu bar, point to Commercial Printing Tools, and then click Color Printing. When the Color Printing dialog box is displayed, click Process colors (**CMYK**). When Publisher displays an information dialog box, click the OK button; then, click the OK button in the Color Printing dialog box.

10. Click File on the menu bar. Point to Pack and Go and then click Take to a Commercial Printing Service on the Pack and Go submenu. Click the Next button in each progressive dialog box. Store the resulting compressed file on your flash drive. When the final dialog box is displayed, click the Finish button.

11. When the wizard completes the packing process, if necessary, click the Print a composite proof check box to display its check mark. The composite will print on two pages.

Extend Your Knowledge

Extend the skills you learned in this chapter and experiment with new skills. You may need to use Help to complete the assignment.

Working with Objects in Brochures

Instructions: Start Publisher. Open the publication, Extend 3-1 Hayes Menu Draft, from the Data Files for Students. See the inside back cover of this book for instructions on downloading the Data Files for Students, or contact your instructor for more information about accessing the required files.

You will make the following changes to the tri-fold, two-sided menu: edit the text boxes, change the pictures, create a WordArt, autofit several text boxes, replace the map, and enter menu items on page 2.

Perform the following tasks:

1. On page 1 of the menu, change the graphic in the left and right panels to a photograph of a hamburger. You may use clip art graphics, or one of your own. If you use a picture you did not take, make sure you have permission to use the graphic.

2. Create a new color scheme with black as the Main color, red as the Accent 1 color, an Accent 2 color based on the dominant color in your hamburger photograph, and a lighter version of that color for Accent 3.

3. Create a WordArt with the text, Hayes, using a style of your choice. Place a copy of the WordArt above the business name text box in the right panel and above the hours text box in the middle panel. Resize the WordArt as necessary.

4. Enter Hayes Hamburgers as the title of the menu. Use the phrase, where every burger is cooked to order, in the business name text box above the title.

5. Enter appropriate hours, address, and phone numbers in the text boxes in the middle and right panels.

6. Use the text in Table 3–8 for the story in the left panel. Autofit all text boxes on page 1.

Table 3–8 Text for Page 1	
Location	**Text**
Left Panel Heading Story	For over 25 years, Camden's has been the most popular hamburger restaurant. Located "Four Blocks from the Beach," we are within walking distance from all downtown hotels as well as the Gardner Convention Center. A local landmark, Camden's is well-known in the Tri-state area for its cooked-to-order burgers and homemade pies.
Left Panel Lower Text Box	We accept most credit cards, including Visa, Mastercard, Discover, and American Express.

7. Click the large background graphic that appears as a watermark on page 1. Move it to the master page.

8. Go to page 2 and replace the fields with your favorite foods and local prices. Move the large background graphic that appears as a watermark to a second master page. Use Help if necessary to create the second master page.

9. Open a Web browser and go to a mapping Web site, such as mapquest.com or maps.google.com. Enter your address, or an address you know of, into the appropriate text boxes of the Web page. When the map displays, choose a printer-friendly version. Press the Print Screen key on your keyboard. Paste the resulting graphic into your Publisher document. Use the crop tool on the Picture toolbar to crop the graphic so it displays only the map. Resize the graphic to fit in the space on page 1, middle pane.

10. Save a copy of the publication with the file name, Extend 3-1 Hayes Menu Revised. Print a copy using duplex printing.

Make It Right

Analyze a publication and correct all errors and/or improve the design.

Correcting Transparency Errors, Illegible Text, and Format Inconsistencies

Instructions: Start Publisher. Open the publication, Make It Right 3-1 Health Plan Brochure Draft, from the Data Files for Students. See the inside back cover of this book for instructions on downloading the Data Files for Students, or contact your instructor for more information about accessing the required files.

The publication is a brochure that has transparency errors, illegible text, and format inconsistencies, as shown in Figure 3–86. You are to correct the errors.

Figure 3–86

Perform the following steps:

1. The official color for Healthy Iowa is a medium purple. Change the color scheme to match more closely the industry color and help brand the brochure.

2. Change all of the graphics to appropriate health care graphics so the brochure is more effective.

3. Wrap the text around all of the graphics so there is no overlap.

4. On page 1 in the shape text, change the font color so that the text is more legible. Autofit the text.

5. CTRL+Drag the upper graphic on page 1 to a location in the workspace. Go to page 2 and drag the copy to a position in the lower part of the left panel.

6. On page 2, copy the formatting from the left panel heading to the other headings on the back page.

7. Right-justify all the prices in the right panel.

8. Correct all spelling and design errors.

9. Save the brochure with the name, Make It Right 3-1 Health Plan Brochure Revised.

In the Lab

Lab 1: Creating a Brochure Layout with One Spot Color

Problem: A large company in the paper industry is planning a seminar for their salespeople. They would like you to create a sample brochure, advertising the event. The theme is "Reach Your Goal." They would like a tri-fold brochure with a graphic related to the paper industry and a large blue logo with white slanted lettering, spelling the word, GOAL. On the inside of the brochure, the manager would like a response form to gain some knowledge of the participants' backgrounds. Note that your finished product is only a design sample; if the recipients like the sample, they will submit text for the other text boxes.

Instructions: Start Publisher and perform the following tasks to create the design sample shown in Figures 3–87a and 3–87b.

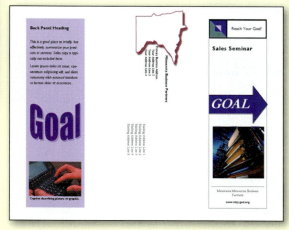

(a)

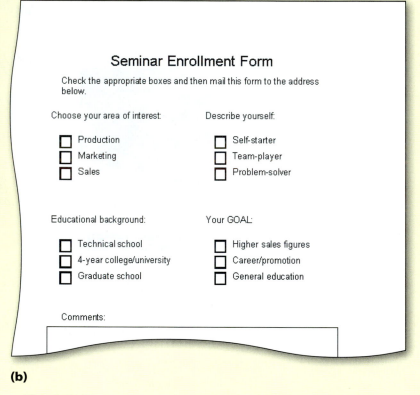

(b)

Figure 3–87

1. From the catalog, choose the Accent Box Informational Brochure. Choose to display the customer address and a response form.

2. Edit the text frames in the right panel as shown in Figure 3–87a. Delete the logo in the middle panel.

3. Double-click the graphic in the front panel. Insert a clip using the keywords, paper mills.

4. Click the AutoShapes button on the Objects toolbar. Point to Block Arrows and then click the Right Arrow shape. In the workspace, shift-drag to create an arrow approximately two inches square. Use the Fill Color button to choose Accent 1.

5. Add the text GOAL, in a white font color, and autofit it. Choose an appropriate style and font effect.

6. Drag the logo to the empty space above the picture.

7. Create a WordArt for the left panel, as shown in Figure 3–87a. Use the Can Down WordArt shape.

8. Go to the master page. On the Insert menu, point to Picture, and then click From File. Insert the file named, Minnesota, from the data disk. Rotate the image by dragging the green rotation handle 90°to the right. Drag the image to the upper-right corner of the center panel.

9. Navigate to page 2. Use the Ignore Master Page command to remove the graphic of the state from page 2.

10. In the Response Form in the right panel of page 2, make the text changes as indicated in Figure 3–87b.

11. Save the publication using the file name, Lab 3-1 GOAL Brochure. Print a copy for your instructor.

In the Lab

Lab 2: Creating a CD Liner

Problem: Your friend has recorded a new CD of his original guitar music. Knowing of your interest in desktop publishing, he has asked you to create the CD liner. You decide to create a publication with two panels, front and back, using Publisher's CD liner template.

Instructions: Perform the following tasks to create the two-panel, two-sided CD liner, as shown in Figures 3–88a and 3–88b on the next page.

1. Start Publisher.

2. In the catalog, click Labels, and then click the CD/DVD Labels link. When Publisher displays the previews, click the CD/DVD Booklet preview.

3. Choose the Glacier color scheme and the Modern font scheme.

4. Edit the text in both panels, as shown in Figure 3–88a.

5. Select the large rectangle border in the right panel. Press CTRL+T to make the rectangle transparent, in preparation for the watermark.

6. Replace the picture in the right panel using the Clip Art task pane. Search using the keyword, guitar.

7. Copy the graphic using the Copy button on the Standard toolbar.

8. On the Insert menu, click Page to insert a new blank page to follow page 1. Click Page 2 on the status bar, if necessary.

9. Paste the picture from page 1. Drag it to the left panel and shift-drag a corner handle, resizing so it fills the entire panel.

10. Create a large text frame in the left panel. Make it transparent so the picture shows through. Use a white font color. Type the text as shown in Figure 3–88b.

11. Go to the master page. Use the Clip Art task pane to search for an appropriate line drawing graphic, similar to the one in Figure 3–88b, for a watermark effect using the keyword, music.

12. Drag the music graphic to the right panel and shift-drag a corner handle, resizing so it fills the entire panel. Close the master page. (*Hint*: Do not forget to use the Ignore Master Page on page 1.)

13. On page 2, using the Design Gallery Object button, insert a Voyage style table of contents. Make it transparent. Edit the table of contents, as shown in Figure 3–88b.

14. Check the spelling and design of the publication. Save the publication on a floppy disk, using the file name, Lab 3-2 Guitar CD Liner.

15. Print a copy of the CD liner, using duplex printing. The default settings will print the liner in the middle of an 8½ × 11-inch piece of glossy paper if possible. Use your printer dialog box to choose to display crop marks. Trim the printout.

Continued >

In the Lab continued

(a)

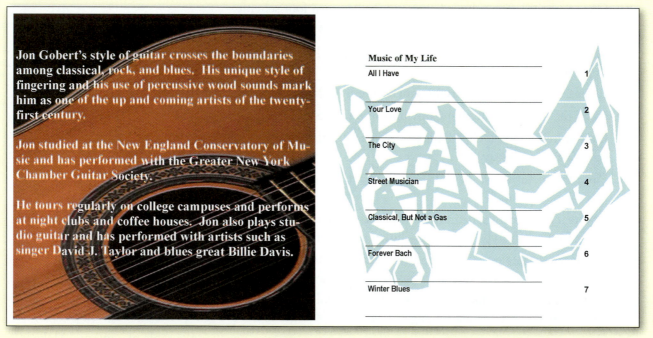

(b)

Figure 3–88

In the Lab

Lab 3: Creating a Travel Brochure

Problem: Alpha Zeta Mu fraternity is planning a ski trip to Sunset Mountain, Colorado, during spring break. They have asked you to design a brochure that advertises the trip. They would like a full-color tri-fold brochure on glossy paper that includes pictures of Sunset Mountain, a sign-up form, and the Alpha Zeta Mu logo. The fraternity plans to use mailing labels when it distributes the brochures.

Instructions: Perform the following tasks to create the brochure, as shown in Figures 3–89a and 3–89b.

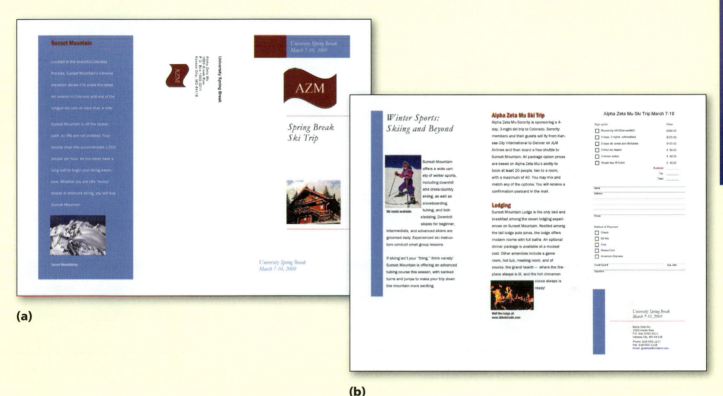

(a)

(b)

Figure 3–89

1. From the catalog, choose the Straight Edge Informational Brochure. Choose a 3-panel display, choose to include the customer address, and select the Sign-up form.

2. Choose the Clay Color scheme and the Textbook font scheme.

3. On Page 1, in the right panel, edit the brochure title, Spring Break Ski Trip, as shown in Figure 3–89a. Delete the tag line and telephone number text boxes in the lower portion of the right panel. Delete the address text box in the center of the middle panel.

4. Table 3–9 on the next page displays the text for the left panel. Enter the text. Press CTRL+A to select all of the text. On the Format menu, click Paragraph. Choose left alignment, and then type 2.5 in the between lines text box. Close the Paragraph dialog box. With the text still selected, click the Font Color button and select White in the color palette. Using Table 3–9 on the next page, edit the text for the middle and right panels. Your fonts may display differently.

Continued >

In the Lab *continued*

Table 3–9 Text for Page 1	
Location	**Text**
Left Panel Heading	Sunset Mountain
Left Panel	Located in the beautiful Colorado Rockies, Sunset Mountain's extreme elevation allows it to boast the latest ski season in Colorado and one of the longest ski runs at more than a mile! Sunset Mountain is off the beaten path, so lifts are not crowded. Four double chairlifts accommodate 1,000 people per hour, so you never have a long wait to begin your skiing adventure. Whether you are into bunny slopes or telemark skiing, you will love Sunset Mountain.
Left Panel Caption	Sunset Mountaintop
Middle Panel	University Spring Break Alpha Zeta Mu 1050 Greek Row P.O. Box 1050-3211 Kansas City, MO 64118
Right Panel	University Spring Break March 7–10, 2009

5. Click Page 2 on the page sorter.
6. Table 3–10 displays the text for the three stories on Page 2. Enter the text and headings, as shown in Figure 3–89b on the previous page. Use the Format Painter button to ensure that the headings use the same style.

Table 3–10 Text for Page 2			
Location	**Text**		
Winter Sports: Skiing and Beyond	Sunset Mountain offers a wide variety of winter sports, including downhill and cross-country skiing, as well as snowboarding, tubing, and bobsledding. Downhill slopes for beginner, intermediate, and advanced skiers are groomed daily. Experienced ski instructors conduct small group lessons. If skiing isn't your "thing," think variety! Sunset Mountain is offering an advanced tubing course this season, with banked turns and jumps to make your trip down the mountain more exciting.		
Left Panel Caption	Ski rental available		
Alpha Zeta Mu Ski Trip	Alpha Zeta Mu Fraternity is sponsoring a 4-day, 3-night ski trip to Colorado. Fraternity members and their guests will fly from Kansas City International to Denver on JLM Airlines and then board a free shuttle to Sunset Mountain. All package option prices are based on Alpha Zeta Mu's ability to book at least 20 people, two to a room, with a maximum of 40. You may mix and match any of the options. You will receive a confirmation postcard in the mail.		
Lodging	Sunset Mountain Lodge is the only bed and breakfast among the seven lodging experiences on Sunset Mountain. Nestled among the tall lodge pole pines, the lodge offers modern rooms with full baths. An optional dinner package is available at a modest cost. Other amenities include a game room, hot tub, meeting room, and of course, the grand hearth — where the fireplace always is lit, and the hot cinnamon cocoa always is ready!		
Middle Panel Caption	Visit the lodge at: www.skicolorado.com		
Order Form Detail	Alpha Zeta Mu Ski Trip March 7–10		
	Round trip MCI/Denver/MCI	$300.00	
	4 days, 3 nights w/breakfast	$325.00	
	3 days ski rental and lift tickets	$125.00	
	2-hour ski lesson	$50.00	
	3-dinner option	$50.00	
	Single-day lift ticket	$40.00	

7. Replace each of the template graphics. Using the Clip Art task pane, search for graphics, similar to the ones shown in Figure 3–89 on page PUB 221, that are related to lodge, mountain, fireplace, and skiing. Replace the placeholder graphics in the brochure.

8. Click the AutoShapes button on the Objects toolbar, point to Stars and Banners, and then click the Wave shape. Drag a wave shape in the scratch area, approximately 1.6 × 1.2 inches in size. Use the Fill Color button to fill the shape with Accent 1 (Dark Red).

9. Add the text, AZM, to the AutoShape, using a white font. Autofit the text.

10. Create a second copy of the shape.

11. With the copy of the grouped shape selected, click Arrange on the menu bar and then click Rotate Right. Drag a corner handle to resize the shape to approximately 1 × .75 inches. Drag the shape to the middle panel, as shown in Figure 3–89a.

12. Check the publication for spelling. Run the Design Checker. Fix any errors.

13. Click Tools on the menu bar and then point to Commercial Printing Tools. Click Color Printing. When the Color Printing dialog box is displayed, click Process colors (CMYK).

14. Check the spelling and design of the publication. Save the publication using the file name, Lab 3-3 Ski Trip Brochure.

15. Print the publication two sided. Fold the brochure and submit it to your instructor.

Cases and Places

Apply your creative thinking and problem solving skills to design and implement a solution.

● EASIER   ●● MORE DIFFICULT

● 1: Youth Baseball League Brochure

Use the Ascent Event brochure template to create a brochure announcing the Youth Baseball League. Pick an appropriate color and font scheme. Type Preseason Sign-Up as the brochure title. Type Youth Baseball League as the Organization name. Type your address and telephone number in the appropriate text boxes. Delete the logo. Replace all graphics with sports-related clip art. Edit the captions to match. The league commissioner will send you content for the stories at a later date. Include a sign-up form on page 2. Edit the sign-up form event boxes as displayed in Table 3–11.

Table 3–11 Sign-Up Form Check Box Content

Event Name	Time	Price
Preschool T-Ball: ages 4 and 5	10:00 a.m.	$35.00
Pee-Wee T-Ball: ages 6 and 7	11:00 a.m.	$35.00
Coach Pitched: ages 8 and 9	1:00 p.m.	$50.00
Intermediate: ages 10 and 11	2:30 p.m.	$50.00
Advanced: ages 12 and 13	4:00 p.m.	$50.00
City Team: audition only	6:00 p.m.	TBA

On a separate piece of paper, make a table similar to Table 3–1 on page PUB 149, listing the type of exposure, kinds of information, audience, and purpose of communication. Turn in the table with your printout.

Continued >

Cases and Places *continued*

● 2: Creating a Menu

Bob Bert of Bert's Beanery has hired you to "spice up" and modernize the look of the restaurant's menu. You decide to use a menu template to create a full-color menu for publication at a local copy shop. Bob wants special attention paid to his famous "Atomic Chili®," which is free if a customer can eat five spoonfuls without reaching for water. You will find the registered trademark symbol in the Symbol dialog box. Bob serves salads, soups, and sandwiches a la carte. He has several family specials, as well as combo meals and a variety of drinks and side dishes.

●● 3: Recreating a Logo

Using the Blank Print Publications link in the catalog, re-create as closely as possible your school or company logo on a full-page publication. Use the AutoShapes button, fill and font colors, text boxes, and symbols to match the elements in your logo. You also may use WordArt. Ask your instructor or employer for clip art files, if necessary. Use the workspace scratch area to design portions of the logo and then layer and group them before dragging them onto the publication.

●● 4: Creating a new Color Scheme

Make It Personal

Create a new color scheme named, My Favorite Colors. Use the Color Scheme task pane to access the Color Schemes dialog box. Choose colors that complement one another. Using the Publisher catalog, create a blank publication. Insert six different AutoShapes and fill each with a color from your color scheme. Create text box captions for each of the AutoShapes, identifying the name of the shape and the color. Print the publication.

●● 5: Exploring Commercial Printing

Working Together

Individually, visit or call several local copy shops or commercial printers in your area. Ask them the following questions: What kind of paper stock do your customers choose for brochures? What is the most commonly used finish? Do you support all three color processes? Will you accept files saved with Microsoft Publisher Pack and Go, or EPS files? What prepress tasks do you perform? Come back together as a group and create a blank Publisher publication to record your answers. Create a table with the Insert Table button on the Objects toolbar. Insert the questions down the left side. Insert the names of the print shops across the top. Fill in the grid with the answers they provide.

E-Mail Feature

Creating an E-Mail Letter Using Publisher

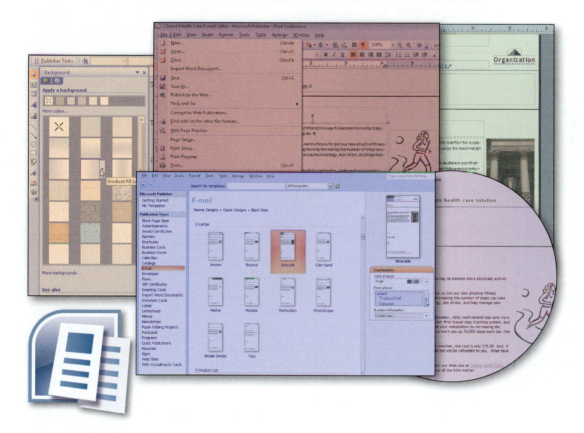

Objectives

You will have mastered the material in this project when you can:

- Select and format an e-mail letter template

- Insert an e-mail hyperlink

- Choose a logo design and add a background

- Preview and send an e-mail message using Publisher

Introduction

E-mail, short for electronic mail, is a popular form of communication to transmit messages and files via a computer network. For businesses, e-mail can be an efficient and cost-effective way to keep in touch with customers. E-mail is used in ways similar to traditional mail. With it, you can send correspondence, business communications, greeting cards, letters, brochures, newsletters, and other types of publications.

Project — E-Mail Message

The project in this feature illustrates how to create and send an e-mail message using Publisher 2007. An **e-mail message** or **e-mail letter** displays traditional correspondence-related text and graphics, as well as hyperlinks, similar to a Web page. All of the objects in an e-mail message are displayed in the body of the message rather than as a separate publication attached to the e-mail.

E-Mail Marketing
Using e-mail for marketing purposes has many benefits, including very little cost, immediate communication, interactivity, and the ability to contact multiple customers. It makes it easy to track positive and negative responses, visits to Web pages, and increases in specific product sales. Considerate and thoughtful e-mail marketing can reinforce positive interaction with your business. There are some disadvantages of e-mail marketing including the possible deletion or filtering by the customer before your message is read, or customers who may become offended by too many e-mails and consider your message spam.

When you send an e-mail message, recipients can read the message using HTML-enabled e-mail programs, such as GMail, AOL, Yahoo!, or the current versions of Microsoft Outlook and Outlook Express. **HTML-enabled e-mail** allows the sender to include formatted text and other visuals to improve the readability and aesthetics of the message. The majority of Internet users can access HTML-enabled mail. With e-mail messages, recipients do not need to have Publisher installed to view e-mail messages because the page you send will be displayed as the body of the e-mail message. Sending a one-page publication by e-mail to a group of customers or friends is an efficient and inexpensive way to deliver a message.

Publisher provides several ways to create an e-mail message. You can use a template, create an e-mail message from scratch, or convert a single page of another publication into an e-mail message, expanding the use of your existing content. Publisher's e-mail message templates are preformatted to the correct page size. The templates use placeholder text and graphics that download quickly and are suitable for the body of an e-mail message.

A second way to create an e-mail message is to send a single page of another publication type as an e-mail message, although some adjustments may need to be made to the width of your publication in order for it to fit in an e-mail message.

When you send an entire publication as an **e-mail attachment**, the recipient must have Microsoft Publisher 2002 or a later version installed to view it. When the recipient opens the attached file, Publisher automatically opens and displays the publication. Unless you convert it, a multipage publication must be sent as an e-mail attachment.

An **e-mail merge** can be created when you want to send a large number of messages that are mostly identical, but you also want to include some unique or personalized information in each message. An e-mail merge creates content that is personalized for each recipient on a mailing list. You will learn about several kinds of merged publications in Chapter 5.

The type of e-mail publication you choose depends on the content and the needs of the recipients. Table 1 describes specific audiences and the appropriate kinds of e-mail publications.

Table 1 Publisher E-Mail Types			
Audience Characteristic	**E-Mail Message**	**E-Mail Merge**	**E-Mail Attachment**
Recipients definitely have Publisher			X
Recipients may not have Publisher	X	X	
Recipients need to read and print the content in its original format			X
Recipients may not have HTML-enabled e-mail	X	X	
Recipients need personalized messages		X	

Figure 1 displays an e-mail message sent to a list of participants or members of a health care plan. The e-mail message includes a colorful heading, a logo, a graphic, and directions for obtaining more information about a fitness initiative sponsored by the health care provider.

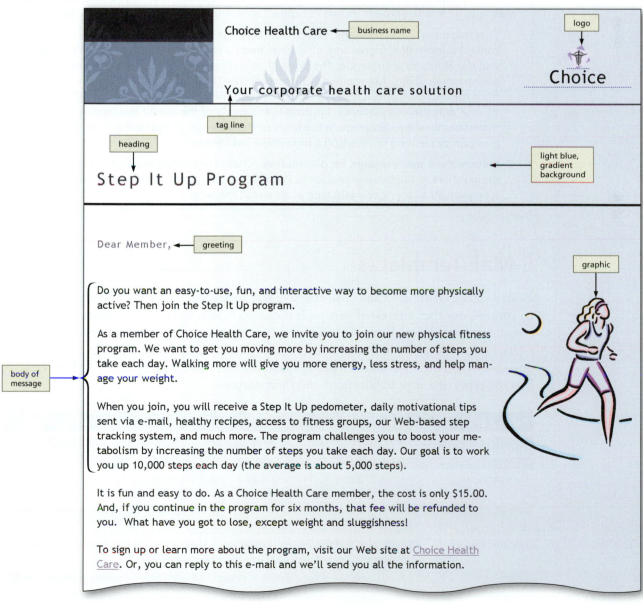

Figure 1

This E-Mail Feature is for instructional purposes only. You do not have to be connected to the Internet or have an e-mail program on your system in order to create the e-mail message. You can create and save the e-mail message on a flash drive rather than send it via e-mail.

Overview

As you read through this feature, you will learn how to create the e-mail message shown in Figure 1 on the previous page by performing these general tasks:

- Edit an e-mail message template.
- Save an e-mail message.
- Preview and send an e-mail message.

Plan Ahead

General Project Guidelines

When creating a Publisher publication, the actions you perform and decisions you make will affect the appearance and characteristics of the finished document. As you create an e-mail message, such as the project shown in Figure 1, you should follow these general guidelines:

1. **Customize the e-mail message.** Your e-mail message should present, at a minimum, your contact information, a greeting, a message body, a salutation, a link to your Web site, and the ability to unsubscribe. The body of your message should present honestly all your positive points. Ask someone else to proofread your message and give you suggestions for improvements. Choose a color scheme, font scheme, page size, and graphic that fit your purpose and audience. Improve the usability of the e-mail message by creating hyperlinks where appropriate in the body of the message. Enhance the look of the e-mail message by creating or inserting a logo and a background.

2. **Prepare the e-mail message for distribution.** Check for spelling errors and run Publisher's design checker. Correct any problems. Preview the publication in a browser and then send it to yourself to see how it will look as an e-mail message.

E-Mail Templates

E-mail can be an efficient and cost-effective way to keep in touch with friends, customers, coworkers, or other interested parties. It is easy to design and send professional-looking e-mail using Publisher. Each of Publisher's design sets features several e-mail publication types, so you can create and send e-mail that is consistent in design with the rest of the business communication and marketing materials that you create using Publisher. Table 2 lists the types of e-mail publications and their purpose.

E-Mail Template	Purpose
Event/Activity	A notice of a specific upcoming activity or event containing a combination of pictures, dates, times, maps, agenda, and the ability to sign up
Event/Speaker	A notice of a specific upcoming event that includes a speaker and usually contains pictures, dates, times, and a map
Featured Product	A publication that provides information about a company and a specific product or service, including graphics and Web page links for more information
Letter	A more personalized document to correspond with one or more people, including specific information on a single topic

Table 2 E-Mail Template Publications

Table 2 E-Mail Template Publications *(continued)*	
E-Mail Template	**Purpose**
Newsletter	A publication that informs interested clientele about an organization or business with stories, dates, contact information, and upcoming events
Product List	A sales-oriented publication to display products, prices, and special promotions, including Web page links for more information

Creating an E-Mail Message

The following steps open an e-mail message template.

To Open an E-Mail Template

- Start Publisher, as described in the steps on page PUB 4 through PUB 5.

- In the catalog, click E-mail.

- In the Newer Designs area, scroll down to the Letter previews and then click the Brocade preview.

- In the Customize area, select the Origin color scheme and the Opulent font scheme (Figure 2).

- Click the Create button.

- If necessary, click the Special Characters button on the Standard toolbar to display paragraph marks.

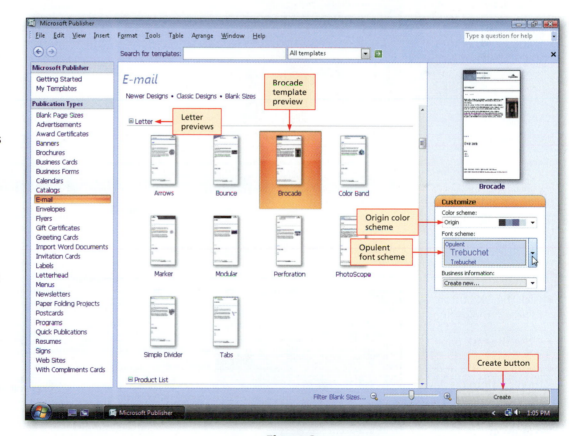

Figure 2

Q&A What if I want to send an e-mail to someone who does not have Publisher?

E-mail messages display in the body of the e-mail and do not require Publisher. If you are sending an attachment and are worried that your recipients may not have Publisher installed on their system, you can send your publication in a different format. Publisher can create PDF files or XPS files, which have free or inexpensive viewers. The files then can be attached to an e-mail message.

To Customize the E-Mail Page Size

The following steps change the page size of the e-mail message.

- In the Format Publication task pane, click the Change Page Size button to display the Page Setup dialog box.

- In the E-mail area, click the Short button to choose a short page format (Figure 3).

Q&A

What are the other settings in the Page Setup dialog box?

As you will learn in a future chapter, you can set the margins and choose various paper sizes and layouts in the Page Setup dialog box. The e-mail sizes include the standard width of 5.818 inches, a long e-mail (up to 66 inches), a short e-mail (up to 11 inches), or a custom size.

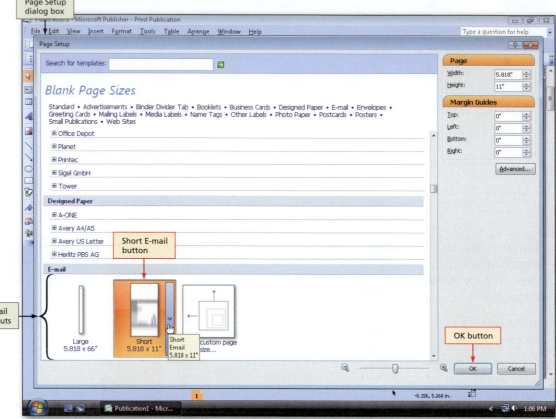

Figure 3

- Click the OK button to accept the settings.

- Close the task pane.

- Zoom to 100% and then scroll to display the upper portion of the page layout (Figure 4).

Figure 4

Editing Text

The text boxes in an e-mail letter template include the business name, the tag line, the heading, the salutation, the body of the letter, the closing, the signature block, and the contact text box at the bottom of the e-mail letter.

To Edit the Headings and Greeting

The following steps edit the placeholder text in the upper portion of the e-mail letter. Your placeholder text may differ from that shown in the figures.

1 Select the placeholder text in the business name text box. Type `Choice Health Care` to replace the text. Select the placeholder text in the tag line text box. Type `Your corporate health care solution` to replace the text.

2 Select the text, Letter, in the heading text box. Type `Step It Up Program` to replace the text. Select the text, Dear Customer, in the salutation text box. Type `Dear Member,` to replace the text (Figure 5).

BTW

E-Mail Templates
E-mail letter templates contain text boxes, logos, hyperlinks, and graphics. To customize the e-mail letter, you replace the placeholder text and graphics with your own content, just as you would in any other template publication.

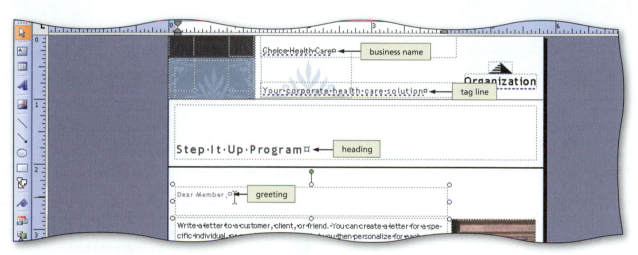

Figure 5

Editing the Body of the E-Mail Letter

Table 3 displays the text for the body of the e-mail letter.

Table 3 Text for Body of E-Mail Letter
Text
Do you want an easy-to-use, fun, and interactive way to become more physically active? Then join the Step It Up program.
As a member of Choice Health Care, we invite you to join our new physical fitness program. We want to get you moving more by increasing the number of steps you take each day. Walking more will give you more energy, less stress, and help manage your weight.
When you join, you will receive a Step It Up pedometer, daily motivational tips sent via e-mail, healthy recipes, access to fitness groups, our Web-based step tracking system, and much more. The program challenges you to boost your metabolism by increasing the number of steps you take each day. Our goal is to work you up 10,000 steps each day (the average is about 5,000 steps).
It is fun and easy to do. As a Choice Health Care member, the cost is only $15.00. And, if you continue in the program for six months, that fee will be refunded to you. What have you got to lose, except weight and sluggishness!
To sign up or learn more about the program, visit our Web site at Choice Health Care. Or, you can reply to this e-mail, and we'll send you all the information.

To Edit the Body of the E-Mail Letter

The following steps replace the text in the body of the e-mail letter.

1 Select the text in the body of the e-mail letter.

2 Enter the text from Table 3 on the previous page, pressing the ENTER key after each paragraph (Figure 6).

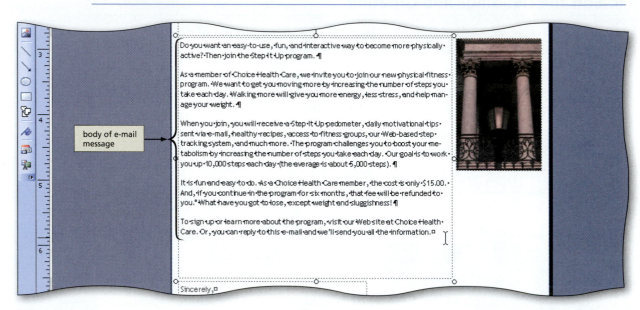

Figure 6

To Edit the Closing Text Boxes

To complete the text box editing in the e-mail letter, the next steps edit the signature block and contact information.

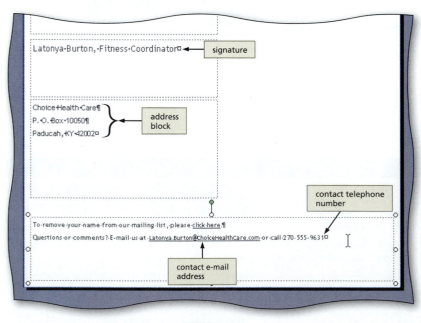

Figure 7

1 Select the text in the signature text box and then type Latonya Burton, Fitness Coordinator to replace the text.

2 Select the text in the name, position, and company text box and then type Choice Health Care to replace the text. Press the ENTER key.

3 Type P. O. Box 10050 as the second line of the address. Press the ENTER key.

4 Type Paducah, KY 42002 to complete the address.

5 In the final text box at the bottom of the page, select the text, someone@example.com. Type Latonya. Bruton@ChoiceHealthCare.com to replace the text.

6 Select the text, or call 555-555-5555. Type or call 270 555-9631 to replace the text (Figure 7).

Creating a Hyperlink

E-mail messages can contain hyperlinks, just as Web pages do. Recall that a hyperlink is a colored and underlined text or a graphic that you click to go to a file, a location in a file, a Web page, or an e-mail address. When you insert a hyperlink, you select the text or object and then click the Insert Hyperlink button on the Standard toolbar. When clicked, hyperlinks can take the viewer to an existing file or Web page, another place in the publication, a new document, or open an e-mail program and create a new message. For a more detailed description of how to insert hyperlinks, see pages PUB 49 through PUB 50 in Chapter 1.

Editing the Hyperlink

In the body of the e-mail letter template, the words, Choice Health Care, should display as a hyperlink to open the company's Web page. In the final text box at the bottom of the page, the words, click here, should display as a hyperlink that opens the user's e-mail program and creates a new message. For a more detailed description of how to insert hyperlinks, see pages PUB 49 through PUB 50 in Chapter 1.

To Edit the Hyperlinks

1 In the body of the e-mail letter template, select the words, Choice Health Care, in the last paragraph.

2 Click the Insert Hyperlink button on the Standard toolbar to display the Insert Hyperlink dialog box.

3 In the Address text box, type `www.choicehealthcare.com` in the Address text box.

4 Click the OK button.

5 Select the text, click here, in the contact information text box at the bottom of the page.

6 Click the Insert Hyperlink button on the Standard toolbar.

7 When the Insert Hyperlink dialog box is displayed, click E-mail Address in the Link to bar on the left.

8 In the E-mail address text box, type `unsubscribe@ChoiceHealthCare.com` as the entry.

9 Click the OK button.

E-Mail Logos and Graphics

Most of the e-mail templates contain both logos and graphics that you can edit to suit your publication. In the upper-right corner of the Brocade e-mail letter template, Publisher displays one of the predesigned logos from the Design Gallery. A **logo** is a recognizable symbol that identifies a person, business, or organization. A logo may be composed of text, a picture, or a combination of symbols. Most Publisher-supplied logos display in templates as a grouped object, combining a graphic and text.

Farther down in the e-mail letter, Publisher displays a graphic that you can change to reflect the purpose of your publication. You edit e-mail graphics in the same way as you edit graphics in other publications. You can select a clip art clip, insert a graphic from a file, or import a graphic from a scanner or digital camera.

To Edit the Logo

The following step edits the graphic and text in the logo of the e-mail letter. Because the purpose of the letter is to inform members of a health care plan about a new fitness program, a graphic representing medicine is appropriate. Not all graphics are appropriate for logos. You need to choose a graphic that will display well in a very small area. Your graphic should not have a lot of fine details. Some large clip art is too big to fit within a small logo and might need to be resized before being used.

- Click the logo to select it. Zoom to 200%. Double-click the graphic within the logo to display the Clip Art task pane.

- When the Clip Art task pane is displayed, search for clip art related to the word, medicine.

- Choose a graphic similar to the one shown in Figure 8.

- Double-click the text, Organization, to select it. Type `Choice` to replace the text.

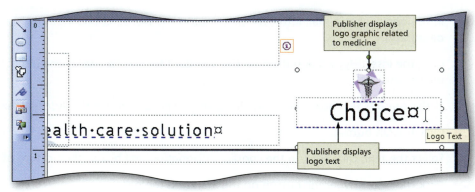

Figure 8

To Edit the Graphic

The next steps edit the graphic that displays next to the body of the letter.

1. Scroll as necessary and then double-click the graphic that displays next to the body of the letter.

2. When the Clip Art task pane is displayed, search for clip art related to the word, fitness.

3. Choose a graphic similar to the one shown in Figure 9.

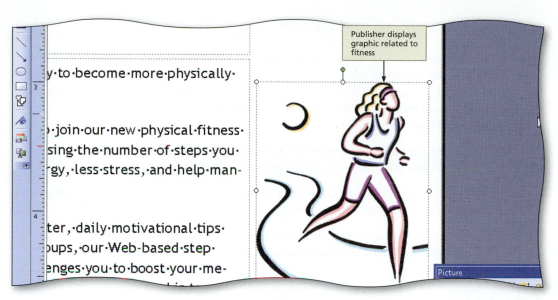

Figure 9

Backgrounds

You can add a **background** to an e-mail or Web publication by applying a color, gradient, picture, texture, or pattern. A background should not be detailed or busy because it displays behind the text and graphics. Simple backgrounds will not add significantly to the download time. If you select a custom picture file for your background texture, make sure it is 20 kilobytes (KB) or smaller. Large picture files will require people who are viewing your Web site to wait a long time for the graphic to download. If you select a picture for a background, the picture is repeated (or tiled) to create the background texture for your Web pages. A background is not the same as a master page. When you add a background, the publication's master page does not change. Avoid changing the background on master pages in e-mail and Web publications. Special effects applied to master pages do not display correctly when they are viewed in some Web browsers.

To Add a Background

The following step adds a background to the e-mail publication.

- Click Format on the menu bar and then click Background to open the Background task pane.

- In the Apply a background area, click the 30% tint of Accent 2 button, and then click the Gradient fill (vertical) preview that displays white on the left and light blue on the right (Figure 10).

Figure 10

To Check for Spelling and Design Errors

BTW

E-Mail Hyphenation
If your e-mail publication contains text with hyphenation, some e-mail programs may insert gaps in the e-mail message, and it may not appear as you intended. To fix the problem, on the Tools menu, point to Language, and then click Hyphenation. In the Hyphenation dialog box, clear the Automatically hyphenate this story check box. Delete any hyphens that remain in your text.

The publication now is complete. Before you send the e-mail message, you should use the Design Checker to check the message for potential issues, such as fonts that do not display well online and text that may be exported as an image — which increases the file size of the e-mail message. The following steps describe how to check the publication for spelling and design errors.

1 Click the Spelling button on the Standard toolbar. Correct any errors. Click the Yes button when Publisher asks you to check the rest of the document.

2 On the Tools menu, click Design Checker. Click the Run e-mail checks (current page only) check box so that it displays a check mark.

3 If you have objects that are positioned slightly off the page, ignore the error message. Correct any other problems and then close the Design Checker task pane.

To Save the E-Mail Letter

The following steps save the e-mail letter. For a detailed example of the procedure summarized below, refer to pages PUB 31 through PUB 33 in Chapter 1.

1 With a USB flash drive connected to one of the computer's USB ports, click the Save button on the Standard toolbar.

2 Type Choice Health Care E-mail Letter in the File name text box to change the file name. Do not press the ENTER key.

3 Navigate to your USB flash drive.

4 Click the Save button in the Save As dialog box to save the publication on the USB flash drive with the file name, Choice Health Care E-mail Letter.

Sending an E-Mail Letter

E-mail letters can be sent to one or more people. Many organizations create a **listserv**, which is a list of interested people with e-mail addresses who want to receive news and information e-mails about the organization. A listserv e-mail is one e-mail sent to everyone on the list. Listserv e-mails always should contain a link to allow recipients to remove their name from the list to prevent receiving future e-mails.

Using the Send E-Mail Command

The steps on the next page describe how to preview and then send an e-mail using Publisher's Send E-mail command. You do not have to send the e-mail, nor do you have to be connected to the Internet to perform the steps.

To Preview and Send a Publication via E-Mail

1

- With the publication displayed, click File on the menu bar and then point to Send E-mail (Figure 11).

Q&A

Do most people prefer to receive a publication as an e-mail attachment?

Whether or not to use an attachment depends on the purpose and the size of the attachment. For immediate viewing, such as an announcement, letter, or card, it is better to send a single page in the body of an e-mail. With an attachment, the person receiving your e-mail will need to have

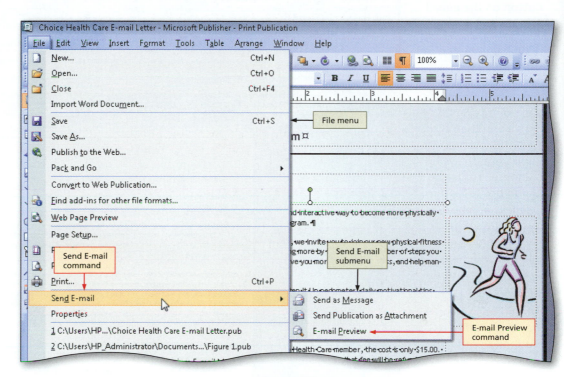

Figure 11

Publisher installed to open and view the publication. Additionally, with a large attachment, you may run the risk of the e-mail being blocked by firewalls and filters at the receiving end.

2

- Click the E-mail Preview command on the Send E-mail submenu (Figure 12).

Experiment

- Scroll through the e-mail letter and try clicking the hyperlinks. The Choice Health Care Web site is fictional and will not open, but the click here hyperlink will display an e-mail dialog box if your system is configured with an e-mail program, such as Microsoft Outlook.

- Click the Close button on any open e-mail window without sending or saving the e-mail.

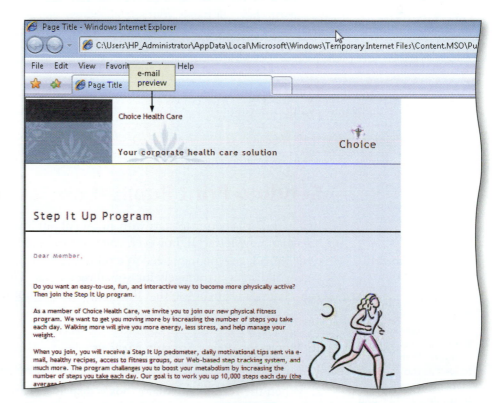

Figure 12

3

- Click the Close button on the e-mail preview.

- If your system is connected to an e-mail program, click File on the menu bar, point to Send E-Mail and then click Send as Message. If Publisher displays a Choose Profile dialog box, click the Profile Name box arrow and select your system's e-mail profile; then click the OK button (Figure 13).

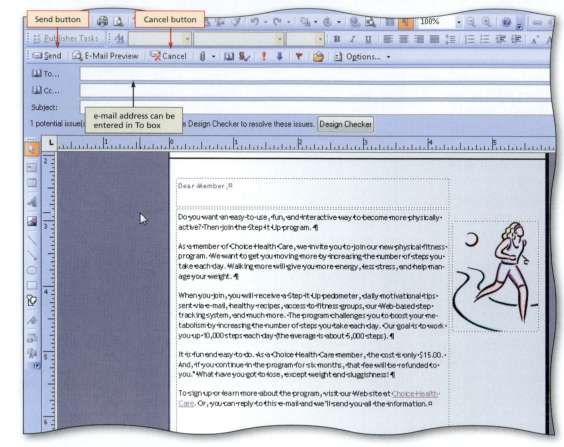

Figure 13

Q&A

What if my system wants to configure Outlook to send an e-mail?

If you are not sure how to configure your system for e-mail, or you do not want to check your e-mail via an e-mail program, click the Cancel button. Configuring your system with an e-mail program is not complicated, however. Windows Vista asks for your name, your e-mail address, and your password. It then determines the kind of e-mail program and connection you need.

4

- If you want to send the e-mail, type your e-mail address in the To box and then click the Send button. To cancel the request, close the window without saving.

BTW

Web Mail
Many e-mail service providers use a Web browser interface, so setting up an e-mail program is not necessary. Corporate and business communications commonly use the Microsoft Outlook e-mail program, which allows access to e-mail addresses for everyone in the company as well as tools to manage other forms of communication and scheduling.

Sending Print Publications as E-Mail Messages

In general, it is better to start with an e-mail publication template such as the e-mail letter or e-mail newsletter. If, however, you want to send a page of another publication as an e-mail message, you may need to modify the width and margins to ensure that the message will display attractively for e-mail recipients. The typical page size of an e-mail message is 5.8×11 inches so that the recipients will not need to scroll horizontally to view the entire width of the message.

To Modify the Paper Size and Margins

1. Click File on the menu bar and then click Page Setup.

2. When the Page Setup dialog box is displayed, if necessary, scroll to the e-mail layouts.

3. Click the Create custom page size preview and then enter the new width and height entries in the Width and Height boxes.

4. Click the OK button.

It is a good idea to send the publication to yourself first to see how it will look before sending it to other recipients.

If you have already created specific print publications that you would like to send electronically, you can convert the publication to a single-page e-mail message. For example, if you create a newsletter for customers, you can send it to your e-mail list as well as distributing it on paper. When you convert your publication, Publisher gives you the options to send the current page or all pages. If you choose to send all pages, Publisher combines the contents of all pages onto one e-mail page.

To Send a Multiple Page Publication as an E-mail Message

1. Open the publication that contains the page or pages that you want to send as an e-mail message.

2. On the File menu, point to Send E-mail, and then click Send as Message.

3. In the Send as Message dialog box, click Send all pages and then click the OK button.

4. Follow the steps.

You can preview this page and rearrange text and graphics. If Publisher cannot determine where to fit some objects, the **Extra Content** task pane will display the objects for you to manually place.

Occasionally, you may encounter unexpected formatting results when sending a page of a publication as an e-mail message. Some of these problems have easy solutions, while others involve the unavoidable loss of formatting. You can take measures to prevent formatting problems as you add and manipulate text and graphics in your publication.

To Quit Publisher

The final step quits Publisher.

1 Click the Close button on the Publisher title bar. If Publisher displays a dialog box, click its No button.

Feature Summary

This feature introduced you to creating an e-mail message by illustrating how to select and format an e-mail template. The feature then showed how to edit both the text boxes and graphics. Next, you learned how to choose a logo design, insert a background, and create an e-mail hyperlink. Finally, the project showed how to preview and send a publication as an e-mail message. The items listed below include all the new Publisher skills you have learned in this chapter.

1. Open an E-Mail Letter Template (PUB 229)
2. Customize the E-Mail Page Size (PUB 230)
3. Edit the Logo (PUB 234)
4. Add a Background (PUB 235)
5. Preview and Send a Publication via E-Mail (PUB 237)

In the Lab

Design and/or create a publication using the guidelines, concepts, and skills presented in this chapter. Labs are listed in order of increasing difficulty.

Lab 1: Creating an E-Mail Featured Product List

Problem: You work for a company that sells music on the Web. Your boss wants you to send an e-mail out to all previous customers advertising the newest songs. You decide to use a Publisher E-mail Featured Product template to design the e-mail message.

Instructions:

1. Start Publisher and choose the e-mail template named Watermark in the Featured Product templates. Select the Aspect color scheme and the Foundry font scheme. Select a short page size.

2. Add a background to your e-mail by using the Background command on the Format menu.

3. Think of a name for your music company and replace it in the heading. Use the phrase, Our Web songs are safe and spyware-free!, as the tag line text.

4. Replace the logo graphic with a piece of clip art. Use the keyword, media, in your search. Replace the logo text with the words, Web Songs.

5. Replace the larger graphic with one picturing an MP3 player. Describe your favorite artist or song in the lower text boxes.

6. Edit the hyperlink at the bottom to reflect your e-mail address.

7. Check the publication for spelling and design errors.

8. Save the publication with the file name, Lab EF-1 Web Songs E-Mail. Preview the e-mail.

In the Lab

Lab 2: Sending a Newsletter as an E-Mail Message

Problem: You created the newsletter shown in Figure 2-1 on page PUB 75. You decide to send the first page of the newsletter as an e-mail publication.

Instructions:

1. Open the file you created in Project 2. (If you did not create the publication in Project 2, see your instructor for a copy.)

2. On the File menu, point to Send E-mail, and then click Send as Message.

3. When Publisher asks if you want to save the publication, click the No option.

4. When Publisher asks if you want to send one page or multiple pages, select one page.

5. Scroll through and identify articles, lists, and graphics from the original newsletter. Delete any objects that you feel are not needed in the e-mail message.

6. In the Format Publication task pane, locate the Extra Content area. Insert two appropriate objects back into the publication.

7. Add a background of your choice.

8. Check the publication for spelling and design errors. If Publisher displays the error that text is not Web-ready, choose to use it in the e-mail message as an image.

9. Save the publication as Lab EF-2 Communiquarium E-Mail. Preview the e-mail and send it to your instructor.

Appendix A
Project Planning Guidelines

Using Project Planning Guidelines

The process of communicating specific information to others is a learned, rational skill. Computers and software, especially Microsoft Office 2007, can help you develop ideas and present detailed information to a particular audience.

Using Microsoft Office 2007, you can create projects such as Word documents, Excel spreadsheets, Access databases, and PowerPoint presentations. Computer hardware and productivity software such as Microsoft Office 2007 minimizes much of the laborious work of drafting and revising projects. Some communicators handwrite ideas in note-books, others compose directly on the computer, and others have developed unique strategies that work for their own particular thinking and writing styles.

No matter what method you use to plan a project, follow specific guidelines to arrive at a final product that presents information correctly and effectively (Figure A–1). Use some aspects of these guidelines every time you undertake a project, and others as needed in specific instances. For example, in determining content for a project, you may decide that a bar chart communicates trends more effectively than a paragraph of text. If so, you would create this graphical element and insert it in an Excel spreadsheet, a Word document, or a PowerPoint slide.

Determine the Project's Purpose

Begin by clearly defining why you are undertaking this assignment. For example, you may want to track monetary donations collected for your club's fundraising drive. Alternatively, you may be urging students to vote for a particular candidate in the next election. Once you clearly understand the purpose of your task, begin to draft ideas of how best to communicate this information.

Analyze Your Audience

Learn about the people who will read, analyze, or view your work. Where are they employed? What are their educational backgrounds? What are their expectations? What questions do they have?

PROJECT PLANNING GUIDELINES

1. DETERMINE THE PROJECT'S PURPOSE
Why are you undertaking the project?

2. ANALYZE YOUR AUDIENCE
Who are the people who will use your work?

3. GATHER POSSIBLE CONTENT
What information exists, and in what forms?

4. DETERMINE WHAT CONTENT TO PRESENT TO YOUR AUDIENCE
What information will best communicate the project's purpose to your audience?

Figure A–1

Design experts suggest drawing a mental picture of these people or finding photographs of people who fit this profile so that you can develop a project with the audience in mind.

By knowing your audience members, you can tailor a project to meet their interests and needs. You will not present them with information they already possess, and you will not omit the information they need to know.

Example: Your assignment is to raise the profile of your college's nursing program in the community. How much do they know about your college and the nursing curriculum? What are the admission requirements? How many of the applicants admitted complete the program? What percent pass the state Boards?

Gather Possible Content

Rarely are you in a position to develop all the material for a project. Typically, you would begin by gathering existing information that may reside in spreadsheets or databases. Web sites, pamphlets, magazine and newspaper articles, and books could provide insights of how others have approached your topic. Personal interviews often provide perspectives not available by any other means. Consider video and audio clips as potential sources for material that might complement or support the factual data you uncover.

Determine What Content to Present to Your Audience

Experienced designers recommend writing three or four major ideas you want an audience member to remember after reading or viewing your project. It also is helpful to envision your project's endpoint, the key fact you wish to emphasize. All project elements should lead to this ending point.

As you make content decisions, you also need to think about other factors. Presentation of the project content is an important consideration. For example, will your brochure be printed on thick, colored paper or transparencies? Will your PowerPoint presentation be viewed in a classroom with excellent lighting and a bright projector, or will it be viewed on a notebook computer monitor? Determine relevant time factors, such as the length of time to develop the project, how long readers will spend reviewing your project, or the amount of time allocated for your speaking engagement. Your project will need to accommodate all of these constraints.

Decide whether a graph, photograph, or artistic element can express or emphasize a particular concept. The right hemisphere of the brain processes images by attaching an emotion to them, so audience members are more apt to recall these graphics long term rather than just reading text.

As you select content, be mindful of the order in which you plan to present information. Readers and audience members generally remember the first and last pieces of information they see and hear, so you should put the most important information at the top or bottom of the page.

Summary

When creating a project, it is beneficial to follow some basic guidelines from the outset. By taking some time at the beginning of the process to determine the project's purpose, analyze the audience, gather possible content, and determine what content to present to the audience, you can produce a project that is informative, relevant, and effective.

Appendix B

Introduction to Microsoft Office 2007

What Is Microsoft Office 2007?

Microsoft Office 2007 is a collection of the more popular Microsoft application software. It is available in Basic, Home and Student, Standard, Small Business, Professional, Ultimate, Professional Plus, and Enterprise editions. Each edition consists of a group of programs, collectively called a suite. Table B-1 lists the suites and their components. **Microsoft Office Professional Edition 2007** includes these six programs: Microsoft Office Word 2007, Microsoft Office Excel 2007, Microsoft Office Access 2007, Microsoft Office PowerPoint 2007, Microsoft Office Publisher 2007, and Microsoft Office Outlook 2007. The programs in the Office suite allow you to work efficiently, communicate effectively, and improve the appearance of the projects you create.

Table B–1

	Microsoft Office Basic 2007	Microsoft Office Home & Student 2007	Microsoft Office Standard 2007	Microsoft Office Small Business 2007	Microsoft Office Professional 2007	Microsoft Office Ultimate 2007	Microsoft Office Professional Plus 2007	Microsoft Office Enterprise 2007
Microsoft Office Word 2007	✓	✓	✓	✓	✓	✓	✓	✓
Microsoft Office Excel 2007	✓	✓	✓	✓	✓	✓	✓	✓
Microsoft Office Access 2007					✓	✓	✓	✓
Microsoft Office PowerPoint 2007		✓	✓	✓	✓	✓	✓	✓
Microsoft Office Publisher 2007				✓	✓	✓	✓	✓
Microsoft Office Outlook 2007	✓		✓				✓	✓
Microsoft Office OneNote 2007		✓				✓		
Microsoft Office Outlook 2007 with Business Contact Manager				✓	✓	✓		
Microsoft Office InfoPath 2007						✓	✓	✓
Integrated Enterprise Content Management						✓	✓	✓
Electronic Forms						✓	✓	✓
Advanced Information Rights Management and Policy Capabilities						✓	✓	✓
Microsoft Office Communicator 2007							✓	✓
Microsoft Office Groove 2007						✓		✓

Microsoft has bundled additional programs in some versions of Office 2007, in addition to the main group of Office programs. Table B–1 on the previous page lists the components of the various Office suites.

In addition to the Office 2007 programs noted previously, Office 2007 suites can contain other programs. Microsoft Office OneNote 2007 is a digital notebook program that allows you to gather and share various types of media, such as text, graphics, video, audio, and digital handwriting. Microsoft Office InfoPath 2007 is a program that allows you to create and use electronic forms to gather information. Microsoft Office Groove 2007 provides collaborative workspaces in real time. Additional services that are oriented toward the enterprise solution also are available.

Office 2007 and the Internet, World Wide Web, and Intranets

Office 2007 allows you to take advantage of the Internet, the World Wide Web, and intranets. The Microsoft Windows operating system includes a **browser**, which is a program that allows you to locate and view a Web page. The Windows browser is called Internet Explorer.

One method of viewing a Web page is to use the browser to enter the Web address for the Web page. Another method of viewing a Web page is clicking a hyperlink. A **hyperlink** is colored or underlined text or a graphic that, when clicked, connects to another Web page. Hyperlinks placed in Office 2007 documents allow for direct access to a Web site of interest.

An **intranet** is a private network, such as a network used within a company or organization for internal communication. Like the Internet, hyperlinks are used within an intranet to access documents, pages, and other destinations on the intranet. Unlike the Internet, the materials on the network are available only for those who are part of the private network.

Online Collaboration Using Office

Organizations that, in the past, were able to make important information available only to a select few, now can make their information accessible to a wider range of individuals who use programs such as Office 2007 and Internet Explorer. Office 2007 allows colleagues to use the Internet or an intranet as a central location to view documents, manage files, and work together.

Each of the Office 2007 programs makes publishing documents on a Web server as simple as saving a file on a hard disk. Once placed on the Web server, users can view and edit the documents and conduct Web discussions and live online meetings.

Using Microsoft Office 2007

The various Microsoft Office 2007 programs each specialize in a particular task. This section describes the general functions of the more widely used Office 2007 programs, along with how they are used to access the Internet or an intranet.

Microsoft Office Word 2007

Microsoft Office Word 2007 is a full-featured word processing program that allows you to create many types of personal and business documents, including flyers, letters, resumes, business documents, and academic reports.

Word's AutoCorrect, spelling, and grammar features help you proofread documents for errors in spelling and grammar by identifying the errors and offering suggestions for corrections as you type. The live word count feature provides you with a constantly updating word count as you enter and edit text. To assist with creating specific documents, such as a business letter or resume, Word provides templates, which provide a formatted document before you type the text of the document. Quick Styles provide a live preview of styles from the Style gallery, allowing you to preview styles in the document before actually applying them.

Word automates many often-used tasks and provides you with powerful desktop publishing tools to use as you create professional looking brochures, advertisements, and newsletters. SmartArt allows you to insert interpretive graphics based on document content.

Word makes it easier for you to share documents for collaboration. The Send feature opens an e-mail window with the active document attached. The Compare Documents feature allows you easily to identify changes when comparing different document versions.

Word 2007 and the Internet   Word makes it possible to design and publish Web pages on the Internet or an intranet, insert a hyperlink to a Web page in a word processing document, as well as access and search the content of other Web pages.

Microsoft Office Excel 2007

Microsoft Office Excel 2007 is a spreadsheet program that allows you to organize data, complete calculations, graph data, develop professional looking reports, publish organized data to the Web, and access real-time data from Web sites.

In addition to its mathematical functionality, Excel 2007 provides tools for visually comparing data. For instance, when comparing a group of values in cells, you can set cell backgrounds with bars proportional to the value of the data in the cell. You can also set cell backgrounds with full-color backgrounds, or use a color scale to facilitate interpretation of data values.

Excel 2007 provides strong formatting support for tables with the new Style Preview gallery.

Excel 2007 and the Internet   Using Excel 2007, you can create hyperlinks within a worksheet to access other Office documents on the network or on the Internet. Worksheets saved as static, or unchanging Web pages can be viewed using a browser. The person viewing static Web pages cannot change them.

In addition, you can create and run queries that retrieve information from a Web page and insert the information directly into a worksheet.

Microsoft Office Access 2007

Microsoft Office Access 2007 is a comprehensive database management system (DBMS). A **database** is a collection of data organized in a manner that allows access, retrieval, and use of that data. Access 2007 allows you to create a database; add, change, and delete data in the database; sort data in the database; retrieve data from the database; and create forms and reports using the data in the database.

Access 2007 and the Internet   Access 2007 lets you generate reports, which are summaries that show only certain data from the database, based on user requirements.

Microsoft Office PowerPoint 2007

Microsoft Office PowerPoint 2007 is a complete presentation graphics program that allows you to produce professional looking presentations. With PowerPoint 2007, you can create informal presentations using overhead transparencies, electronic presentations using a projection device attached to a personal computer, formal presentations using 35mm slides or a CD, or you can run virtual presentations on the Internet.

PowerPoint 2007 and the Internet   PowerPoint 2007 allows you to publish presentations on the Internet or other networks.

Microsoft Office Publisher 2007

Microsoft Office Publisher 2007 is a desktop publishing program (DTP) that allows you to design and produce professional quality documents (newsletters, flyers, brochures, business cards, Web sites, and so on) that combine text, graphics, and photographs. Desktop publishing software provides a variety of tools, including design templates, graphic manipulation tools, color schemes or libraries, and various page wizards and templates. For large jobs, businesses use desktop publishing software to design publications that are **camera ready**, which means the files are suitable for production by outside commercial printers. Publisher 2007 also allows you to locate commercial printers, service bureaus, and copy shops willing to accept customer files created in Publisher.

Publisher 2007 allows you to design a unique image, or logo, using one of more than 45 master design sets. This, in turn, permits you to use the same design for all your printed documents (letters, business cards, brochures, and advertisements) and Web pages. Publisher includes 70 coordinated color schemes; 30 font schemes; more than 10,000 high-quality clip art images; 1,500 photographs; 1,000 Web-art graphics; 340 animated graphics; and hundreds of unique Design Gallery elements (quotations, sidebars, and so on). If you wish, you also can download additional images from the Microsoft Office Online Web page on the Microsoft Web site.

Publisher 2007 and the Internet   Publisher 2007 allows you easily to create a multipage Web site with custom color schemes, photographic images, animated images, and sounds.

Microsoft Office Outlook 2007

Microsoft Office Outlook 2007 is a powerful communications and scheduling program that helps you communicate with others, keep track of your contacts, and organize your schedule. Outlook 2007 allows you to view a To-Do bar containing tasks and appointments from your Outlook calendar. Outlook 2007 allows you to send and receive electronic mail (e-mail) and permits you to engage in real-time communication with family, friends, or coworkers using instant messaging. Outlook 2007 also provides you with the means to organize your contacts, and you can track e-mail messages, meetings, and notes with a particular contact. Outlook's Calendar, Contacts, Tasks, and Notes components aid in this organization. Contact information is available from the Outlook Calendar, Mail, Contacts, and Task components by accessing the Find a Contact feature. **Personal information management (PIM)** programs such as Outlook provide a way for individuals and workgroups to organize, find, view, and share information easily.

Microsoft Office 2007 Help

At any time while you are using one of the Office programs, you can interact with **Microsoft Office 2007 Help** for that program and display information about any topic associated with the program. Several categories of help are available. In all programs, you can access Help by pressing the F1 key on the keyboard. In Publisher 2007 and Outlook 2007, the Help window can be opened by clicking the Help menu and then selecting Microsoft Office Publisher or Outlook Help command, or by entering search text in the 'Type a question for help' text box in the upper-right corner of the program window. In the other Office programs, clicking the Microsoft Office Help button near the upper-right corner of the program window opens the program Help window.

The Help window in all programs provides several methods for accessing help about a particular topic, and has tools for navigating around Help. Appendix C contains detailed instructions for using Help.

Collaboration and SharePoint

While not part of the Microsoft Office 2007 suites, SharePoint is a Microsoft tool that allows Office 2007 users to share data using collaborative tools that are integrated into the main Office programs. SharePoint consists of Windows SharePoint Services, Office SharePoint Server 2007, and, optionally, Office SharePoint Designer 2007.

Windows SharePoint Services provides the platform for collaboration programs and services. Office SharePoint Server 2007 is built on top of Windows SharePoint Services. The result of these two products is the ability to create SharePoint sites. A SharePoint site is a Web site that provides users with a virtual place for collaborating and communicating with their colleagues while working together on projects, documents, ideas, and information. Each member of a group with access to the SharePoint site has the ability to contribute to the material stored there. The basic building blocks of SharePoint sites are lists and libraries. Lists contain collections of information, such as calendar items, discussion points, contacts, and links. Lists can be edited to add or delete information. Libraries are similar to lists, but include both files and information about files. Types of libraries include document, picture, and forms libraries.

The most basic type of SharePoint site is called a Workspace, which is used primarily for collaboration. Different types of Workspaces can be created using SharePoint to suit different needs. SharePoint provides templates, or outlines of these Workspaces, that can be filled in to create the Workspace. Each of the different types of Workspace templates contain a different collection of lists and libraries, reflecting the purpose of the Workspace. You can create a Document Workspace to facilitate collaboration on documents. A Document Workspace contains a document library for documents and supporting files, a Links list that allows you to maintain relevant resource links for the document, a Tasks list for listing and assigning To-Do items to team members, and other links as needed. Meeting Workspaces allow users to plan and organize a meeting, with components such as Attendees, Agenda, and a Document Library. Social Meeting Workspaces provide a place to plan social events, with lists and libraries such as Attendees, Directions, Image/Logo, Things To Bring, Discussions, and Picture Library. A Decision Meeting Workspace is a Meeting Workspace with a focus on review and decision-making, with lists and libraries such as Objectives, Attendees, Agenda, Document Library, Tasks, and Decisions.

Users also can create a SharePoint site called a WebParts page, which is built from modules called WebParts. WebParts are modular units of information that contain a title bar and content that reflects the type of WebPart. For instance, an image WebPart would contain a title bar and an image. WebParts allow you quickly to create and modify a SharePoint site, and allow for the creation of a unique site that can allow users to access and make changes to information stored on the site.

Large SharePoint sites that include multiple pages can be created using templates as well. Groups needing more refined and targeted sharing options than those available with SharePoint Server 2007 and Windows SharePoint Services can add SharePoint Designer 2007 to create a site that meets their specific needs.

Depending on which components have been selected for inclusion on the site, users can view a team calendar, view links, read announcements, and view and edit group documents and projects. SharePoint sites can be set up so that documents are checked in and out, much like a library, to prevent multiple users from making changes simultaneously. Once a SharePoint site is set up, Office programs are used to perform maintenance of the site. For example, changes in the team calendar are updated using Outlook 2007, and changes that users make in Outlook 2007 are reflected on the SharePoint site. Office 2007 programs include a Publish feature that allows users easily to save file updates to a SharePoint site. Team members can be notified about changes made to material on the site either by e-mail or by a news feed, meaning that users do not have to go to the site to check to see if anything has been updated since they last viewed or worked on it. The search feature in SharePoint allows users quickly to find information on a large site.

Appendix C
Microsoft Office Publisher 2007 Help

Using Microsoft Office Publisher Help

This appendix shows how to use Microsoft Office Publisher Help. At any time while you are using one of the Microsoft Office 2007 programs, you can use Office Help to display information about all topics associated with the program. To illustrate the use of Office Help, this appendix uses Microsoft Office Publisher 2007. Help in other Office 2007 programs responds in a similar fashion.

In Office 2007, Help is presented in a window that has Web browser-style navigation buttons. Each Office 2007 program has its own Help home page, which is the starting Help page that is displayed in the Help window. If your computer is connected to the Internet, the contents of the Help page reflect both the local help files installed on the computer and material from Microsoft's Web site. As shown in Figure C–1, four methods for accessing Publisher's Help are available:

1. Microsoft Office Publisher 'Type a question for help' text box near the upper-right corner of the Publisher window
2. Microsoft Office Publisher Help button on the Standard toolbar
3. Microsoft Office Publisher Help command on the Help menu
4. Function key F1 on the keyboard

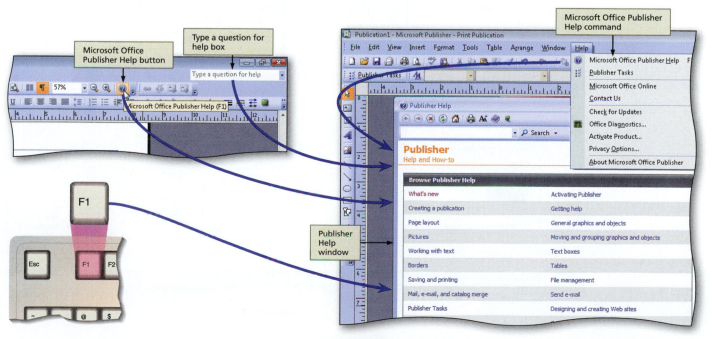

Figure C–1

To Open the Publisher Help Window

The following steps open the Publisher Help window and maximize the window.

1

• Start Microsoft Publisher, if necessary. Press F1 to open the Publisher Help window (Figure C–2).

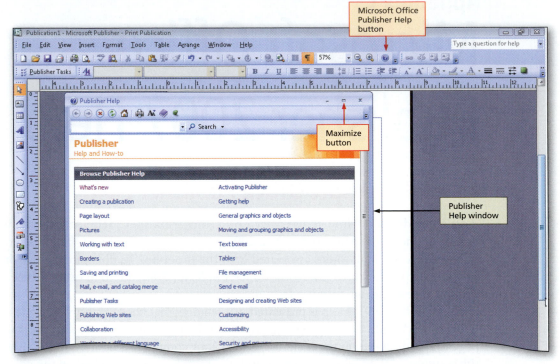

Figure C–2

2

• Click the Maximize button on the Help title bar to maximize the Help window (Figure C–3).

Figure C–3

The Publisher Help Window

The Publisher Help window provides several methods for accessing help about a particular topic, and also has tools for navigating around Help. Methods for accessing Help include searching the help content installed with Publisher, or searching the online Office content maintained by Microsoft.

Figure C–3 shows the main Publisher Help window. To navigate Help, the Publisher Help window includes search features that allow you to search on a word or phrase about which you want help; the Connection Status button, which allows you to control where Publisher Help searches for content; toolbar buttons; and links to major Help categories.

Search Features

You can perform Help searches on words or phrases to find information about any Publisher feature using the 'Type words to search for' text box and the Search button (Figure C–4a).

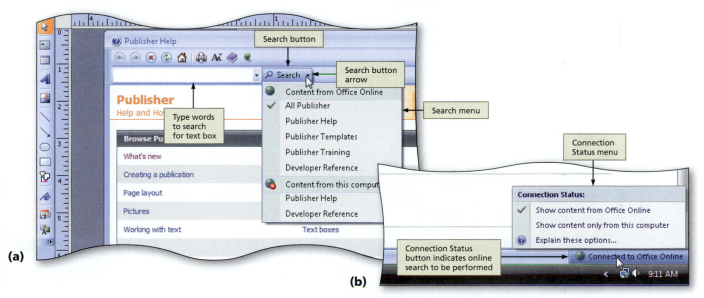

Figure C–4

Publisher Help offers the user the option of searching the online Help Web pages maintained by Microsoft or the offline Help files placed on your computer when you install Publisher. You can specify whether Publisher Help should search online or offline from two places: the Connection Status button on the status bar of the Publisher Help window, or the Search button arrow on the toolbar. The Connection Status button indicates whether Help currently is set up to work with online or offline information sources. Clicking the Connection Status button provides a menu with commands for selecting online or offline searches (Figure C–4b). The Connection Status menu allows the user to select whether Help searches will return content only from the computer (offline), or content from the computer and from Office Online (online).

Clicking the Search button arrow also provides a menu with commands for an online or offline search (Figure C–4a). These commands determine the source of information that Help searches for during the current Help session only. For example, assume that your preferred search is an offline search because you often do not have Internet access. You would set Connection Status to 'Show content only from this computer'. When you have Internet access, you can select an online search from the Search menu to search Office Online for information for your current search session only. Your search will use the Office Online resources until you quit Help. The next time you start Help, the Connection Status once again will be offline. In addition to setting the source of information that Help searches for during the current Help session, you can use the Search menu to further target the current search to one of four subcategories of online Help: Publisher Help, Publisher Templates, Publisher Training, and Developer Reference. The local search further can target one subcategory, Developer Reference.

In addition to searching for a word or string of text, you can use the links provided on the Browse Publisher Help area (Figure C–3 on page APP 10) to search for help on a topic. These links direct you to major help categories. From each major category, subcategories are available to further refine your search.

Finally, you can use the Table of Contents for Publisher Help to search for a topic the same way you would in a hard copy book. The Table of Contents is accessed via a toolbar button.

Toolbar Buttons

You can use toolbar buttons to navigate through the results of your search. The toolbar buttons are located on the toolbar near the top of the Help Window (Figure C–5). The toolbar buttons contain navigation buttons as well as buttons that perform other useful and common tasks in Publisher Help, such as printing.

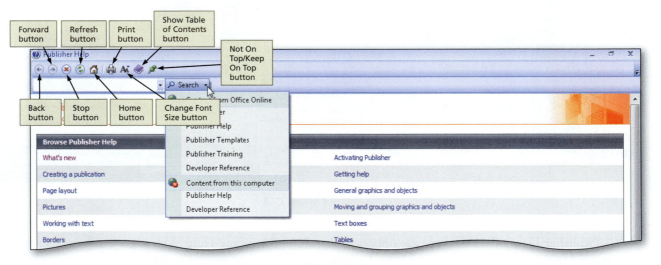

Figure C–5

The Publisher Help navigation buttons are the Back, Forward, Stop, Refresh, and Home buttons. These five buttons behave like the navigation buttons in a Web browser window. You can use the Back button to go back one window, the Forward button to go forward one window, the Stop button to stop loading the current page, and the Home button to redisplay the Help home page in the Help window. Use the Refresh button to reload the information requested into the Help window from its original source. When getting Help information online, this button provides the most current information from the Microsoft Help Web site.

The buttons located to the right of the navigation buttons — Print, Change Font Size, Show Table of Contents, and Not On Top — provide you with access to useful and common commands. The Print button prints the contents of the open Help window. The Change Font Size button customizes the Help window by increasing or decreasing the size of its text. The Show Table of Contents button opens a pane on the left side of the Help window that shows the Table of Contents for Publisher Help. You can use the Table of Contents for Publisher Help to navigate through the contents of Publisher Help much as you would use the Table of Contents in a book to search for a topic. The Not On Top button is an example of a toggle button, which is a button that can be switched back and forth between two states. It determines how the Publisher Help window behaves relative to other windows. When clicked, the Not On Top button changes to Keep On Top. In this state, it does not allow other windows from Publisher or other programs to cover the Publisher Help window when those windows are the active windows. When in the Not On Top state, the button allows other windows to be opened or moved on top of the Publisher Help window.

You can customize the size and placement of the Help window. Resize the window using the Maximize and Restore buttons, or by dragging the window to a desired size. Relocate the Help window by dragging the title bar to a new location on the screen.

Searching Publisher Help

Once the Publisher Help window is open, several methods exist for navigating Publisher Help. You can search for help by using any of the three following methods from the Help window:

1. Enter search text in the 'Type words to search for' text box
2. Click the links in the Help window
3. Use the Table of Contents

To Obtain Help Using the Type words to search for Text Box

Assume for the following example that you want to know more about symbols. The following steps use the 'Type words to search for' text box to obtain useful information about symbols by entering the word, symbol, as search text. The steps also navigate in the Publisher Help window.

1

• Type symbol in the 'Type words to search for' text box at the top of the Publisher Help window.

• Click the Search button arrow to display the Search menu (Figure C-6).

• If it is not selected already, click All Publisher on the Search menu to select the command. If All Publisher is already selected, click the Search button arrow again to close the Search menu.

Q&A

Why select All Publisher on the Search menu?

Selecting All Publisher on the Search menu ensures that Publisher Help will search all possible sources for information on your search term. It will produce the most complete search results.

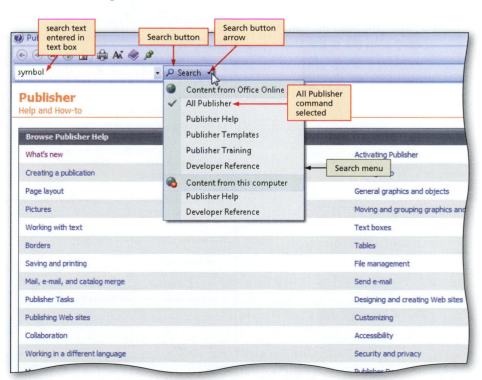

Figure C–6

2

- Click the Search button to display the search results (Figure C–7).

Q&A

Why do my results differ?

If you do not have an Internet connection, your results will reflect only the content of the Help files on your computer. When searching for help online, results also can change as material is added, deleted, and updated on the online Help Web pages maintained by Microsoft.

Q&A

Why were my search results not very helpful?

When initiating a search, keep in mind to check the spelling of the search text and to keep your search very specific, with fewer than seven words, to return the most accurate results.

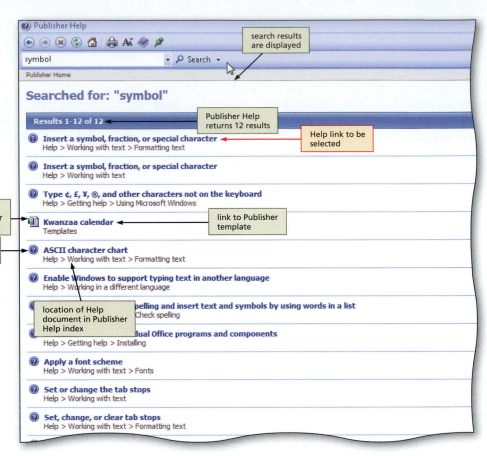

Figure C–7

3

- Click the 'Insert a symbol, fraction, or special character' link to open the Help document associated with the link in the Help window (Figure C–8).

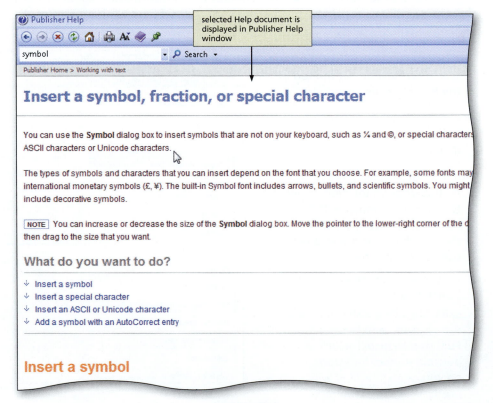

Figure C–8

4

- Click the Home button on the taskbar to clear the search results and redisplay the Publisher Help home page (Figure C–9).

Figure C–9

To Obtain Help Using the Help Links

If your topic of interest is listed in the Browse Publisher Help area, you can click the link to begin browsing Publisher Help categories instead of entering search text. You browse Publisher Help just like you would browse a Web site. If you know in which category to find your Help information, you may wish to use these links. The following steps find the symbol Help information using the category links from the Publisher Help home page.

1

- Click the 'Working with text' link to open the 'Working with text' page.

- Click the 'Insert a symbol, fraction, or special character' link to open the Help document associated with the link (Figure C–10).

Q&A

What does the Show All link do?

In many Help documents, additional

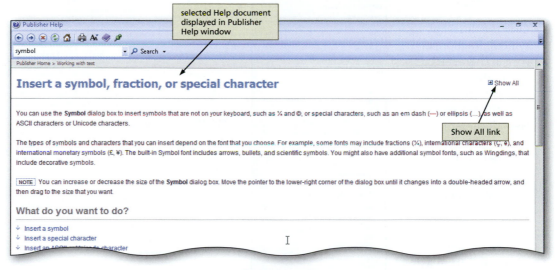

Figure C–10

information about terms and features is available by clicking a link in the document to display additional information in the Help document. Clicking the Show All link opens all the links in the Help document that expand to additional text.

To Obtain Help Using the Help Table of Contents

A third way to find Help in Publisher is through the Help Table of Contents. You can browse through the Table of Contents to display information about a particular topic or to familiarize yourself with Publisher. The following steps access the symbol Help information by browsing through the Table of Contents.

- Click the Home button on the toolbar.

- Click the Show Table of Contents button on the toolbar to open the Table of Contents pane on the left side of the Help window. If necessary, click the Maximize button on the Help title bar to maximize the window (Figure C–11).

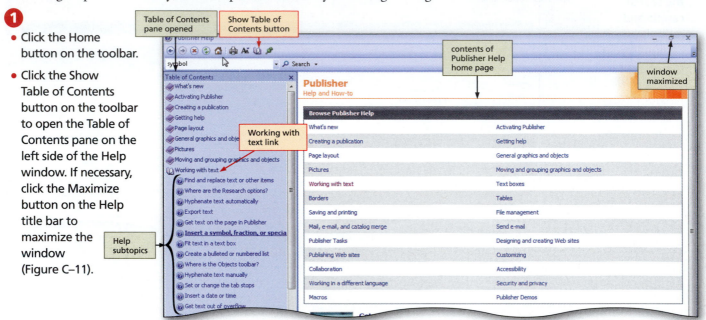

Figure C–11

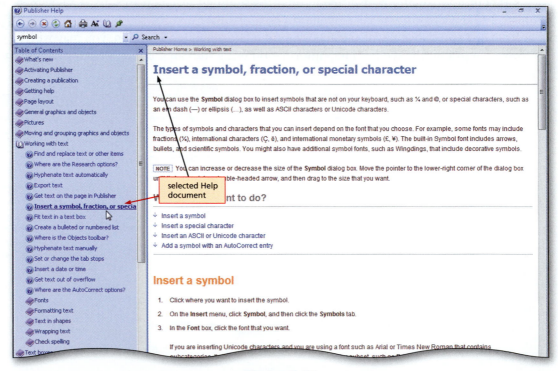

- Click the 'Working with text' link in the Table of Contents pane to view a list of Help subtopics.

- Click the 'Insert a symbol, fraction, or special character' link in the Table of Contents pane to view the selected Help document in the right pane (Figure C–12).

Q&A

How do I remove the Table of Contents pane when I am finished with it?

The Show Table of Contents button acts as a toggle switch. When the Table of Contents pane is visible, the button changes to Hide Table of Contents. Clicking it hides the Table of Contents pane and changes the button to Show Table of Contents.

Figure C–12

Obtaining Help while Working in Publisher

Often you may need help while working on a document without already having the Help window open. For example, you may be unsure about how a particular command works, or you may be presented with a dialog box that you are not sure how to use. Rather than opening the Help window and initiating a search, Publisher Help provides you with the ability to search directly for help.

Figure C–13 shows a dialog box with a Help button in it. Pressing the F1 key or clicking the Help button in the title bar while the dialog box is displayed opens a Help window. The Help window contains help about that dialog box, if available. If no help file is available for that particular dialog box, then the main Help window opens.

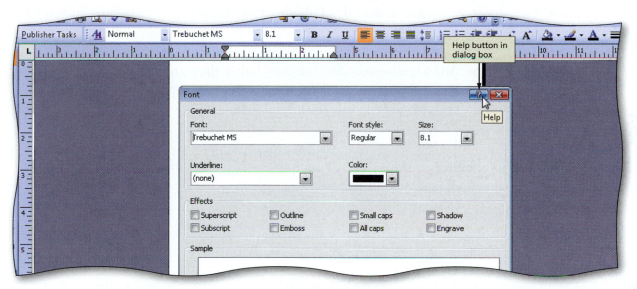

Figure C–13

Use Help

1 Obtaining Help Using Search Text

Instructions: Perform the following tasks using Publisher Help.

1. Use the 'Type words to search for' text box to obtain help about crop marks. Use the Connection Status menu to search online help if you have an Internet connection.

2. Click Print crop marks in the list of links in the search results. Double-click the Microsoft Office Publisher Help window title bar to maximize it. Read and print the information. At the top of the printout, write down the number of links Publisher Help found.

3. Use the Search menu to search for help offline. Repeat the search from Step 1. At the top of the printout, write down the number of links that Publisher Help found searching offline. Submit the printouts as specified by your instructor.

4. Use the 'Type words to search for' text box to search for information online about adjusting line spacing. Click the 'Add a line between text columns' link in the search results. If necessary, maximize the Microsoft Office 2007 Publisher Help window. Read and print the contents of the window. Close the Microsoft Office Publisher Help window. Submit the printouts as specified by your instructor.

5. For each of the following words and phrases, click one link in the search results, click the Show All link, and then print the page: tables; date; print preview; word count; and borders. Submit the printouts as specified by your instructor.

2 Expanding on Publisher Help Basics

Instructions: Use Publisher Help to better understand its features and answer the questions listed below. Answer the questions on your own paper, or submit the printed Help information as specified by your instructor.

1. Use Help to find out how to customize the Help window. Change the font size to the smallest option and then print the contents of the Microsoft Office Publisher Help window. Change the font size back to its original setting. Close the window.

2. Press the F1 key. Search for information about charts, restricting the search results to Publisher Templates. Print the first page of the Search results.

3. Search for information about charts, restricting the search results to Publisher Help files. Print the first page of the Search results.

4. Use Publisher Help to find out what happened to the Office Assistant, a feature in the previous version of Publisher. Print out the Help document that contains the answer.

Appendix D
Publishing Office 2007 Web Pages to a Web Server

With the Office 2007 programs, you use the Save As command on the Office Button menu or the Save As command on the File menu in Publisher to save a Web page to a Web server using one of two techniques: Web folders or File Transfer Protocol. A **Web folder** is an Office shortcut to a Web server. **File Transfer Protocol** (**FTP**) is an Internet standard that allows computers to exchange files with other computers on the Internet.

You should contact your network system administrator or technical support staff at your Internet access provider to determine if their Web server supports Web folders, FTP, or both, and to obtain necessary permissions to access the Web server. If you decide to publish Web pages using a Web folder, you must have the Office Server Extensions (OSE) installed on your computer.

Using Web Folders to Publish Office 2007 Web Pages

When publishing to a Web folder, someone first must create the Web folder before you can save to it. If you are granted permission to create a Web folder, you must obtain the Web address of the Web server, a user name, and possibly a password that allows you to access the Web server. You also must decide on a name for the Web folder. Table D–1 explains how to create a Web folder.

Office 2007 adds the name of the Web folder to the list of current Web folders. You can save to this folder, open files in the folder, rename the folder, or perform any operations you would to a folder on your hard disk. You can use your Office 2007 program or Windows Explorer to access this folder. Table D–2 explains how to save to a Web folder.

Table D–1 Creating a Web Folder
1. In applications with ribbons, click the Office Button and then click Save As or Open. In applications with menus, click Save As or Open on the File menu.
2. When the Save As dialog box (or Open dialog box) appears, click the Tools button arrow, and then click Map Network Drive... When the Map Network Drive dialog box is displayed, click the 'Connect to a Web site that you can use to store your documents and pictures' link.
3. When the Add Network Location Wizard dialog box appears, click the Next button. If necessary, click Choose a custom network location. Click the Next button. Click the View examples link, type the Internet or network address, and then click the Next button. Click 'Log on anonymously' to deselect the check box, type your user name in the User name text box, and then click the Next button. Enter the name you want to call this network place and then click the Next button. Click to deselect the 'Open this network location when I click Finish' check box, and then click the Finish button.

Table D–2 Saving to a Web Folder
1. In applications with ribbons, click the Office Button, click Save As. In applications with menus, click Save As on the File menu.
2. When the Save As dialog box is displayed, type the Web page file name in the File name text box. Do not press the ENTER key.
3. Click the Save as type box arrow and then click Web Page to select the Web Page format.
4. Click Computer in the Navigation pane.
5. Double-click the Web folder name in the Network Location list.
6. If the Enter Network Password dialog box appears, type the user name and password in the respective text boxes and then click the OK button.
7. Click the Save button in the Save As dialog box.

Using FTP to Publish Office 2007 Web Pages

When publishing a Web page using FTP, you first must add the FTP location to your computer before you can save to it. An FTP location, also called an **FTP site**, is a collection of files that reside on an FTP server. In this case, the FTP server is the Web server.

To add an FTP location, you must obtain the name of the FTP site, which usually is the address (URL) of the FTP server, and a user name and a password that allows you to access the FTP server. You save and open the Web pages on the FTP server using the name of the FTP site. Table D–3 explains how to add an FTP site.

Office 2007 adds the name of the FTP site to the FTP locations list in the Save As and Open dialog boxes. You can open and save files using this list. Table D–4 explains how to save to an FTP location.

Table D–3 Adding an FTP Location
1. In applications with ribbons, click the Office Button and then click Save As or Open. In applications with menus, click Save As or Open on the File menu.
2. When the Save As dialog box (or Open dialog box) appears, click the Tools button arrow, and then click Map Network Drive... When the Map Network Drive dialog box is displayed, click the 'Connect to a Web site that you can use to store your documents and pictures' link.
3. When the Add Network Location Wizard dialog box appears, click the Next button. If necessary, click Choose a custom network location. Click the Next button. Click the View examples link, type the Internet or network address, and then click the Next button. If you have a user name for the site, click to deselect 'Log on anonymously' and type your user name in the User name text box, and then click Next. If the site allows anonymous logon, click Next. Type a name for the location, click Next, click to deselect the 'Open this network location when I click Finish' check box, and click Finish. Click the OK button.
4. Close the Save As or the Open dialog box.

Table D–4 Saving to an FTP Location
1. In applications with ribbons, click the Office Button and then click Save As. In applications with menus, click Save As on the File menu.
2. When the Save As dialog box is displayed, type the Web page file name in the File name text box. Do not press the ENTER key.
3. Click the Save as type box arrow and then click Web Page to select the Web Page format.
4. Click Computer in the Navigation pane.
5. Double-click the name of the FTP site in the Network Location list.
6. When the FTP Log On dialog box appears, enter your user name and password and then click the OK button.
7. Click the Save button in the Save As dialog box.

Customizing Microsoft Office Publisher 2007

This appendix explains how to change the screen resolution in Windows Vista to the resolution used in this book. It also describes how to customize the Publisher toolbars and menus.

Changing Screen Resolution

Screen resolution indicates the number of pixels (dots) that the computer uses to display the letters, numbers, graphics, and background you see on the screen. When you increase the screen resolution, Windows displays more information on the screen, but the information decreases in size. The reverse also is true: as you decrease the screen resolution, Windows displays less information on the screen, but the information increases in size.

The screen resolution usually is stated as the product of two numbers, such as 1024×768 (pronounced "ten twenty-four by seven sixty-eight"). A 1024×768 screen resolution results in a display of 1,024 distinct pixels on each of 768 lines, or about 786,432 pixels. The figures in this book were created using a screen resolution of 1024×768.

The screen resolutions most commonly used today are 800×600 and 1024×768, although some Office specialists set their computers at a much higher screen resolution, such as 2048×1536.

To Change the Screen Resolution

The following steps change the screen resolution to 1024×768 to match the figures in this book.

- If necessary, minimize all programs so that the Windows Vista desktop appears.

- Right-click the Windows Vista desktop to display the Windows Vista desktop shortcut menu (Figure E–1).

Figure E–1

• Click Personalize on the shortcut menu to open the Personalization window.

• Click Display Settings in the Personalization window to display the Display Settings dialog box (Figure E–2).

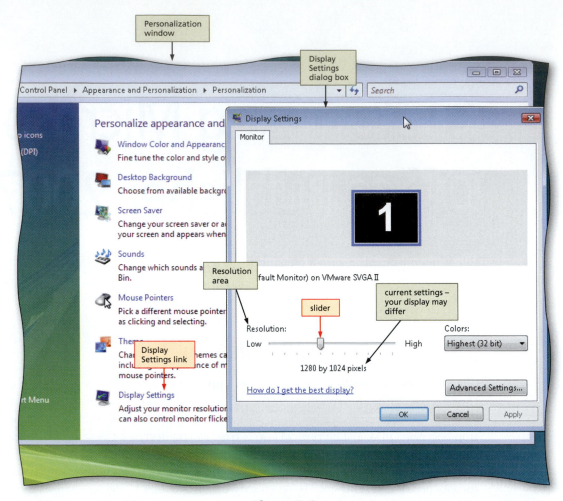

Figure E–2

• If necessary, drag the slider in the Resolution area so that the screen resolution is set to 1024 × 768 (Figure E–3).

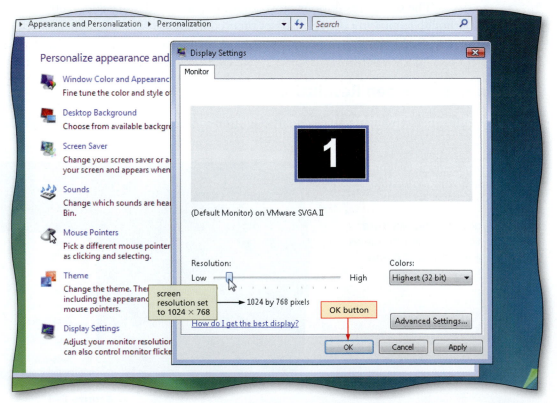

Figure E–3

4
- Click the OK button to set the screen resolution to 1024 × 768 (Figure E–4).

5
- Click the Yes button in the Display Settings dialog box to accept the new screen resolution.

- Click the Close button to close the Personalization Window.

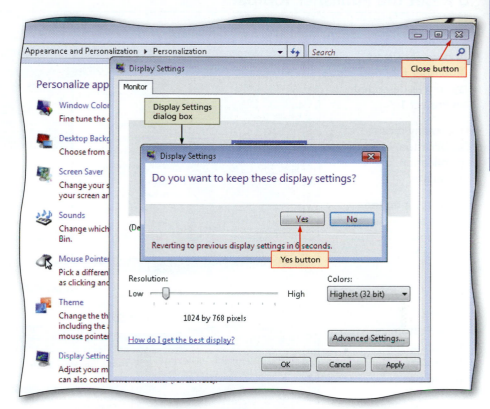

Figure E–4

BTW

Display Settings
If you do not want to change the screen resolution after seeing it applied, you either can click the No button in the inner Display Settings dialog box, or wait for the timer to run out, at which point Windows Vista will revert to the original screen resolution.

Customizing the Publisher Toolbars and Menus

Publisher customization capabilities allow you to reset toolbars and menus, create custom toolbars by adding and deleting buttons, and personalize menus based on their usage. Each time you start Publisher, the toolbars and menus display using the same settings as the last time you used it. The figures in this book were created with the Publisher toolbars and menus set to the original, or installation, settings.

Resetting the Publisher Toolbars

If in the past, buttons or commands were added or removed on any Publisher toolbars, you quickly can restore the original settings. The following steps reset the six toolbars that initially display in Publisher. The six toolbars include the following:

- Standard toolbar
- Formatting toolbar
- Connect Text Boxes toolbar
- Menu Bar
- Objects toolbar
- Publisher Tasks toolbar

To Reset the Publisher Toolbars

- If necessary, start Publisher for your system as described in Project 1.

- Open any recent publication, blank publication, or template.

- Click Tools on the menu bar to display the Tools menu (Figure E–5).

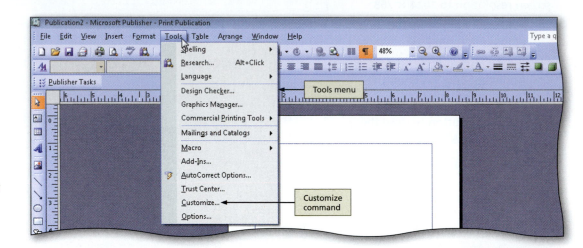

Figure E–5

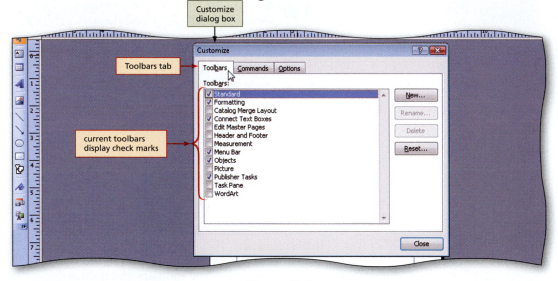

Figure E–6

- Click Customize to display the Customize dialog box.

- In the Customize dialog box, click the Toolbars tab, if necessary. (Figure E–6).

- In the Toolbars list, if necessary, click Standard to select it.

- Click the Reset button to reset the toolbar (Figure E–7).

- Click the OK button in the Microsoft Office Publisher dialog box to confirm the changes.

- Follow steps 1 through 3 to reset each of the other toolbars that display a check mark in the list.

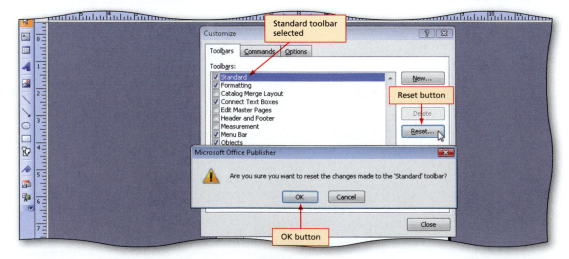

Figure E–7

Editing Toolbars

You can add, delete, or rearrange the commands and buttons on Publisher toolbars. You might want to promote commands that you use frequently to a higher position in the menu. Or you might want to move a button from one toolbar to another to facilitate your use of the button. You even can create new toolbars and menus and populate them with buttons from the list or buttons that you create using macros. On the Commands sheet in the Customize dialog box, the commands are grouped by category or purpose on the left and listed individually on the right.

Another way to edit toolbars is to change the way the buttons look or behave. For example, you can create a button that automatically opens a browser and goes to a specific Web address.

BTW

New Toolbars
If you want to create a new toolbar, click the New button (shown in Figure E–7) to display a dialog box where you can name the new toolbar. Once the new toolbar is created, you can use the Commands sheet to add or remove buttons on the new toolbar.

To Edit Toolbars

The following steps rearrange commands on the File menu and then reset them back to the default order.

1
- With the Customize dialog box still displayed, click the Commands tab.

- If necessary, click File in the Categories list (Figure E–8).

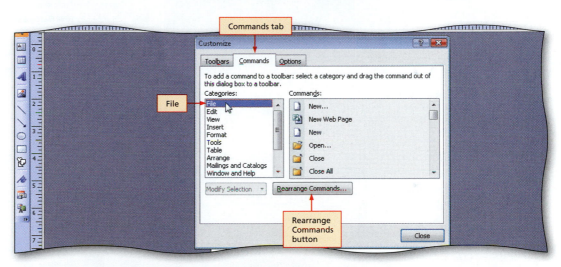

Figure E–8

2
- Click the Rearrange Commands button to display the Rearrange Commands dialog box (Figure E–9).

 How do I rearrange other menus or toolbars?

At the top of the Rearrange Commands dialog box, you can select Menu Bar or Toolbar by clicking the desired option button. You then can choose a specific menu or toolbar by clicking the box arrow. Publisher will change the list of Controls based on your choices.

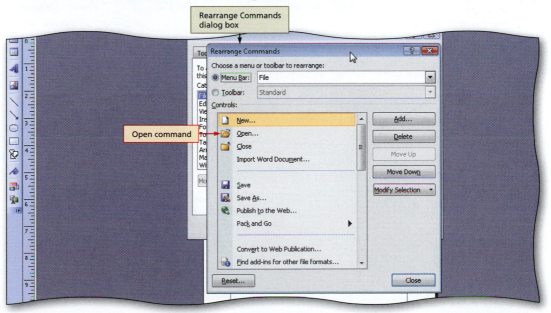

Figure E–9

3

- Click Open in the Controls list and then click the Move Up button to rearrange the commands (Figure E–10).

Q&A

What does the Modify Selection button do?

The Modify Selection button offers you many choices to edit each button and menu command. You can choose a different name, image, or text; edit, copy, or paste images; insert a new separator line to begin a group; or assign a hyperlink. If you change the name or assign a hyperlink, the screen-tip also changes.

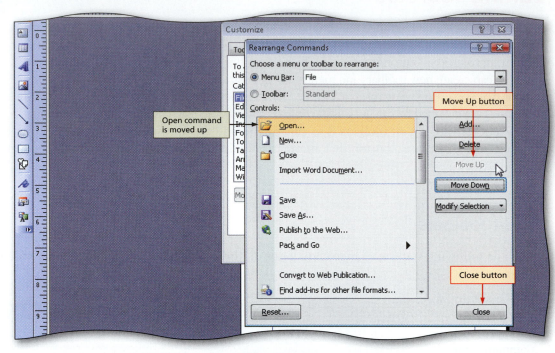

Figure E–10

4

- Click the Close button in the Rearrange Commands dialog box and then click File on the Publisher menu bar to view the rearrangement (Figure E–11).

5

- In the Customize dialog box, click the Rearrange Commands button again, and then click the Reset button to restore the original order.

- When Publisher displays the Microsoft Office Publisher dialog box, click the OK button to confirm the changes.

- Click the Close button in the Rearrange Commands dialog box.

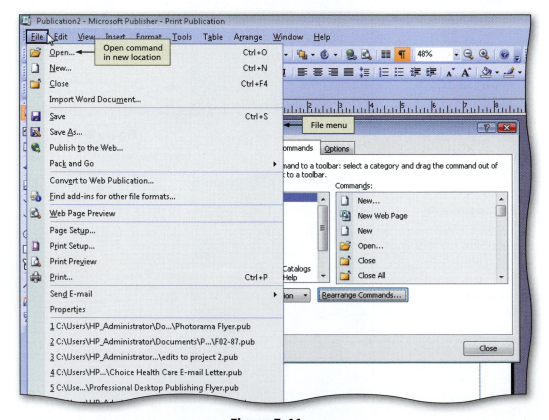

Figure E–11

Resetting the Publisher Menu Usage

On an initial installation, Publisher displays the entire menu when you click a menu command. You can customize or personalize the menus to display the more popular menu commands or recently used commands in a short menu; a More Commands button allows you access to the longer menu. You can reset the short menu and toolbar usage, and you can choose to display the Standard and Formatting toolbars on one row or two.

Adding New Commands

Using the **Commands sheet** in the Customize dialog box, you can add buttons to toolbars and commands to menus. To add buttons, click a category name in the Categories list and then drag the command name in the Commands list to a toolbar. To add menu commands, click a category name in the Categories list, drag the command name in the Commands list to a menu name and then to the desired location in the menu.

To Reset the Publisher Menu Usage

The following steps reset the menu or toolbar usage.

1
- With the Customize dialog box still displayed, click the Options tab (Figure E–12).

2
- Click the Reset menu and toolbar usage data button. If Publisher displays a dialog box asking you to confirm the reset, click the Yes button.

3
- Click the Close button in the Customize dialog box.

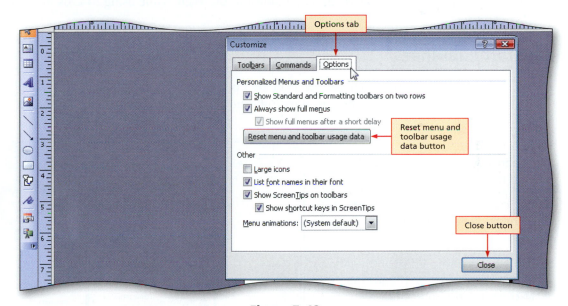

Figure E–12

Other Ways

1. On toolbar, click Toolbar Options button, point to Add or Remove Buttons, click Customize, on Options sheet click Reset menu and toolbar usage data, click Yes.

2. Right-click toolbar, click Customize, on Toolbars sheet click Reset menu and toolbar usage data, click Yes.

Short Menus
If you choose to display short menus, Publisher retains a record of the commands that you select on menus and toolbars. When you click a command on a menu or a button on a toolbar, the Microsoft Office program records your action and makes the command or button always visible to you. The More Commands button at the bottom of menus, and the Toolbar Options button at the end of toolbars display commands and buttons used less frequently. As you choose the less frequently used commands or buttons, Publisher promotes them to the short menu or to the toolbar display.

Appendix F
Steps for the Windows XP User

For the XP User of this Book

For most tasks, no differences exist between using Office 2007 under the Windows Vista operating system and using an Office 2007 program under the Windows XP operating system. With some tasks, however, you will see some differences, or need to complete the tasks using different steps. This appendix shows how to start Publisher, save a publication, open a publication, insert pictures and text, import a Word Document, and publish to the Web, while using Microsoft Office under Windows XP.

To Start Publisher

The following steps, which assume Windows is running, start Publisher based on a typical installation. You may need to ask your instructor how to start Publisher for your computer.

1

• Click the Start button on the Windows taskbar to display the Start menu.

• Point to All Programs on the Start menu to display the All Programs submenu.

• Point to Microsoft Office on the All Programs submenu to display the Microsoft Office submenu (Figure F–1).

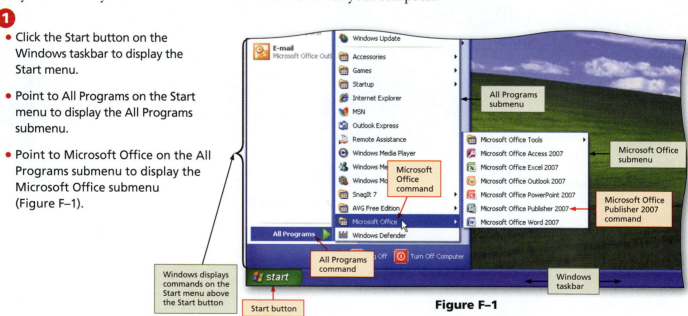

Figure F–1

2

- Click Microsoft Office Publisher 2007 to start Publisher and display the catalog (Figure F–2).

- If the Publisher window is not maximized, click the Maximize button next to the Close button on its title bar to maximize the window.

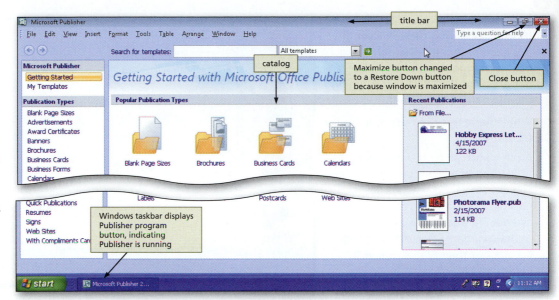

Figure F–2

Other Ways

1. Double-click Publisher icon on desktop, if one is present

2. Click Microsoft Office Publisher 2007 on Start menu

To Save a Document

After editing, you should save the document. The following steps save a document on a USB flash drive using the file name, Horseback Riding Lessons Flyer.

1

- With a USB flash drive connected to one of the computer's USB ports, click the Save button on the Standard Toolbar to display the Save As dialog box (Figure F–3).

Q&A

Do I have to save to a USB flash drive?

No. You can save to any device or folder. A **folder** is a specific location on a storage medium. You can save to the default folder or a different folder. You also can create your own folders, which is explained later in this book.

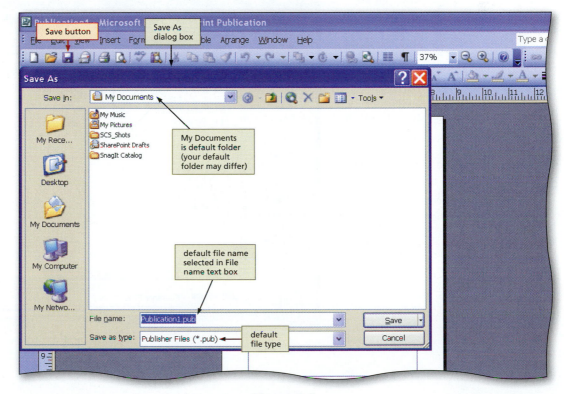

Figure F–3

2

- Type the name of your file (Horseback Riding Lessons Flyer in this example) in the File name text box to change the file name. Do not press the ENTER key after typing the file name (Figure F–4).

Q&A What characters can I use in a file name?

A file name can have a maximum of 255 characters, including spaces. The only invalid characters are the backslash (\), slash (/), colon (:), asterisk (*), question mark (?), quotation mark ("), less than symbol (<), greater than symbol (>), and vertical bar (|).

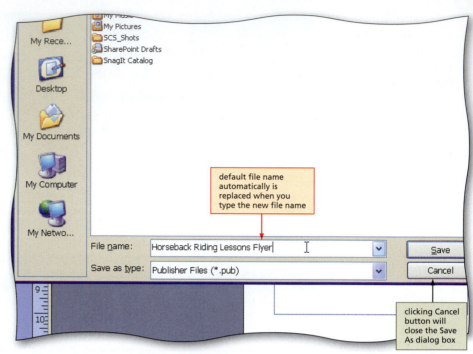

Figure F–4

3

- Click the Save in box arrow to display a list of available drives and folders (Figure F–5).

Q&A Why is my list of files, folders, and drives arranged and named differently from those shown in the figure?

Your computer's configuration determines how the list of files and folders is displayed and how drives are named. You can change the save location by clicking shortcuts on the **My Places bar**.

Q&A How do I save the file if I am not using a USB flash drive?

Use the same process, but be certain to select your device in the Save in list.

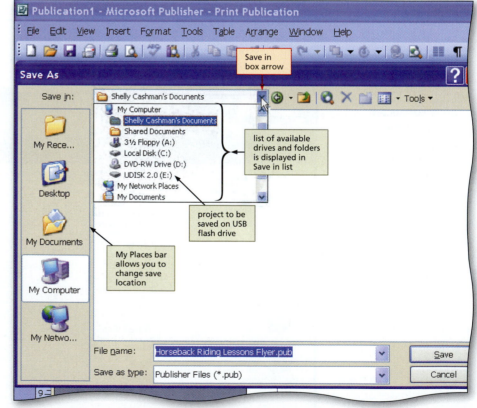

Figure F–5

4

- Click UDISK 2.0 (E:) in the Save in list to select the USB flash drive, Drive E in this case, as the new save location (Figure F–6).

- Click the Save button to save the document.

Q&A

What if my USB flash drive has a different name or letter?

It is very likely that your USB flash drive will have a different name and drive letter and be connected to a different port. Verify the device in your Save in list is correct.

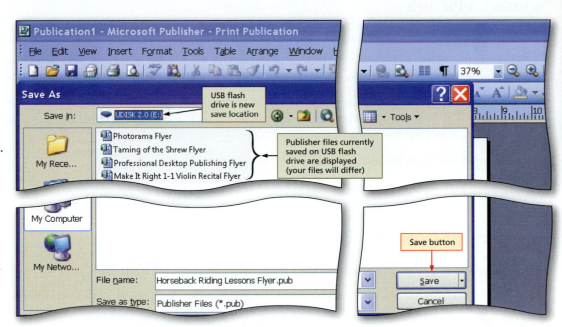

Figure F–6

Other Ways
1. On File menu, click Save, type file name, select drive or folder, click Save button
2. Press CTRL+S, type file name, select drive or folder, click Save button

To Open a Publication

The following steps open the Horseback Riding Lessons Flyer file from the USB flash drive.

1

- With your USB flash drive connected to one of the computer's USB ports, click File on the menu bar to display the File menu.

- Click Open on the File menu to display the Open Publication dialog box.

- If necessary, click the Look in box arrow and then click UDISK 2.0 (E:) to select the USB flash drive, Drive E in this case, in the Look in list as the new open location.

- Click Horseback Riding Lessons Flyer to select the file name (Figure F–7).

- Click the Open button to open the document.

Q&A

How do I open the file if I am not using a USB flash drive?

Use the same process, but be certain to select your device in the Look in list.

Figure F–7

Other Ways
1. On File menu, click file name in Recent Documents list
2. Press CTRL+O, select file name, press ENTER

To Insert a Picture

The following steps insert a picture, which, in this example, is located on a USB flash drive.

1 Go to the page where you want the picture to be located. If you want to replace a current picture, select the picture. On the Insert menu, point to Picture, and then click From File to display the Insert Picture dialog box.

2 With your USB flash drive connected to one of the computer's USB ports, if necessary, click the Look in box arrow and then click UDISK 2.0 (E:) to select the USB flash drive, Drive E in this case, in the Look in list as the device that contains the picture. Select the file name of the picture file.

3 Click the OK button in the dialog box to insert the picture.

To Insert Text from a File

The following steps insert text from a file located on the USB flash drive.

1 Select the text box where you want to insert the text. On the Insert menu, click Text File to display the Insert Text dialog box.

2 With your USB flash drive connected to one of the computer's USB ports, if necessary, click the Look in box arrow and then click UDISK 2.0 (E:) to select the USB flash drive, Drive E in this case, in the Look in list as the device that contains the file. Click to select the file name.

3 Click the OK button in the dialog box to insert the text.

To Import a Word Document

The following steps import a Word document from a file located on the USB flash drive.

1 Select the text box where you want to display the Word document. On the File menu, click Import Word Document to display the Import Word document dialog box.

2 With your USB flash drive connected to one of the computer's USB ports, if necessary, click the Look in box arrow and then click UDISK 2.0 (E:) to select the USB flash drive, Drive E in this case, in the Look in list as the device that contains the file. Click to select the file name.

3 Click the OK button to import the Word file into the selected text box.

To Publish to the Web

The following steps publish the current publication to the Web.

1 With a Web publication open in the Publisher workspace, on the File menu, click Publish to the Web to begin the process. If Publisher displays an information dialog box about Web hosting, click the OK button to display the Publish to the Web dialog box.

2 If necessary, click the Save in box arrow and then click My Network Places in the Save in list as the new open location.

3 Double-click the Web folder name in the Network Location list. If the Enter Network Password dialog box appears, type the user name and password in the respective text boxes and then click the OK button.

4 Click the Save button in the Publish to the Web dialog box.

Index

Quick Reference Summary

In the Microsoft Office Publisher 2007 program, you can accomplish a task in a number of ways. The following table provides a quick reference to each task presented in this textbook. The first column identifies the task. The second column indicates the page number on which the task is discussed in the book. The subsequent four columns list the different ways the task in column one can be carried out.

Microsoft Publisher 2007 Quick Reference Summary

Task	Page Number	Mouse	Menu Bar	Shortcut Menu	Keyboard Shortcut
Add Text	PUB 194			Add text	
AutoCorrect Options	PUB 166	Point to smart tag | click AutoCorrect Options button			
AutoFit Text	PUB 18		Format | AutoFit Text		
Automatic Saving	PUB 158		Tools | Options | Save tab		
Backgrounds	PUB 235	Apply a Background on Background task pane	Format | Background		
Best Fit	PUB 195			Change Text | AutoFit Text | Best Fit	
Bullets	PUB 26, PUB 114	Bullets button on Standard toolbar	Format | Bullets and Numbering		
Center	PUB 48	Center button on Formatting toolbar	Format | Paragraph	Change Text | Paragraph	CTRL+E
Change Pages	PUB 83	Page icon on status bar	Edit | Go to Page		CTRL+G
Close Task Pane	PUB 17	Close button on task pane title bar			
Color Scheme	PUB 9	Color scheme box arrow in Customize area	Format | Color Schemes		
Commercial Printing Tool	PUB 211		Tools | Commercial Printing Tools		
Continued Notices	PUB 95	Double-click text box | Text Box tab	Format | Text Box | Text Box tab	Format Text Box | Text Box tab	
Convert to Web Publication	PUB 53		File | Convert to Web Publication		
Copy	PUB 119	Copy button on Standard toolbar	Edit | Copy	Copy	CTRL+C
Custom Color Schemes	PUB 154	Create new color scheme link on Format Publication task pane	Format | Color Schemes | Create new color scheme link		

Microsoft Publisher 2007 Quick Reference Summary (continued)

Task	Page Number	Mouse	Menu Bar	Shortcut Menu	Keyboard Shortcut
Delete Objects	PUB 28, PUB 158		Edit | Delete Object	Delete Object	DELETE
Delete Pages	PUB 83		Edit | Delete Page	Delete Page	
Design Checker	PUB 51		Tools | Design Checker		
Design Gallery Objects	PUB 117	Design Gallery Object button on Objects toolbar	Insert | Design Gallery Object		
Edit Story in Microsoft Word	PUB 98		Edit | Edit Story in Microsoft Word	Change Text | Edit Story in Microsoft Word	
Fill Color	PUB 191	Fill Color button on Formatting toolbar		Format AutoShape | Colors and Lines tab	
Font Color	PUB 102	Font Color button arrow on Formatting toolbar			
Font Effect	PUB 178		Format | Font	Change Text | Font	
Font Scheme	PUB 163	Style box arrow on Formatting toolbar	Format | Font Schemes	Change Text | Font	
Font Size	PUB 47	Font Size box arrow on Formatting toolbar	Format | Font	Change Text | Font	
Format Painter	PUB 169	Format Painter button on Standard toolbar			
Formatting Marks	PUB 24, PUB 81	Special Characters button on Standard toolbar	View | Special Characters		CTRL+SHIFT+Y
Help	PUB 58	Microsoft Office Publisher Help button on Standard toolbar	Help | Microsoft Office Publisher Help		F1
Import Text	PUB 89, PUB 92		Insert | Text File	Change Text | Text File	
Insert Graphic	PUB 110	Picture Frame button on Objects toolbar | Clip Art	Insert | Picture | Clip Art		
Insert Hyperlink	PUB 49, PUB 233	Insert Hyperlink button on Standard toolbar	Insert | Hyperlink	Hyperlink	CTRL+K
Insert Page Numbers	PUB 124	Insert Page Number button on Header and Footer toolbar	Insert | Page Numbers		
Line Color	PUB 192	Line Color button on Formatting toolbar		Format AutoShape | Colors and Lines tab	
Line Spacing	PUB 181	Line Spacing button on Formatting toolbar	Format | Paragraph	Change Text | Paragraph	
Line/Border Style	PUB 192	Line/Border Style button on Formatting toolbar		Format AutoShape | Colors and Lines tab	
Master Page	PUB 198	View master pages link on Apply Master Page task pane	View | Master Page		CTRL+M
Master Page, Ignore	PUB 205		View | Ignore Master Page		
Move	PUB 122	Point to border and drag			Select object | ARROW KEY

Microsoft Publisher 2007 Quick Reference Summary *(continued)*

Task	Page Number	Mouse	Menu Bar	Shortcut Menu	Keyboard Shortcut
Nudge	PUB 122		Arrange | Nudge		Select object | ALT+ARROW KEY
Open Publication	PUB 42	Open button on Standard toolbar	File | Open		CTRL+O
Pack and Go Wizard	PUB 212		File | Pack and Go | Take to a Commercial Printing Service		
Page Options	PUB 82	Page Options on Format Publication task pane			
Page Size	PUB 238	Change Page Size button on Format Publication task pane	File | Page Setup		
Paste	PUB 119	Paste button on Standard toolbar	Edit | Paste	Paste	CTRL+V
Picture Toolbar	PUB 187		View | Toolbars | Picture	Show Picture Toolbar	
Print	PUB 40, PUB 134	Print button on Standard toolbar	File | Print		CTRL+P
Print Preview	PUB 207	Print Preview button on Standard toolbar	File | Print Preview		
Publication Properties	PUB 38		File | Properties		
Publish to the Web	PUB 55		File | Publish to the Web		
Publisher Tasks	PUB 130	Publisher Tasks button on Standard toolbar			
Quit Publisher	PUB 41	Close button on Publisher title bar	File | Exit	Microsoft Publisher button on Windows taskbar | Close	ALT+F4
Replace Graphic	PUB 34	Picture Frame button on Objects toolbar	Insert | Picture | Clip Art	Change Picture	
Resize Graphic	PUB 112, PUB 197	Format Picture button on Picture toolbar | Picture tab	Format | Picture | Picture tab	Format Picture | Picture tab	SHIFT+drag handle
Save	PUB 40	Save button on Standard toolbar	File | Save		CTRL+S
Save As	PUB 31, PUB 52		File | Save As		CTRL+S
Select All	PUB 20, PUB 86		Edit | Select All		CTRL+A
Select Block of Text	PUB 104	Drag text			Click beginning, SHIFT+click end
Select Characters	PUB 104	Drag character(s)			SHIFT+ARROW KEY
Select Graphic	PUB 104	Click graphic			
Select Paragraph	PUB 104	Triple-click paragraph or double-click left margin			
Select Paragraphs	PUB 104	Drag left margin			
Select Picture within Grouped Object	PUB 104	Click picture | Click picture again			

Microsoft Publisher 2007 Quick Reference Summary *(continued)*

Task	Page Number	Mouse	Menu Bar	Shortcut Menu	Keyboard Shortcut
Select Row	PUB 104	Click left of row in table			
Select Rows	PUB 104	Drag left of rows in table or triple-click left of table			
Select Sentence	PUB 104	Drag text			
Select Text	PUB 22				Click beginning, SHIFT+click end
Select Word	PUB 104	Double-click word			
Select Words	PUB 104	Drag words			
Send Publication via E-Mail	PUB 237		File	Send E-mail		
Shape	PUB 190	Click AutoShapes button on Objects toolbar	Insert	Picture	Autoshapes		
Spell Check	PUB 30, PUB 127	Spelling button on Standard toolbar	Tools	Spelling	Spelling	Proofing Tools	Spelling	F7
Style, Apply	PUB 176	Styles box arrow on Formatting toolbar			
Style, New	PUB 174	New Style button on Styles task pane			
Styles	PUB 172	Styles button on Formatting toolbar	Format	Styles		
Template	PUB 7, PUB 150	Click template preview in catalog			
Text Box	PUB 46	Text Box button on Objects tool bar	Insert	Text Box		
Text Wrap	PUB 187	Text Wrapping button on Picture toolbar			
Transparent Object	PUB 187, PUB 206				CTRL+T
Web Page Preview	PUB 57	Web Page Preview button on Standard toolbar	File	Web Page Preview		
WordArt, Format	PUB 202	WordArt Shape button on WordArt toolbar			
WordArt, Insert	PUB 201	Insert WordArt button on Objects toolbar			
Zoom	PUB 8	Zoom Out or Zoom In button on Standard toolbar	View	Zoom	Zoom	F9